BACON
DISFIGURED

Darren Ambrose

Joan Copjec

Sacha Golob

Dany Nobus

Aaron Schuster

Ben Ware

Jamieson Webster

Alenka Zupančič

BACON DISFIGURED

EDITED BY BEN WARE

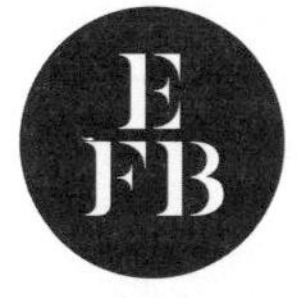

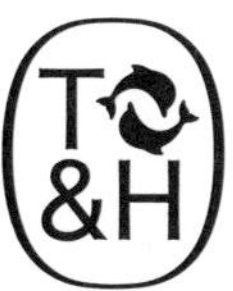

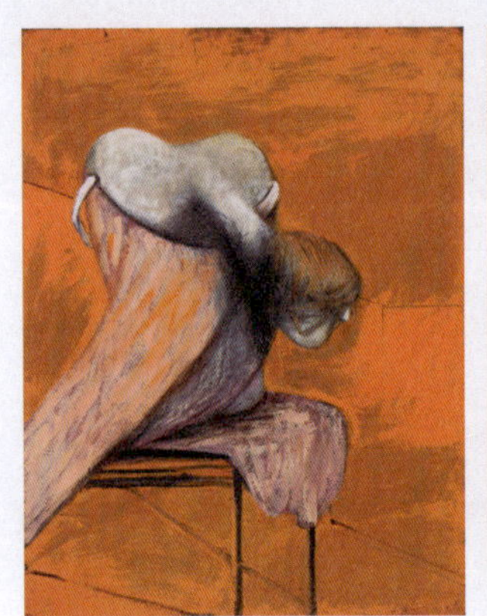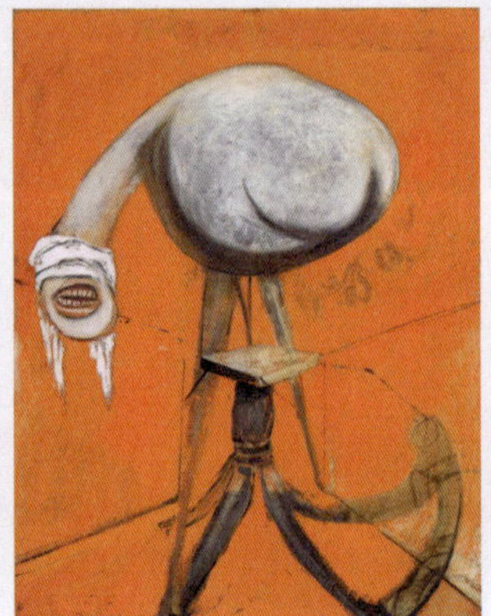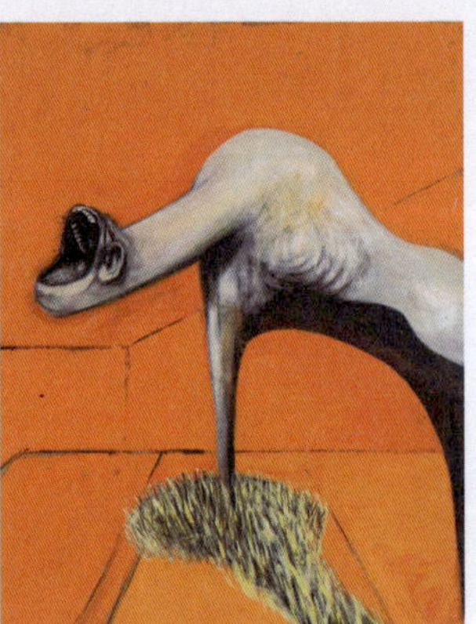

fig. 1 *Three Studies for Figures at the Base of a Crucifixion, 1944*

INTRODUCTION

To disfigure is to wound an appearance: to mar, to distort, to undo the coherence of a form. Disfiguration deprives the person, image, or thing of its recognisability, twisting it out of shape. It can occur as an unwanted effect, or as a deliberate – sometimes creative – act. If to figure is to calculate, to decipher, to render intelligible, then disfigure suggests the unmaking of sense, the introduction of a surplus that eludes accounting. In this respect, disfiguration falls into the orbit of the monstrous and the sublime: that towards which the human mind is inescapably drawn, but from which it simultaneously recoils.

The cultural imagination is replete with examples of disfigurement and different responses to it. In David Lynch's film *The Elephant Man* (1980), the severely disfigured John Merrick is rescued from a circus freak show, only to be presented to the London medical establishment as a 'perverted and degraded version of a human being' – something contrary to nature. In Edgar Allan Poe's short story 'The Tell-Tale Heart', the unnamed narrator is driven mad by a disfigured old man, specifically by his eye: 'one of his eyes resembled that of a vulture – a pale blue eye with a film over it.'[1] At the centre of both narratives is the overpowering anxiety that disfigurement provokes. While Merrick is eventually assimilated into Victorian high society, he remains forever a spectacle, an object to be nervously stared at. Poe's narrator, in gothic contrast, kills the old man – in what turns out to be an act of both murder and symbolic suicide – believing this is the only way to rid himself of the torture of the evil 'eye' ('I').

Psychoanalysis provides us with a different perspective. In German, disfigurement translates as *Entstellung* – a word which can also mean distortion, displacement, or misrepresentation. *Entstellung* is the term that Freud uses to describe the overall effect of the dream-work – the transformation of the latent dream-thoughts into the manifest dream content. For Freud, 'dreams are nothing other than a particular *form* of thinking', and 'it is the *dream-work* which creates that form, and it alone is the essence of dreaming.'[2] What really matters with respect to the dream, then, is not its latent content, but rather its form: why have the dream-thoughts been *disfigured* in this way, why have they been *distorted* into the form of a dream?[3] Yet the dream is never simply what is dreamt, but also its telling; and any elaboration – any 'figuring out' of the dream – is also a disfiguring, the creative reshaping of a text. The speaking subject on the analyst's couch is, consequently, as much implicated in the process of *Entstellung* as the dreamer during the dream.

Jacques Lacan returns to the notion of disfiguring, giving it an explicitly violent twist. Disfiguration is, in one sense, the very condition of being: one becomes a subject only by being *subjected* to language. Subjects, however, do not dwell harmoniously in language; they are, as Lacan says, 'captured and tortured' by it, wounded and split by the signifier.[4] This act of disfiguration extends to the practice of psychoanalysis itself. The consulting room, for Lacan, is a kind of slaughterhouse, wherein the work of 'dismembering' (*démembrement*) is carried out by those who know how to 'cut at the joints' (*couper dans les articulations*).[5] But if the analyst is a good butcher, expertly segmenting his patients, then the aim is always an avowedly ethical one: to intervene in the discourse of the analysand in order to open up the unconscious. The disfiguring cut thus turns out to be the very fissure through which the subject's truth might finally appear.

Bacon famously remarks that he is always 'moved' by images of slaughterhouses and meat: 'we are potential carcasses. If I go into a butcher's shop I always think it's surprising that I wasn't there instead of the animal.'[6] Gilles Deleuze describes Bacon as 'a butcher', with an intense 'pity for the flesh'.[7] In what sense should this be understood? Bacon radically disfigures his figures, making them all but unrecognisable. This, however, is no mere stylistic gesture – it is the expression of a deeply held aesthetic vision. For Bacon, the essence of a subject can only be found in the distorted recording of its appearance. His disfigurations are therefore, as he himself says, attempts to bring back the intensity of the subject's reality and to communicate this as 'rawly' as possible: 'the image must be twisted if it is to make a renewed assault upon the [spectator's] nervous system.'[8]

Yet Bacon accomplishes more than he thinks. He doesn't just capture subjects in isolation; he also makes visible the real social and economic forces operating on and through them, mutilating their very nature. *Look what the world has made of us*, Bacon's figures appear to silently exclaim. But such realities cannot be captured through conventional realism. Bertolt Brecht was right: 'the situation is now…so complex that a simple "reproduction of reality" says less than ever about reality itself.'[9] Representing the effects of the social structure on the subject will therefore require, as Bacon demonstrates, not accuracy but a kind of monstrous distortion – one which intends to make the spectator *shudder*.

What Bacon does to the figure, radical interpretation does to Bacon: twisting, fragmenting, disfiguring, cutting, defacing, and overhauling him, transforming his work into something strange but still living – something yet to be fully discovered. This kind of interpretation does not go in search of what Bacon's paintings 'really mean'; rather, it attends to their enigmatic character, tarrying with their aesthetic and historical complexity. Its aim, like that of psychoanalysis itself, is to produce associations, which open up new aesthetic and subjective truths.

All the essays in this volume follow Bacon's own method: they distort the artist's work, pushing it far beyond its usual appearance, but through this distortion they bring the work back to the reader and viewer as a new kind of event.[10] Each author, in different ways, blasts Bacon out of his familiar contexts, placing him in unexpected dialogues – with Kant, Marx, Nietzsche, Freud, Genet, Canguilhem, Adorno, Lacan, and many others. In his final published work, *Moses and Monotheism*, Freud remarks that the distortion of a text resembles a murder.[11] The essays in *Bacon Disfigured*, however, disfigure Bacon precisely in order to bring him back to life.

Ben Ware

1 Edgar Allan Poe, 'The Tell-Tale Heart', in *The Portable Edgar Allan Poe* (London: Penguin, 2006), p. 187.

2 Sigmund Freud, *The Interpretation of Dreams*, in *The Standard Edition of the Complete Psychological Works of Sigmund Freud*, Volume V, trans. James Strachey (London: Vintage, 2001), pp. 506-07.

3 On this point, see Slavoj Žižek, *The Sublime Object of Ideology* (London: Verso, 1989), pp. 3-9.

4 Jacques Lacan, 'An Address: Freud in the Century', *The Seminar of Jacques Lacan, Book III: The Psychoses*, trans. Russell Grigg (London: Routledge, 1993), p. 243.

5 Jacques Lacan, 'The Other's Desire', *The Seminar of Jacques Lacan, Book V: Formations of the Unconscious*, trans. Russell Grigg (London: Polity, 2017), p. 377.

6 David Sylvester, *The Brutality of Fact: Interviews with Francis Bacon* (London: Thames & Hudson, 2016), p. 53.

7 Gilles Deleuze, *Francis Bacon: The Logic of Sensation*, trans. Daniel W. Smith (London: Bloomsbury, 2016), pp. 17 & xii.

8 Michael Peppiatt, 'On Intuition and Sensation' (Bacon's Early Statements), in *Francis Bacon: A Self-Portrait in Words* (London: Thames & Hudson, 2024), p. 26.

9 Bertolt Brecht cited in Anthony Squiers, *Bertolt Brecht's Adaptations and Anti-capitalist Aesthetics Today* (Leiden: Brill, 2025), p. 150.

10 Sylvester, op. cit., p. 46.

11 Sigmund Freud, *Moses and Monotheism*, in *The Standard Edition of the Complete Psychological Works of Sigmund Freud*, Volume XXIII, trans. James Strachey (London: Vintage, 2001), p. 43.

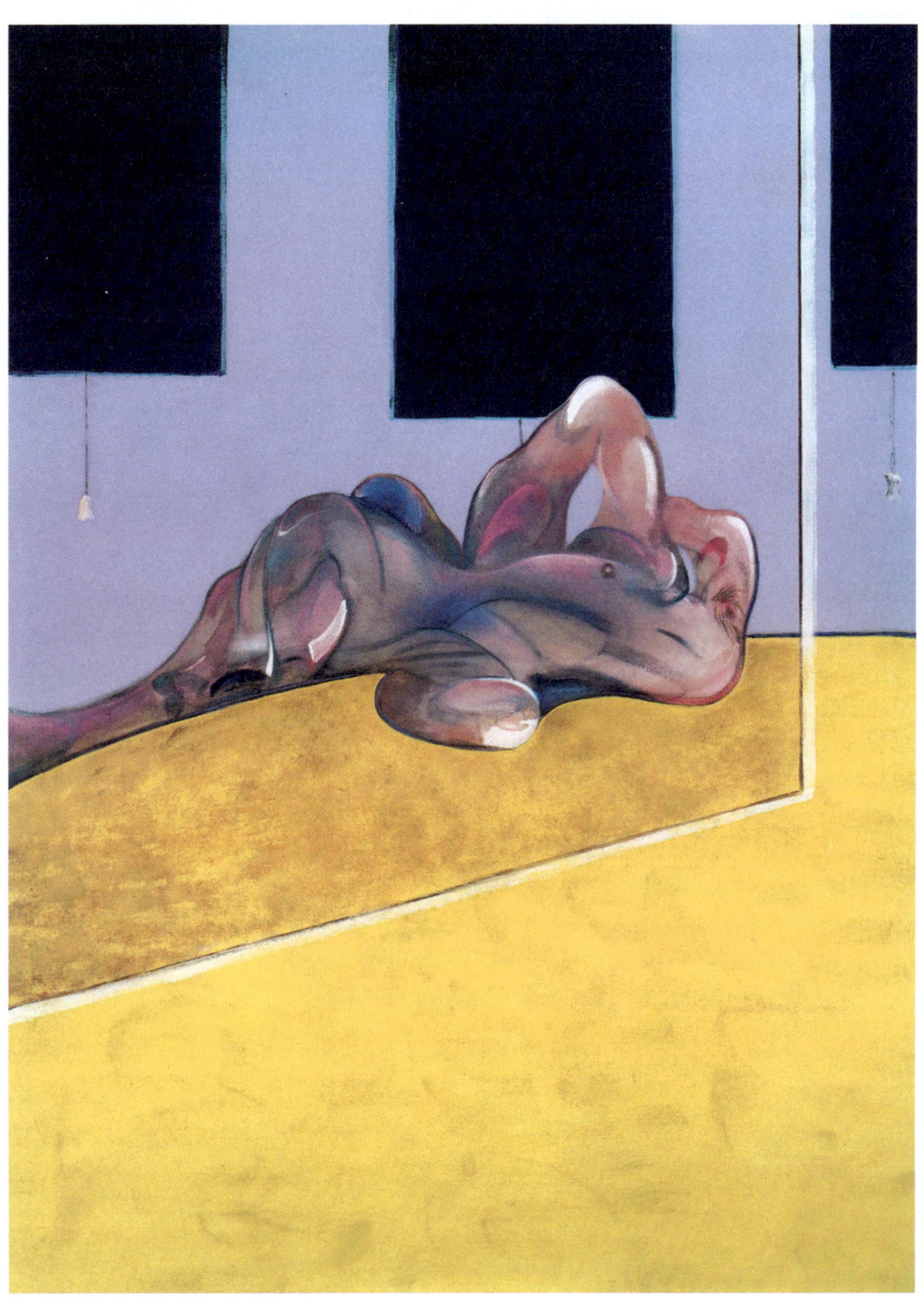

fig. 2 *Lying Figure in a Mirror*, 1971

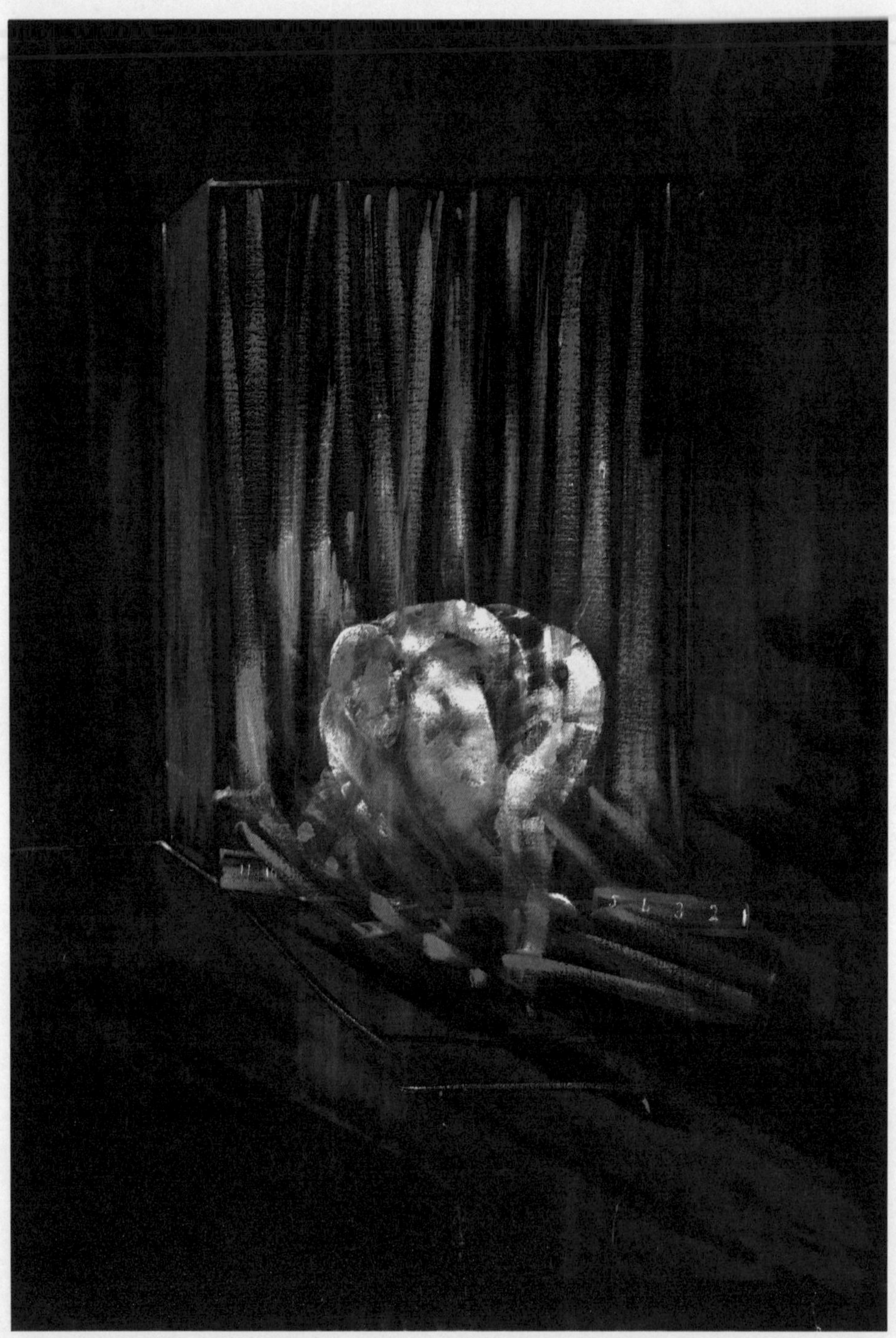

fig. 3   *Study for Nude*, 1951

BACON'S CORPUS – THE BODY AS FRAGMENTARY TOUCHING

Darren Ambrose

Reinvented Realism

In his collected interviews with David Sylvester[1], as well as in numerous other interviews, Francis Bacon repeatedly insisted upon his anti-illustrational[2] and non-narrative intentions. Again and again he stressed that it was not his intention to tell stories or to reproduce appearances, but to push painting towards what he called 'extreme points of realism' – a reinvented practice of realism beyond representation, where extreme bodily deformation and disfiguration in painting became the means for conveying the immediate violence of lived sensation.

In an interview with Sylvester from 1966, while discussing the anti-illustrational nature of his work, Bacon reflects upon the figurative and illustrational achievements in the work of Velázquez, who was obviously an important painter for him:

> In Velasquez it's a very, very extraordinary thing that he has been able to keep it so near to what we call illustration and at the same time so deeply unlock the greatest and deepest things that man can feel…But of course so many things have happened since Velasquez that the situation has become much more involved and much more difficult, for very many reasons. And one of them, of course, which has never actually been worked out, is why photography has altered completely this whole thing of figurative painting, and totally altered it.[3]

By contrasting the 'recording' function undertaken by Velázquez – a function later absorbed by photography and still conditioned by certain 'religious possibilities' – with the contemporary situation that follows Nietzsche's 'death of God', Bacon says that we arrive at the realisation that we are accidental and groundless. We must therefore, in his words, 'play the game without reason'. In such circumstances it is now a matter of struggling against the traps of becoming a merely illustrational painter, producing irrelevant and derivative work. As Bacon argues, the task is one of *reinventing realism* or nothing at all. At this very moment in the 1966 interview, reflecting on the need for a reinvented form of realism, he begins to talk about the need to introduce and survey something he calls a 'graph' into the marks he made when painting the figure:

> The marks are made, and you survey the thing like you would a sort of *graph*. And you see within this graph the possibilities of all types of fact being planted. This is a difficult thing: I'm expressing it badly. But you see, for instance, if you think of a portrait, you maybe at one time have put the mouth somewhere, but you suddenly see through this graph that the mouth could go right across the face. And in a way you would love to be able in a portrait to make a Sahara of the appearance – to make it so like, yet seeming to have the distances of the Sahara.[4] [fig. 30]

The utilisation of a 'graph' is precisely described by Bacon as a means for producing disfiguration, which is seen as a route towards reinventing realism. It is also here that Bacon links the newly invented forms of emergent realism to the operations of chance and accident:

> Does one know why very often, or nearly always, the accidental images are the most real? Perhaps they've not been tampered with by the conscious brain and therefore come across in a much more raw and real sense than something which has been tampered with by consciousness...We're so saturated with all the arts, through all the means of reproducing them and seeing them and everything, that the saturation point has come so strongly that one just longs for new images and new ways by which reality can be created. After all, man wants invention, he doesn't want to go on and on and on just reproducing the past...We can't go on and on reproducing Renaissance or nineteenth-century art or anything else. You want something new. Not an illustrative realism but a realism that comes about through a real invention of a new way to lock reality into something completely arbitrary.[5]

The 'Graph': Chaos and Disfiguration

This particular moment in the interview provides Gilles Deleuze with one of the most crucial conceptual entry points for understanding Bacon's practice of disfiguration in his philosophical study *Francis Bacon: The Logic of Sensation*.[6] Deleuze interprets Bacon's remarks on the 'graph' as signalling the introduction of what he terms the diagram – a manual intervention that injects catastrophe into the pictorial field. At the heart of his 1981 book is a claim regarding Bacon's controlled manipulation of chaos, accident and chance in reinventing realism. His account offers a compelling account of the dynamics of control and accident at work in Bacon's method.[7]

In his book this is crystallised into the concept of the 'diagram'. The diagram names the sudden appearance of chaos within the act of painting: the eruption of accidental or involuntary marks, smears, scrubbings, and erratic gestures that violently disrupt the pre-existing optical organisation of the canvas. For Deleuze, this operation is essential to Bacon's art because it dislocates the figurative and representational coordinates that always already haunt the painter's surface before any image has yet emerged. The diagram, in this sense, is the painter's strategy for breaking through the tyranny of illustration, introducing a moment of productive disorder that allows sensation – rather than depiction – to take form. The 'diagram' captures a type of process undertaken by Bacon to utilise the immanent *catastrophe* confronting all acts of painting.[8] It is a germinal zone of operative catastrophe disrupting conventional representational habits in painting, and forcing the painter to reorganise sensation anew. It marks a threshold where figuration gives way to the emergence of the Figure, an intensive field of sensation that directly affects the viewer's nervous system. The 'diagram' functions as a material mechanism for soliciting and then mastering chaos, and is the painter's way of forcing new possibilities to emerge from the collapse of the representational order. In this sense, the 'diagram' provides a philosophical framework for explaining how and why Bacon's acts of *disfiguration* are produced – how his painting extracts sensation from the field of chaos through a disciplined negotiation of chance. Deleuze's reading conceptualises the way Bacon turns the violence of accident into a productive force, transforming the painted body into an event of sensation rather than an object of representation. Bacon's approach to catastrophe represents a singularly original one, involving a set of painterly techniques for soliciting chance and accident. These techniques emerge as part of Bacon's 'diagram' and operate to germinate and mediate with chaos. Through the 'diagram', his Figures are relentlessly disfigured by this controlled introduction of chaos into the painterly realm. Out of the deliberate handling of painterly chaos summoned by the 'diagram', Bacon produces durably affective Figures placed in proximity with intense thresholds at the field of chaos. It is this process of intense disfiguration which gives us such profoundly violent sensations of life.

This concentration upon the 'diagram' is extremely significant since the Bacon Deleuze tries to establish here is one who comes to occupy a third 'middle way' of utilising the diagram in the history of contemporary painting – 'neither optical like abstract painting, nor manual like action painting.'[9] However, Deleuze's entire approach is seriously undermined once one begins to go back and examine exactly what Bacon said in the original interviews with Sylvester. As we previously saw, Bacon specifically uses the word 'graph'.[10] In the 1976 French translation of the interviews[11] originally published in English, the translators Michel Leiris and Michael Peppiatt translate 'graph' as 'sorte de diagramme', where Bacon's original term could have perhaps more accurately been translated as 'la graphe'. It is as if they have treated 'la graphe' and 'diagramme' as synonyms. But are they? This French translation of the interviews would have been the one read by Deleuze in preparation for, and indeed used fairly extensively throughout, *The Logic of Sensation*. In his original 1981 text Deleuze indeed writes – 'C'est ce que Bacon appelle un *Diagramme*.'[12] When it came to be subsequently translated into English in 2003, the translator Daniel Smith translates this line as 'This is what Bacon calls a "graph" or a "diagram".'[13] So Smith is at pains here to indicate that the use of the term 'diagram' in Deleuze actually relates more specifically to the term 'graph' by Bacon.

I think the slippage here is not insignificant – as well as the 'graph' Bacon proposes to survey at certain moments in painting, there are in fact multiple forms of 'graph' at play in Bacon's process for producing figural disfiguration – photo*graphs*, radio*graphs*, mimeo*graphs*, psycho-*graphs*, rather than *diagrams* as such. Each of these *graphs* would need their own subsequent precise study. From a careful reflection on Bacon's actual words here, it seems as if the survey of the 'graph' involves very precise, careful and deliberate 'intentions' regarding the fragmentary spacing of marks (to make something have the space of a Sahara) and deliberate and suggestive *disfiguration* (a moving or stretching of the mouth from one point to another) – we need to understand the point being made here by Bacon's use of the term *graph*, a specific type of *diagram* used to measure and mark points of *difference* and *change*, rather than a *diagram* per se.[14]

Given the current ubiquity of Deleuze's philosophical approach to Bacon,[15] one needs to ask the question whether his account of a 'diagrammatic' procedure, i.e. as consisting entirely in the so-called disturbances and injections of chaos, is sufficient to explain the pronounced bodily disfiguration in Bacon's paintings? Does it actually provide a sufficient conceptual frame for understanding how Bacon's acts of disfiguration are carried out and are able to produce an intensely affective *sense*? Does Bacon's procedure for producing disfiguration in painting involving a 'graph' (or, indeed, multiple graphs) entail something more than operations of chance and accident? Here I will argue that Deleuze's account of the 'diagram' is seriously flawed and needs to be supplanted. Given the centrality of this notion to Deleuze, it is also my belief that his work on Bacon as a whole has become somewhat over-familiar, and has ended up framing or trapping Bacon's work within a set of well-trodden, and, dare I say it, now clichéd ideas. While retaining considerable resources for thinking about Bacon's work on its own terms (or, often, *in* its own (i.e. Bacon's) terms), Deleuze's book contains much that risks reducing Bacon's paintings to accompanying illustrations for his own conceptual apparatus.

Perhaps now is the time then to introduce some disruptive and disfiguring challenges to Deleuze, and part of this will involve looking again more closely at Bacon's methodology of *fragmentation* and *disfiguration*, and the sheer deliberation consequent to the introduction of what he calls 'the *graph*'. At this point I want to bring this articulation of '*extreme points of realism*' into dialogue with Jean-Luc Nancy's thinking, specifically his presentation of the body as *fragmentary touching of sense*. I will argue that Nancy's work intersects differently and more succesfully than Deleuze's with how 'disfiguration' forms the cornerstone of a reinvented realism in his paintings. Bacon is actually directly cited and discussed, albeit briefly, throughout a number of Nancy's philosophical texts, including his essay devoted to Bacon called 'Disfiguration' in the jointly authored book *Being Nude*;[16] his essay 'On Painting (and) Presence' in the collection *The Birth to Presence*,[17] along with his books *Portrait*,[18] *The Muses*,[19] *A Finite Thinking*,[20] and *Corpus*.[21] The abbreviated observations in the short essay written directly about Bacon are significantly enriched by being first brought into contact with a broader grasp of the major elements of Nancy's ontological claims. And they are also significantly expanded by having a grasp of his philosophy of the fragmentary body in *Corpus*. What follows will thus introduce and explain a little about Nancy's philosophy, before concluding with an examination of the short essay Nancy wrote on Bacon, in collaboration with Frederico Ferrari, in 2006.

Nancy's Ontology: Sense, Touching, Bodies

Throughout Nancy's philosophical work, but particularly in his book *Being Singular Plural*, there runs an overarching concern with the question of what meaning is – or more precisely, how meaning *happens*. How is it that the world, and we ourselves as part of that world, are open and available as meaning? For Nancy, meaning [*le sens*] is not to be understood as signification or representation, as if it were a system of signs referring to an external truth. Rather, meaning is the very sense of being – the way existence exposes itself as a world that is always already shared. Meaning, Nancy writes, 'does not come to beings from the outside, nor does it spring from an interiority of being; it is the very sharing, the very communication of being'.[22]

In this way, Nancy articulates that meaning is inextricably bound up with what he calls the 'we-world' [*monde du nous*], a collective and co-constitutive being-with [être-*avec*], derived from Heidegger's notion of *Mitsein*.[23] Existence is not a collection of isolated substances that later enter into relation; rather, relation is the very structure of being itself. 'Being,' Nancy writes, 'is always being-with'.[24] The world, then, is never a single, unified, or totalised whole – such myths of unity, Nancy suggests, belong to metaphysics and theology and are no longer credible.[25] Instead, the world is constituted through the sharing out [*partage*] of sense: a distribution or division through which beings are both singular and plural.

Sense, for Nancy, exists only as a vast and dynamic circulation – a movement that is always relational, always exposed, and always in excess of closure. This circulation of meaning 'goes in all directions at once, without any progression or linear path, bit by bit and case by case'.[26] It has neither origin nor final fulfilment, because sense is not something to be achieved or completed; it is the ongoing unfolding of coexistence itself. Meaning is thus never given once and for all but continually arises in the spacing and sharing that constitute the world as plural. In this sense, Nancy's ontology of being-with articulates a world whose sense is distributed rather than unified, a world that is plural in its very principle.

If meaning is the sharing out of existence, then this sharing occurs as contact – as the plural and *fragmentary touching* of beings in their exposure to one another. There is contiguity but not continuity: a world of plural, finite beings whose proximity never fuses into unity. In place of a single ordered whole, Nancy conceives being as a network of contacts, where sense circulates from one singular being to another, each touching upon others without ever forming a closed totality. 'All of being is in touch with all of being,' he writes, 'but the law of touching is separation'.[27] This paradox – that being is at once in contact and in separation – defines the structure of sense itself. The world is not a homogeneous medium where things merge or dissolve into one another; there is no neutral continuum that absorbs differences. Rather, being consists of heterogeneous surfaces that touch without fusing, that make sense in and through their very separation. [fig. 32]

Meaning [*le sens*], then, is nothing other than the spacing and contact of singular beings – the point of tension where contiguity and separation coincide. Sense arises not in the fusion of beings but in their exposure to one another. As Nancy puts it, 'sense is what happens at the limit, at the limit between bodies'.[28] The human being, too, must be understood as a product of such differential contact: a body that exists only through its relation to other bodies, through the heterogeneous borders that both separate and expose it. The discrete singularity of a human body is thus not a self-contained substance but a composition – a corpus – of multiple, contiguous differences. 'The body,' Nancy writes, 'is a corpus of parts, traits, forces, tensions, and rhythms'.[29] My body, your body: each is a plurality of openings, clefts, channels, and energies, continually traversed by other bodies and yet never reducible to a seamless whole. To be is to be in touch – in contact and in separation – within the plural circulation of being itself.

The body is the site where the ontology of sense most vividly takes place. It is not a closed substance but a limit – a finite, exposed site where being is continually touched and opened to the outside. It is made up of a series of limits to sense; it exists only as exposure at these limits, in the repetition of its plural contacts. A singular body is always, as Nancy writes, a 'catalogue'[30] – what he calls a corpus – of contiguous traits rather than a definable or fixed unity. Each singularity is a body, and every body is a singularity: bodies, their states, movements, densities, and rhythms all participate in the plural circulation of being. Ontology is an ontology of bodies, of every body, whether animate or inanimate, sentient or inert, thinking or extended, living or lifeless. [fig. 29]

Above all, 'body' means what is outside – what is always outside itself, next to, against, nearby, with another body. The body exists at its limit, and this limit is never self-contained but always shared. Nancy's ontology rejects the metaphysical idea of the integral, fixed, self-identical body – the kind presupposed in classical theology and philosophy – and replaces it with a notion of disintegrated bodies marked by multiple, fragmentary alterities. The body, reconceived as corpus, is fundamentally *being-exscribed*: written or projected outside itself, at the borders of sense.

This process of exscription [*excription*] – Nancy's reworking of both inscription and exteriority – names the movement by which the body ceaselessly places itself outside its own limits, outside its supposed unity or integrity. 'Being-exscribed', Nancy writes, 'means that the body takes place at the limit, as limit'.[31] The body, is a limit that opens. It is *disfigured* in the act of existing, stretched across the spacing of sense, exposed to what is not itself. The body is not a closed form but an opening *onto* the outside and *as* the outside. It is the unstable limit that constantly pulls itself outward in its very being. In this way, *Corpus* reconceptualises the body. Nancy deliberately replaces *le corps* [the body] with *corpus* - a catalogue of singularities that evoke bodies without essentialising them. What it means to be a body is not fixed but continually rearticulated through a multiplicity of corpi, or bodily lists, whose singular traits may repeat from one catalogue to the next but always in new combinations. For Nancy, 'the body is a skin variously folded, refolded, unfolded, multiplied, invaginated, exogastrulated, orificed, evasive, invaded, stretched, relaxed, excited, distressed, tied, untied'.[32] Such language underscores that the body is not an essence but a process – a being continually written on, opened, and displaced.

The body gives us its realism – its concrete existence – precisely by being at and as its boundary. The realism of the body is not interiority or substance, but exscription: the fact that being takes place only at the border, in contact, in exposure, in the plural limits of sense.

Operating at multiple thresholds, the body is always alienated from itself – exposed to itself as other. Every body is constituted through its multiple limits by being exscripted. Each body divides and relates to itself and to others along such mobile and shifting borders. Rather than securing the fixed identity of a self outside time, the corpus records these multiple fault lines and discontinuities that aggregate into a process of temporal selving. The body never ceases to self – it continually inscribes and exscribes itself across its limits. Nancy writes that 'we need a corpus', not a logic, 'to account for this selving – an enumeration of an empirical logos, without transcendental reason, a list of gleanings, in random order and completeness, an ongoing stammer of bits and pieces.'[33]

For Nancy, the body as catalogue is 'a collection of pieces, bits, members, zones, states, functions. Heads, hands and cartilage, burnings, smoothnesses, spurts, sleep, digestion, goosebumps, excitation, breathing, digesting, reproducing, mending, saliva, synovia, twists, cramps, and beauty spots. It's a collection of collections, a corpus corporum, whose unity remains a question for itself'.[34] This inventory is not poetic excess but a philosophical gesture: a refusal of the metaphysical fantasy of organic unity. The corpus is plural, dispersed, empirical, and contingent – a realism grounded in exposure rather than essence.

The realism of *Corpus* is not that of representation or correspondence, but of contact – a realism of exposure, where every being exists only through the spacing and touching that both connects and separates it from others.

Taken together, Nancy's thought in *Being Singular Plural* and *Corpus* articulates an ontology in which meaning, being, and realism are inseparable from plural exposure. Sense is not an ideal content but the event of touching and separation – the continual coming-into-relation of finite beings. The body, in this context, is the privileged site where this event of sense takes place: where being both encounters and exceeds itself. Every being is real precisely insofar as it is outside itself, at the border where it meets what it is not. This 'reinvented realism' is therefore a realism of relation without fusion, an ontology in which the world consists not of substances or essences but of singular pluralities – beings in touch, coexisting at their limits, sharing in the endless circulation of sense.

Interestingly, in Bacon's 1984 interview, Sylvester puts it to him that Giacometti understands the living presence he tries to paint as an attempt to trap the *gaze* of the person – which Bacon rejects by arguing that the face, as well as the body, is made up of *infinitely more parts* than just the gaze:

> I don't think it's just the gaze. There's all your flesh, your skin… you've got your nose, your mouth, your teeth, your tongue, your everything, your lips.[35]

Bacon's own sense of a shifting visceral plurality, and his rejection of an essentially unified and fused unity of something like Giacometti's sense of 'the gaze', definitely places him into proximity with Nancy. [fig. 52]

'Disfiguration' – Nancy and Bacon

In the short text on Bacon called 'Disfiguration', Nancy and Ferrari write in direct reference to the painting *Study for Nude* (1951), which they credit as 'one of Bacon's first nudes'.[36] [fig. 3], [fig. 15]

Nancy and Ferrari begin by discussing the revolutionary photographic work of Eadweard Muybridge and Étienne-Jules Marey, and argue that it is largely thanks to their chronophotographic work that a new form of realism (a new *photographic realism*) emerges where 'the enigmatic relation that exists between figure and time, that is, the problem of a figure's movement and the way in which it is in motion, becomes fundamental and evident.'[37] Despite having a significant influence on Degas and being at the heart of Futurism and Cubism, 'probably only with Bacon…was Muybridge's heritage really taken up, thought all the way through, and thereby re-invented.'[38] With Bacon's painting it is as if in moving, the figure has become dissociated from itself, leaving only a *trace* of itself at each point of touch in the space being traversed. The figure is reduced/alienated (exscripted), to, as Bacon describes it, a 'trace of human presence', as if human presence always only gives itself as a *trace* or a *collection* of traces. For Bacon, it is no longer possible – in contrast with Muybridge – to put this figure in focus, to somehow freeze it in motion (via photography) and give a figure in movement a unified and integral form. 'There is no longer any need for sequence to set it into motion', Nancy and Ferrari write, 'because the figure itself is movement.'[39] The gesture in Muybridge is reversed. Liberated from cognitive or illustrative obligations previously explored and developed, the figure now moves differently from photography within the space of painting. Its movement is that of traces of fragmentary touches and withdrawals that simultaneously connect and separate it from itself and its borders in time. For Bacon there no longer is any 'natural realism' to be legitimately pursued in painting the figure. The 'game' must be 'deepened'.[fig. 4], [fig. 5]

For Nancy and Ferrari, in Bacon's early figurative paintings, the painter assumes and then thoroughly reinvents the photographic realism of Muybridge by reconceiving the figure's relationship to time. The figure in Bacon's paintings alienates itself from its natural, proper, photographic form – it exscripts itself – as it moves through space, entering another register of spatial and temporal relation within painting. In this passage from photography to paint, the body leaves only a series of traces of itself: reduced, stretched, spaced, thickened, and distorted into a collection of temporal residues. The figure is not presented as a stable or continuous identity but as a series of coagulated and inchoate marks – an assemblage of traces that visualise the body's confrontation with time.

Bacon's painting, according to Nancy and Ferrari, remains figurative only insofar as it shows 'the movement that a body completes in order to become a figure', the process 'through which a naked body, in movement, succeeds in shattering the clichés of the Human Figure and exposes it to the extremes of time, to birth, and to death'.[40] Bacon's practice becomes an 'infinite study' of finitude in painting – an endless series of repetitions, reductions, and disfigurations by which he seeks to let naked reality show itself. The painter's task is to compel the real to appear, to force the figure to give itself over to time, exposure, and transformation.

In this nudity, a reinvented realism emerges – one irreducible to any traditional realism or logic of representation. The real is not something fixed and available (outside time) to be transposed into a representational form or reproduced photographically; rather, the real is realised in painting, as the figure is exposed to finitude and spacing, continually unfolding as a plurality of singular traces. Bacon's figures are always in the process of disfiguring themselves: rupturing, folding, and undoing their apparent stability. The painting reveals a realism grounded not in depiction but in sustained deformation – a realism of contact, distortion, and exscription:

It is really the material of the nude – of the body, which is no more human than animal – that, more forcefully than any other subject, allows the disfiguring of figuration in order to make a figure and its movement appear. The pictorial gesture is skinned, stripped, of all narrative, anatomical, classificatory, semantic, symbolic, or sanctifying intent. What appears is the simple presence of the real, its figural side: the nudity of a body.[41] [fig. 24], [fig. 25]

Bacon's invocation of the 'graph' can be understood as precisely his own articulation of this practice – a way of describing how he manipulates and distorts the fixity of the figure through processes of spacing, folding, and tracing. Crucially, for example, it is an approach amenable to the current understanding of how Bacon utilised photographs in his paintings.[42] This stands in stark contrast to Deleuze's reading of Bacon's diagram as a 'catastrophic' system of manual accidents and chance encounters. Nancy's understanding of Bacon's disfiguration reveals, by contrast, a form of deliberate deconstruction: what Bacon himself called the 'execution of detail'. Through repetitive, experimental acts of reduction, folding, and distortion, Bacon propagates movement and disturbance within the figure. The body's 'proper fixity' and 'spatiotemporal continuity' are not undone through chaos or accident but through the touching movements of exscription: tracing, spacing, folding, repetition, layering, and grafting. Each gesture is a deliberate articulation of sense – a painterly thinking of finitude, through which Bacon, like Nancy, redefines realism as the exposure of being at its limit. As Nancy and Ferrari observe, 'painting is precisely the praxis at the heart of which the real realises itself by becoming a figure exposed to time.'[43]

Bacon's painting performs, in visual form, what Nancy's ontology of sense and exscription articulates in thought. The painted figure, like the body in *Corpus*, exists only through its exposure to 'the excess of time',[44] through the plural and fragmentary touches that constitute its finitude. In Bacon's hands, the canvas becomes the surface upon which this ontology of fragmentary touch takes place: a field of contact where sense both emerges and withdraws. The figure is exscribed – cast outside itself – as it encounters time, motion, and decay, and in doing so it reveals that the real is nothing other than this very movement of exteriorisation. Bacon's realism is not one of representation or resemblance but one of exposure: a realism of the limit, of separation-touch, where the body, as painting, comes into contact with its own dissolution. Bacon's 'infinite study of finitude' coincides with Nancy's reinvented realism – a realism that thinks of the real not as presence or substance, but as the ceaseless spacing, touching, and disfiguring through which being continually comes to sense: [fig. 28]

This is the nudity of an art in which the true nature of all realist art emerges: the real is never a given; the real is realised. Painting is precisely the praxis at the heart of which the real realises itself by becoming a figure exposed to time. And because of this exposure to the excesses of time, each figure...is always in the process of disfiguring itself. The restlessness of time sets atremble the immobility that reigns in the mirror of the representation and propagates movement there. After this shock, after this rupture of spatiotemporal continuity, one can use the term figure only for this form (of life) that, stripped of everything, accepts the suspension of its proper fixity, its impassibility, and exposes itself to the continual disconfiguration of itself, to the continual exceeding of the body in relation to the self that is the body's self. Only then can the act and the naked body become figure and realise themselves.[45] [fig. 18]

What Nancy's work ultimately suggests, more broadly, is the extent to which Bacon's paintings of bodies can themselves be approached as a corpus – a painted catalogue of the body's inflections, openings, penetrations, 'twists, spasms, wounds, folds, reflections, tensions, contractions, expansions, eruptions, gatherings, excretions, livings, and dyings'.[46] In this sense, Bacon's work enacts what Nancy calls the exscription of the body: the process by which the body continually writes itself outside itself 'on the surface of the canvas, right at the skin',[47] dislocating and redistributing its own limits. The painted body is not an image of unity but a collection of singularities, a catalogue of contiguities in which sense and matter touch at multiple points of separation. [fig. 38]

In this light, the 'graph' that Bacon describes in his interviews is not simply the random incursion of chaos or catastrophe, as Deleuze's interpretation suggests, but the painterly operation of exscription: the systematic, mark-by-mark displacement of bodies, organs, and parts into adjacent, touching spaces; the gradual folding, twisting, and spacing of corporeal sense. Bacon's practice embodies the execution of detail Nancy attributes to the realist gesture of exscription – the slow building of a corpus as a new realism, the mark-by-mark alienation and distortion of extreme *points* of sense rather than its destruction by chance and accident.

In this way, Bacon's canvases constitute 'a whole corpus of images stretched from body to body – local colours and shadows, fragments, grains, areolas, lumules, nails, hairs, tendons, skulls, ribs, pelvises, bellies, meatuses, foams, tears, teeth, droolings, slits, blocks, tongues, sweat, liquors, veins, pains, and joys, and me, and you'.[48] Through this catalogue of bodily traces, Bacon's painting performs the very movement Nancy identifies as the realism of exposure: a realism grounded in the exscription of the body, in the ceaseless articulation of fragmented touch and separation through which being – and painting – continually comes to sense.

1 David Sylvester, *The Brutality of Fact: Interviews with Francis Bacon 1962-1979*, 3rd edn. (London: Thames & Hudson, 1987).

2 The definition of the word illustration is 'visual explanation', a diagram that makes something clear. Etymologically it is derived from the Latin 'illustrationem' - a vivid representation in writing, literally an enlightening, from 'in' + 'lustrare' - 'to make bright', to 'illuminate'.

3 Ibid., p. 28.

4 Ibid., p. 56.

5 Ibid., p. 179.

6 Gilles Deleuze, *Francis Bacon: The Logic of Sensation*, trans. Daniel W Smith (London: Continuum, 2003).

7 For a more detailed account of this see Darren Ambrose, 'Deleuze's Bacon: Automatism and the Pictorial Fact', in *Francis Bacon: Critical and Theoretical Perspectives*, ed. Rina Arya (Bern: Peter Lang AG, 2012).

8 For a more detailed account of this see *Deleuze On Painting: Courses, March – June 1981* (Minneapolis: University of Minnesota Press, 2025), especially Lecture 1 on 'Catastrophe and Diagram': 'The diagram functions as a kind of cleanup zone that creates catastrophe on the painting, that is, erasing all the previous cliches, even if they were only virtual.' (p. 24)

9 Ibid.

10 A graph is a diagram with lines used to show the relationship between two things, often to show the changes in some quantity. It is from the Greek 'graphos' – meaning writing – from 'graphe', 'writing' - 'to write, express by written characters'; 'to represent by lines drawn'.

11 David Sylvester, *Francis Bacon: L'Art De L'impossible: Entretiens Avec David Sylvester*, 2 vols., trans. Michel Leiris and Michael Peppiatt (Geneva: Editions d'Art Albert Skira, 1976).

12 Deleuze, *Francis Bacon: Logique de la sensation*, (Paris : Editions de la Difference, 1981), Vol. 1, p. 65. Diagram, from the Greek 'digramma' – a geometric figure, that which is marked out by lines – 'diagraphein' – to mark out by lines, delineate – from 'dia' – meaning 'across', 'between', 'through' + 'graphein' – meaning 'write', 'mark', 'draw', 'description of', originally to 'scrape', 'scratch', 'carve'. A diagram is a symbolic representation of information using visualisation techniques. A graphic design that explains rather than represents, especially a drawing that shows arrangements and relations (as of parts).

13 Deleuze, op. cit., p. 100.

14 There is an irony here regarding Deleuze's comment at the beginning of his chapter on the 'diagram' in *The Logic of Sensation*, that 'We do not listen closely enough to what painters have to say.' (p. 99).

15 As Ben Ware has observed, 'Deleuze's reading has now become the hegemonic philosophical approach to Bacon.' (Ben Ware, 'Looking the Negative in the Face: Modernist Painting After Affect' in *Francis Bacon: Painting, Philosophy, Psychoanalysis* (*Francis Bacon Studies* Vol. II) (London: Thames & Hudson and The Estate of Francis Bacon, 2019), p. 156, note 24.

16 Jean-Luc Nancy & Federico Ferrari, *Being Nude: The Skin of Images* (New York: Fordham University Press, 2014).

17 Jean-Luc Nancy, *The Birth to Presence* (Stanford, Calif.: Stanford University Press, 1993).

18 Jean-Luc Nancy, *Portrait* (New York: Fordham University Press, 2018).

19 Jean-Luc Nancy, *The Muses* (Stanford, Calif.: Stanford University Press, 1997).

20 Jean-Luc Nancy, *A Finite Thinking* (Stanford, Calif.: Stanford University Press, 2003).

21 Jean-Luc Nancy, *Corpus*, trans. Richard A. Rand (New York: Fordham University Press, 2008).

22 Jean-Luc Nancy, *The Sense of the World* (Minneapolis: University of Minnesota Press, 2008), p. 7.

23 See Martin Heidegger's *Being and Time,* trans. John Macquarrie & Edward Robinson (London: SCM Press, 1962).

24 Jean- Luc Nancy, *Being Singular Plural* (Stanford, Calif.: Stanford University Press, 2000), p. 30.

25 Jean-Luc Nancy, *The Inoperative Community,* (Minneapolis: University of Minnesota Press, 1991), p. 35.

26 Nancy, *Being Singular Plural*, op. cit., p. 82.

27 Nancy, *Corpus*, op. cit., p. 5.

28 Nancy, *Being Singular Plural*, op. cit., p. 97.

29 Nancy, *Corpus*, op. cit., p. 12. Corpus is from the Latin word 'corpus', meaning the body. Also a collection of writing; a body of work; the main body, section, or substance. The names of body parts. The main body of mass of a structure. Synonyms include collection; catalogue; compilation; aggregation.

30 Ibid., p. 13.

31 Ibid., p. 23. The word 'exscription' was invented by Nancy.

32 Ibid., p. 14.

33 Ibid., p. 17.

34 Ibid., p. 14.

35 Francis Bacon in Martin Harrison, 'Lost Words: Unpublished Bacon' in *Francis Bacon Retrieved: Lost Words/New Writing* (*Francis Bacon Studies* Vol. V) (London: Thames & Hudson and The Estate of Francis Bacon, 2025), p. 123.

36 There is the earlier nude painted in 1949, *Study of the Human Body* (1949) (CR-49-08), and there are two other 'nude' paintings by Bacon executed earlier in 1950, *Study for a Figure* (1950) (CR-50-03) and *Painting* (1950) (CR-50-06).

37 Nancy and Ferrari, op. cit., p. 23. Marey's and Muybridge's chronophotography was a technique developed for capturing a number of phases of a figure's movement in time and space.

38 Ibid., pp. 23-24.

39 Ibid., p. 24.

40 Ibid.

41 Ibid., p. 25. Note Nancy's reference to Jean-Francois Lyotard's notion of the 'figural' to evoke the disruptive power of Bacon's Figures. See J-F. Lyotard, *Discours, figure* (Paris: Klincksieck, 1971), in English as *Discourse, Figure*, trans. Antony Hudek & Mary Lydon (Minneapolis: University of Minnesota Press, 2019).

42 For a more detailed account of how Bacon handled and utilised photographs as part of a pictorial strategy of folding, tracing, incorporation and disfiguring, see M. Harrison, *In Camera: Francis Bacon – Photography, Film and the Practice of Painting* (London: Thames & Hudson, 2005), Marcel Finke, *Prekäre Oberflächen: Zur Materialität des Bildes und des Körpers am Beispiel der künstlerischen Praxis Francis Bacons* (Berlin: Deutscher Kunstverlag, 2015) and Katharina Gunther, *Francis Bacon: In the Mirror of Photography - Collecting, Preparatory Practice and Painting* (Berlin: De Gruyter, 2022).

43 Nancy and Ferrari, op. cit., p. 24.

44 Ibid.

45 Ibid.

46 Nancy, *Corpus*, op. cit., p. 155.

47 Nancy and Ferrari, op. cit., p. 24.

48 Nancy, Ibid. p. 121.

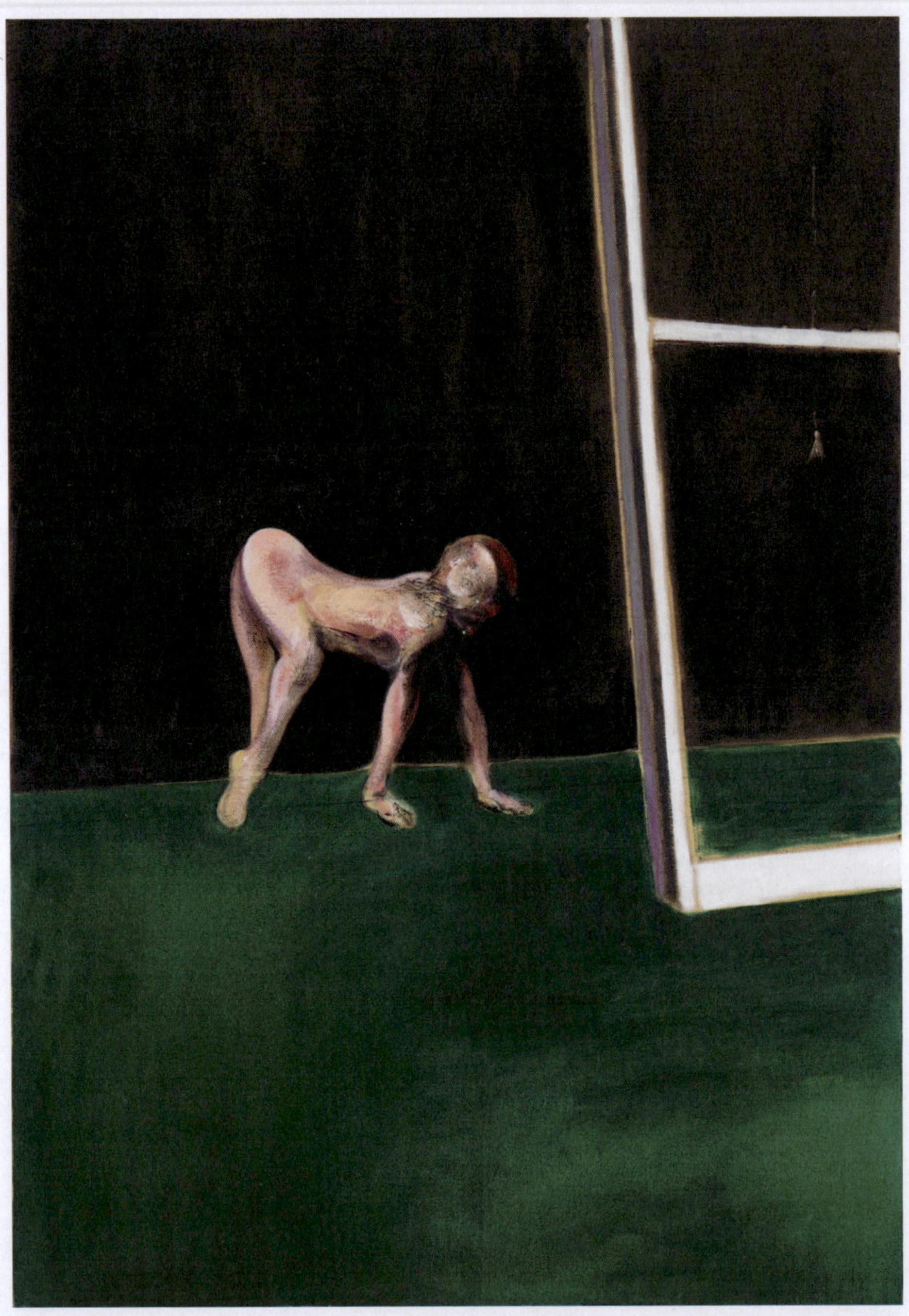

fig. 4   *Paralytic Child Walking on all Fours (from Muybridge)*, 1961   **24**

CREATIVE MUTILATION: OF MONSTERS AND MILIEUX

Joan Copjec

Flesh

Back to the camera, shoulders jutting back and forth, a young woman runs up a street only to be halted mid-run by two members of the Komiteh, the religious Iranian police force founded after the revolution, charged with patrolling the behaviour of citizens and forcing their adherence to fundamentalist dictates. Pulling up beside her in a police van, one of the men sternly admonishes the young woman and orders her to desist from her inappropriate behaviour. Set in Tehran, this scene from the graphic, autobiographical film, *Persepolis* (Marjane Satrapi, 2007), displays the sadistic relish with which formerly powerless men were suddenly authorised to clamp down hard, especially on women, who flouted the codes of modesty. This young woman – caught *in flagrante*, caught in other words, 'running like a girl' – is taken aback by the reprimand and stares uncomprehendingly at the officers as if to demand an explanation.[1] She is given one: 'When you run, your ass jiggles; it's immodest,' the man in charge responds, registering through his choice words the depth of his revulsion.

The film is filled with humour, some of which is self-deprecating, but its primary target is the men who are depicted as snot-nosed, stupidly self-serving, and sadistic. In the scene above the words *ass* and *jiggle* redound on the man who utters them; they expose his puerile vulgarity. The humour of the scene stems not solely from its own visual and verbal logic, but also from an association it evokes, wittingly or unwittingly. *Persepolis* moves back and forth between Paris and Tehran as it follows the exile and return home of the female protagonist, who becomes culturally disoriented. As does the viewer, who cannot help discerning in the words of the crude officer another source of humour. For, despite their lack of philosophical refinement, they sound eerily similar to others penned by Jean-Paul Sartre. All transpires as if the crude officer were ventriloquising the following passage from *Being and Nothingness*:

> The *obscene* appears when the body adopts postures [that] entirely strip it of its acts and...reveal the inertia of the flesh. The sight of a naked body from behind is not obscene. But certain involuntary

waddlings of the rump are obscene. This is because it is...only the legs which are acting for the walker, ...the rump [on the other hand] is like an isolated cushion...carried by the legs and...balanced by obedience to the laws of weight. It cannot be justified by the situation; on the contrary, it [the rump] is entirely destructive of any situation since it has the passivity of a thing and since it is made to rest like a thing upon the legs. Suddenly it is revealed as an unjustified facticity; it is *de trop* like every contingent...it is naked even if material covers it, for it no longer shares in the transcendence-transcended of the body in action.[2]

The difference between the non-obscene naked body and the obscene waddling rump relies on the assumption that merely being unclothed does not in itself expose a body's flesh for a body is robed at birth in a grace that veils it. Grace is an obscure supposition: it constitutes and makes visible the body's freedom, its ability to transcend outside forces such as gravity, a fractured foot, or disruptions of the digestive tract.

It is from Bergson that Sartre inherited the idea that 'the graceful act, insofar as it reveals the body as a precision instrument, furnishes [us] at each instant with [a] justification for existing.'[3] Flesh disappears when intentional consciousness turns the body into a honed instrument. Thus, 'the supreme coquetry and supreme challenge of grace is to exhibit the body unveiled, with no clothing, with no veil except grace itself. The most graceful body is the naked body whose acts enclose it with an invisible garment.'[4] In Sartre's view, naked dancers and athletes provided ideal illustrations of this transcendence of their flesh.

One can imagine media theorists wanting to add Eadweard Muybridge's photographs of nude men and women engaged in a variety of graceful activities to Sartre's list. If these photographs do not strike observers as lewd, it is because – one might say, following Sartre – the human figures in them assume the 'supreme challenge of grace' by veiling their bodies in purposeful action. The various objects of sport, industry, and domesticity – dumbbells, spades, saws, hammers, water jugs – are all props of these actions. In her study of Muybridge's photographs, however, Linda Williams noted long ago that there is a difference between the male and female figures pictured in them. For, despite the fact that they are engaged in similar activities, the women do not appear to be as fully absorbed in their actions as the men. Often the women seem to be distracted by other concerns, such as the need to support their breasts while running. This protective gesture against 'jiggling' has, however, no parallel in the photographs of walking or running men, who remain completely oblivious – as Williams duly notes – to their 'bouncing genitals'.[5] As we watch the women in Muybridge's photographs struggling to hold onto their grace while they perform their various tasks, we cannot help being reminded of Sartre's argument.

Let us pause here to say that this essay is only obliquely about Sartre and his conception of grace's relation to freedom. Its primary concern is Francis Bacon, who was himself keenly interested in Muybridge's photographs – though not in grace. Several of his paintings cite Muybridge by name in their titles. Two prime examples are *The Paralytic Child Walking on All Fours (from Muybridge)* (1961) [fig. 4] and *After Muybridge – Woman Emptying a Bowl of Water and Paralytic Child on All Fours* (1965), [fig. 5] in which the child's rump sticks up conspicuously in the air. *De trop*, useless, a graceless, *paralytic* child. Neither a dancer nor an athlete, he. What is it that interested Bacon in these photographs and how is this interest manifest in his work? In countless interviews the painter shows no particular interest in what the figures in photographs are doing. His interest focuses on the apparatus itself; he speaks mainly about the seriality of the photographs and we find ample confirmation of this interest in the triptychs he often paints. It is apparent, however, that the painter's fascination with the inventor and his photo-graphic contraption was fundamental and went beyond this.

In *Francis Bacon: The Logic of Sensation* – perhaps the most erudite and influential reading of Bacon's work to date – Gilles Deleuze mentions the artist's fascination with Muybridge several times but his own interests lie elsewhere.[6] *The Logic of Sensation's* agenda is double; while offering a forceful analysis of Bacon's remarkable oeuvre, it seeks at the same time to rescue flesh from its association with unfreedom. While Sartre is never named, flesh appears prominently in Deleuze's argument, but this time it is in the flesh, as it were, no longer hidden by grace, nor by Levinas's alternative, a face. Bacon paints heads, Deleuze insists, stripped of any cover. (p. 6) In his introduction to the English edition of his *The Logic of Sensation*, Deleuze provides a useful sketch of his basic thesis:

> Bacon's bodies, heads, Figures are of flesh, and what fascinates him are the invisible forces that model flesh or shake it. [...] [Bacon attempts] to make... forces visible through their effects on flesh... There is, before anything else, a force of inertia that is of flesh itself: with Bacon, flesh, however firm, descends from bones; it falls...away from them.... What fascinates Bacon is not movement, but its effect on an immobile body.... [He aims] to make spasm visible. (p. xxix)

Visible in this sketch is Deleuze's determination to overturn Sartre's characterisation of flesh as inert in favour of a redefinition of it as a

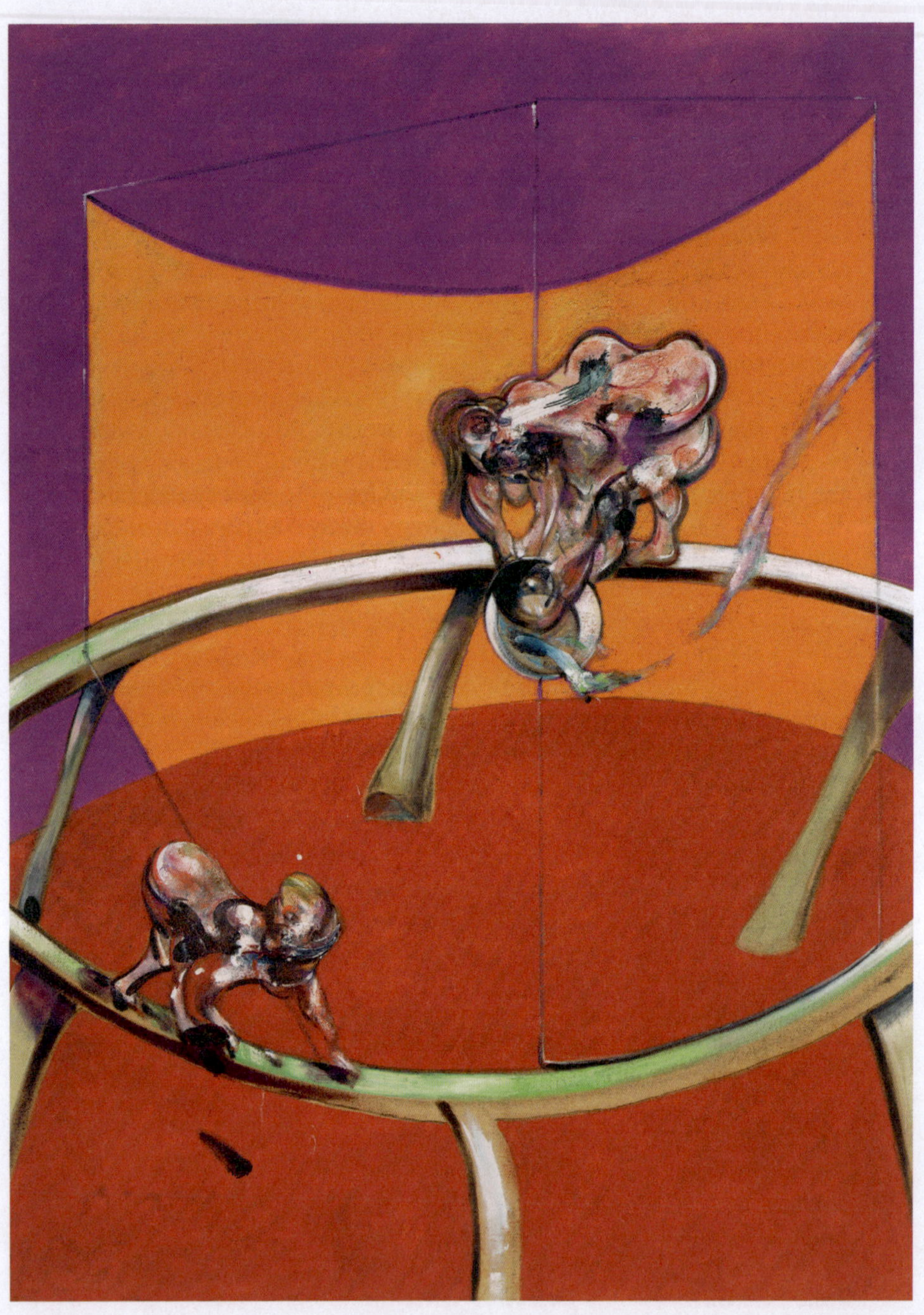

fig. 5 *From Muybridge 'The Human Figure in Motion':*
Woman Emptying a Bowl of Water / Paralytic Child Walking on All Fours, 1965 **28**

vitalising force of inertia. If flesh falls from bones in Bacon's paintings, it is not because some entropic force, such as gravity or a problem of the digestive tract, causes flesh to sag, to relax the tension needed to hold the Figure firm. We are prompted by Deleuze to imagine, instead, an *active* fall, performed while one's hands reach upward. Rather than hamper action, the fall of flesh heightens effort and tension. (p. 67) Beyond this obvious confrontation with Sartre one can detect others. Consider the following staccato sentence: 'Forces acting on the body, and "affective athleticism", a scream breath.' (p. 40) *"Affective athleticism"* plainly evokes and distances itself from the athleticism of the graceful dancers and athletes whom Sartre deemed to be ideal illustrations of a transcendence of the flesh. Far from transcending the flesh, affective athleticism, as Deleuze defines it, conveys the flesh. 'A vital emotion – sensation' – rifles through the body tearing off the face and leaving only flesh and nerves in its wake.

In order to redeem Sartre's negative conception of flesh, Deleuze has to infuse it with tension, make it tremble, enliven it. *Sensation* is the term Deleuze gives to the invisible source of this infusion. Invisible, as it is, sensation makes itself known only through the effects it has on the Figures – the tremblings, rhythms and distortions that save them from becoming frozen in a stasis. The Figures are what sustain, or hold together in an unstable form, the violent assaults of sensation. They bear the brunt of the rhythmic assaults of sensation without giving way to complete demolition. A problem arises, however, with the term *sensation,* which, along with other violent terms that orbit it, smacks of sensationalism. Deleuze is aware of this and makes a point of disentangling the two terms. Sensation does not illustrate anything outside itself, but simply 'becomes real'. In other words, the '*cruelty* that is linked to it is linked [not]...to the representation of something horrible, 'not to a scenario of cruel behaviour', but to 'nothing other than the action of forces upon the body'. (p. 40)

Deleuze makes reference to an exchange between Bacon and Sylvester in which Bacon insists that his concerns lie not in the nature of feelings expressed in any given image, but in the nature of the image as such. Deleuze endorses Bacon's stance while reemphasising his own view: 'If we presuppose an ambivalence in the Figure itself, it would refer to feelings the Figure would experience in relation to represented things...to a narrated story. But there are no feelings in Bacon: there are only affects.' (p. 35)

The statements of Bacon and Deleuze are clarifying. To pose the question of the image's function is to suggest that it has one and does not merely represent an already existing reality beyond it. And the distinction between feelings and affect (which is, as Deleuze indicates, synonymous with sensation) is critical. Affect, anxiety, is not prompted by external objects (snorting horses, for example) but by an internal, non-objectifiable object and it does not deceive, but is a matter of certainty. While these valid points justify the distinction between Figures and figuration – that is, Deleuze's argument that Bacon's Figures are isolated from any visual or narrative environment in which they would be situated and defined – it does not, to my mind, justify the claim that the Figures are isolated. Nor does it justify Deleuze's contention that the disfigured Figures in Bacon's paintings can only be seen as monsters 'from the point of view of figuration .... [but] from the point of view of the Figures themselves these are only rhythms.'(p. xxxiii)

Gaze, Mouth, Scream: Views from the Side of Psychoanalysis

While Lacan never offered a reading of Bacon's paintings directly, he dealt with several issues central to them. He noted, for example, that at traumatic moments there emerges in the visible field an object he refers to as a *gaze*. Significantly, he introduces this concept in response to 'one of the most brilliant passages of *L'Etre et le Neant*.'[7] For Lacan as for Sartre, the gaze is not an object that is actually seen; but one that is known only through its effects. It is something *imagined* in response to a disturbance that triggers it: a rustling of leaves, footsteps in the corridor, for example, whatever serves as of proof of the existence of others outside the subject. Lacan, however, de-psychologises Sartre's conception of the imagination, claiming that the subject responds to the *real*, to an objective glitch or hole in the world outside. To imagine is here is to become alert to something that cannot be seen.

Other crucial important differences follow. In *Being and Nothingness* the encounter of the subject with the gaze of another induces shame in the subject, who is thereby reduced to a mere body, a pile of *inert flesh*. Here the split is conceived as occurring between the gaze of the other and the subject subjected to it and who is thereby stripped of his freedom. Lacan regards the split differently and explains it thus: 'I propose that the interest the subject takes in *his own split* is bound up with that which determines it – namely, a privileged object, which has emerged from some primal separation, from some *self-mutilation* induced by the very approach of the real, whose name, in our algebra, is the *object a*.'[8]

In Sartre's scenario, it is a voyeur crouched while looking through a keyhole who is caught off guard by the gaze. Lacan does not allow this detail to slip by, but points out that the pose alerts us to the voyeur's *desire*. There is something the voyeur desires, aches to see through the keyhole, but cannot see. For what the encounter with the gaze does is expose the voyeur's sense of auto-conception, of self-appropriation, as merely an illusion.

One sees how close the Lacanian scenario of the encounter with the gaze comes to the description Deleuze offers of Bacon's Figures, mouths wide open, bombarded by sensation. In each case the Figure is mutilated, forced to bear a violent inner tension. Forced to cry out. Yet this is not the final word in Lacan's telling, for affect often functions as a prelude to desire and/or courage. Anxiety, the certainty of our not-knowing, produces a 'state of emergency in life' to which the subject responds with a force commensurate to the force of the blow. Abruptly confronted with the *certainty* of our non-knowing, one does not inevitably collapse.

In a recent essay, 'Of a Gaze, The Strangeness', Jacques-Alain Miller returns to the question of the gaze and its relation to flesh to distinguish the position of Lacan less from Sartre's than from that of his phenomenologist friend, Merleau-Ponty (who, like Deleuze, attempted to rescue flesh from the devaluation to which Sartre submitted it). Miller points to a problem he perceives with German psychology and phenomenology in general: both discount the dimension of enunciation. As a result, their 'accounts of experience [appear] totally innocent and harmless'.[9] Thus, when something seems to go awry in perception, phenomenologists are left with no other option than to 'find a cripple' or a 'monster' to account for the problem. Misperception becomes the fault of a damaged perceiver. Psychoanalysis avoids this error because it embeds the subject, the instance of enunciation, not outside but within the perceptual field. The placement of the subject within the enunciation leads to – and accounts for – the 'vacillation in [the subject's] relationship to perceptive reality, [it creates] a dissonant tone, far from accord and harmony.'[10] As Miller puts it, in psychoanalysis, 'the monsters are us.' The perceiving subject, as such, is a monster and perception is never innocent.

Miller's essay lends credence to and enhances Deleuze's reading in ways that are apparent, most notably in its implied dismissal of Sartre's devalorisation of flesh. But it also buttresses my own reluctance to accept Deleuze's twin injunctions against 1) setting Bacon's Figures in a space, since this would jeopardise their singularity; or 2) embellishing or 'imaginarising' the Figures by alluding to them as monsters, when they are, in fact, 'rhythms and nothing else'. If Deleuze forbids the use of the term *monster* it is because he regards it as merely descriptive. And if monsters are not reducible to this...?

Zoopraxiscopes and the Vitality of Error

Before confronting these points of contention directly, it will be useful to take a quick tour through questions of technology, beginning with the photographs of Muybridge's photographs with which Bacon was fascinated. In this he was not alone; Degas, Duchamp, Sol LeWitt, and Hollis Frampton and Marion Faller, among other artists were also highly influenced by these proto-cinematic images. We noted earlier that Bacon's tendency to construct series of paintings was inspired by the stop-action series of Muybridge's photographs. The gaps between the images are critical. Unlike Étienne-Jules Marey, to whom he is often compared, Muybridge was uninterested in closing the gaps between the still photographs in order to create the illusion of a flowing river of time or a continuous space. Jonathan Crary accurately describes Muybridge's agenda as:

> a dismantling of the apparent continuities of movement and of time, …his work is one instance of a larger decoupling of empirical verisimilitude from a 'reality effect.'[...] No relations of causal necessity link the positions and sections that are presented in sequence, only an imprecise and disjunct sense of before and after. [...] The breakthrough of Muybridge's work in 1878 was its deployment of machinic high speeds for the creation of perceptual units beyond the capacities of human vision, and their subsequent abstract arrangement outside the terms of any subjective experience.[11]

The pre-cinematic apparatus Muybridge invented – and to which he gave the name *zoopraxiscope* – was a rotating glass disc on which the photographs turned around in a circle. We actually see this apparatus in several of Bacon's paintings, including the two we mentioned earlier: *Paralytic Child Walking on All Fours* [fig. 4] and *Woman Emptying a Bowl of Water and Paralytic Child Walking on All Fours*. [fig. 5] We should also state at this point that Muybridge's photographs were not limited to nude men and women engaged in activities that absorbed them fully or partially. It is well known that Muybridge photographed running horses and other animals. And, finally, but significantly – though this is a lesser known or commented upon fact – he also photographed disabled people, not unlike Bacon's paralytic child.[12] Physiological and morphological monsters swirled around on his zoopraxiscope with some regularity. As its name implies, this apparatus gave spectators *a glimpse of life at work.*

Crary seems almost automatically to assume that the abstract components of the Muybridge machine – the gridded or black backgrounds he used and the undisguised breaks in movement – threatened modern life by packaging it into mechanised bits. The result: assembly lines to which living beings became tied and the reduction of temporality to clock time. While one cannot deny that capitalist forms of abstraction had begun to threaten modern life, it must be acknowledged that modern technology *adds* to life by injecting new *ideas* into life. Deleuze emphasises the second alternative; he contends that one of his goals in *The Logic of Sensation* is to pay homage to Bacon as an artist who 'in the name of an intense life, can call for a more intense life.[...] an increasingly powerful Figure of life.' (p. 53) Fine; but we must remember that life is a contentious concept and that Bergson, one of its most famous champions in the modern era regarded abstraction as a threat to life, even as he began to recognise the necessity of technology, 'means other than life', as necessary for the prolongation of life.

A number of questions emerge in the interviews and elsewhere regarding the difference between abstract art and figurative art (or: representation). Bacon is unwilling to place himself on one side or the other, nor to acknowledge that the difference is worth contemplating. He sees his own work as a kind of solecism, as an art of painting in an age of modern technology and is mindful of the grammatical oddities his work creates *per force*. Yet he regards his work, as participating, nevertheless, in the era in which it is made. He admits to relying on photographs of the people he paints either exclusively or along with his own eyes. To understand why he adopts this strategy, it is enough to attend to his response to one of Sylvester's questions about his interest in photographs. Bacon responds, 'I think one's sense of appearance is assaulted all the time by photography and by film. So, when one looks at something, one's not only looking at it directly, but...through the assault that has already been made by photography and film'.[13] *Assault* appears twice in the response, emphasising the capacity of photographs to create a surplus effect unavailable to our naked eyes. 'Through the photographic image I find myself beginning to wander into the image and unlock what I think of as its reality more than I can by looking at it [...] Photographs are not only points of reference; they're often triggers of ideas.'[14] One must not miss the two key points in this reply 1) Bacon 'wanders into' the images; he 'embeds [himself] not outside but *within* the perceptual field', to borrow the words of Miller cited earlier; and 2) the phrase often used to describe Bacon's artistic intent, to 'unlock sensation', is linked to what that intent produces: new ideas. Photographs do not lead necessarily to a deadening of life by capturing and stilling a part of it; on the contrary, they have the capacity to go beyond the inadequacies of our senses, to 'bring *life* to shadows'.[15]

Life. Not reality. The two pose different questions, but they have a relation which Lacan characterises succinctly: because of its precarious nature, 'reality...only manages to affirm itself at the margins'. And 'if reality is precarious, it is because life renders it so'.[16] When Bacon speaks to Sylvester of his desire to 'keep the vitality of the accident and yet preserve a continuity', he is effectively elaborating Lacan's argument.[17] For, if photographs allow us to see what we could not see without them, it is not because they function like a pair of glasses by allowing us to see what was there before we donned them. The photographs unlock a new reality that collides with the old one.

Phenomeno-technology

Along with a handful of other French philosophers, Gaston Bachelard is known for his forceful dismissal of the supposed conflict between the empirical and the conceptual, or between life and technology, as a chimera. He coined the hyphenated term, *phenomeno-technology,* to efface the hard break between technology and life, between the conceptual and the empirical. Bachelard puts it this way: 'A truly scientific phenomenology [...] takes its instruction from construction. Wonderworking reason designs its own miracles. Science conjures up a world, by means not of magic...but of rational impulses immanent to mind.... Scientific work makes rational entities real, in the full sense of the word.[18] For Bachelard and his colleagues, science and technology are materially engaged in bringing phenomena into the world. Electricity is a simple example. While electric phenomena are found in nature – in lightning and static electricity – we do not find there any stable, continuous current of electricity. We can no longer imagine life without it. Our everyday reality is aways already informed by thought.

Bachelard sometimes referred to his theory as 'applied rationalism' in order to distinguish it from the position of positivists who considered science to be purely objective. As Mary Tiles points out, Bachelard elaborated this theory at a time when scientific objectivity founded itself on a principled rejection of the knowing subject. He carved out a new path by formulating a principled rejection of his own: 'We have as our task to show that rationalism is in no way linked with the *imperialism* of the subject, that it cannot be formed in an *isolated* consciousness....Technological materialism corresponds essentially to a transformed reality, a reality which has received the human mark par excellence, the mark of rationalization.'[19] Rather than celebrating the death of the subject, as others were doing at the time, Bachelard insisted on its redefinition: a subject is *necessarily supposed*, that is: it is an inconspicuous but necessary part of the operation of reality. The subject cannot be situated above reality, as a transcendental subject, nor outside it as a mere observer, but only within it. This position, as Miller pointed out, is that of the subject as monster.

In keeping with this conception of the relation between abstraction and empirical reality, Bachelard and his colleagues rejected philosophy's status as the queen of the sciences. They charged it with a more modest mission: take up the issues that that emerged in the sciences.[20] But while Bachelard and others chose to focus on issues emerging in mathematics, physics and chemistry, Canguilhem chose to study biology: *the science of life*. This choice presented a different challenge than those faced by his colleagues. He formulated the nature of that challenge in a single line, 'The thought of the living must take from the living the idea of the living.'[21] If Descartes became one of his most frequent targets, it was because Canguilhem held this pre-eminent philosopher up as an exemplary proponent of the position he sought to overthrow. For, Descartes attempted to think the subject – a *living being* – on the model of machines. Canguilhem refrained from simply reversing the terms; instead, he argued that the terms *living beings* and *machines* did not constitute a simple opposition in which one or the other vied for, or attempted to retain, the upper hand. Like his colleagues he focused on the irresolvable tensions that bound the terms.

The Monster That Therefore I Am

From the volumes of Canguilhem's writings I have chosen to focus – not by chance – on a brief essay that seems at first improbable, dwelling as it does on a topic outside the concerns of biology and scientific reason in general. Canguilhem's essays and books usually offer accounts of the historical changes in biological concepts and practices: the reflex, biological cells, epistemological approaches to physiology, practices of animal experimentation, and so on. The essay I selected – which also provides a fascinating history of its subject from classical antiquity up until the present – focuses on monsters! Yes, monsters. Even Canguilhem admits – twice in the essay – that 'life is poor in monsters'.[22] It therefore comes as no surprise that the overwhelming majority of the monsters on which he comments are not drawn from life, but on fantastical creatures, products of the imagination. This prompts an obvious question: what do monsters have to do with the science of biology, with life itself? Behind this another question, one that has been waiting impatiently, begs to be addressed – what light does it throw on Bacon's paintings?

The essay, 'Monstrosity and the Monstrous', shifts back and forth in a complex manner between the two concepts named in the title. The essay's argument is that the two became entangled with each other in various ways throughout history. We can separate them, nevertheless, by providing basic definitions of each. *Monstrosity* is a matter of size and morphology; monsters tend to be over-large and/or misshapen. But Canguilhem is quick to insist that we must – and do – distinguish between the large size of a monster and that of an enormous boulder, say. An outsized boulder is judged to be so merely in metric terms; it is measurably larger than the average rock, yet we are not inclined to describe it as a monster. As Canguilhem puts it, there are 'no mineral' nor 'mechanical' monsters.[23] This point licenses Canguilhem's thesis: monstrosity situates itself exclusively in the domain of *biological life* and we, therefore, 'must include in the definition of the monster its nature as living being. The monster is a living being with negative value.'[24] The concept of the *monstrous,* on the other hand, belongs to the order of behaviour, of wrong doing, legally or socially defined. It is one's actions that can be labelled *monstrous.*

An interruptive comment: that these two terms are assumed not only to operate alongside each other, but also to become enmeshed, is not an observation mandated by the seemingly anecdotal topic of the monster. It emerges from a fundamental conviction Canguilhem took from Bachelard: life is inherently technical or: 'to live is to attach value to life's purposes and experiences; ...it is to prefer certain methods, circumstances and directions to others. Life is the opposite of indifference to one's surroundings.'[25] To speak of life as technical is to refuse to define what it *is* and to examine instead the various norms – the various ways or techniques – living beings invent for themselves.

This said, we can return to the point where we broke off: Canguilhem's claim is that a monster is 'a living being with negative value'. This claim does not rob but affirms the monster's value. Canguilhem begins by alluding to a grey area in the matter of size that presented itself at a specific historical moment when the gigantism of mythological giants came under scrutiny. Were these giants merely outsized humans or were they something else entirely, that is: monsters? This is how Canguilhem responds to the question: 'If man is defined by a certain limitation of forces and functions, then the man who, by his size, escapes these limitations is no longer a man. To say he is no longer one is also to say he still is one.'[26] Now, it is nearly impossible not to hear in this last statement an echo of Robert Antelme's striking proposition in *The Human Race,* 'He can kill a man, but he can't change him into something else'.[27] In the following paragraph Canguilhem seems to confirm our suspicion by mentioning a different writer who argued that what valorises living beings is 'their consistency as a species'.

The echo removes monsters from the realm of fairy tales or, as I am suggesting, from the realm of figuration. First, we are forced to face a concrete and horrific instance in which the monstrous became entangled with monstrosity, in the specific historical form of the Nazi death camps whose cruelties Antelme barely survived at the hands of those who wished to assure the consistency of the species by doing away with those who did not, in their estimation, belong to it. That the human species is not consistent over time – nor at any given moment – but disrupted by contingencies that produce differences – is a fact of life living beings do not wish to acknowledge. The precarious nature of reality is not easily tolerated. Antelme's stolid insistence that 'there is no ambiguity: we're still men, and we shall not end otherwise than as men' exposes the holocaust as a fantasy formed out of 'resistance to deformation and a struggle for the integrity of form'.[28] Yet, while he inserts these oblique allusions to give us a glimpse or what he refers to as 'radical fear', Canguilhem opens his essay in a mundane manner. He evokes our basic confidence – distilled from our experiences of 'seeing wild roses blooming on bushes, tadpoles turning into frogs, mares suckling foals' – in the fact that 'the same engenders the same'.[29] This confidence is so ingrained in us, he quietly points out, that any 'morphological divergence' or any 'appearance equivocal as to its species' breeds in us a 'radical fear'. The mundane nature of the experiences of continuity may not seem to justify the extreme nature of the effect caused by their being thrown into doubt, but Canguilhem is adamant on this point. The effect *is* radical. It strikes us at our core, for it teaches us that we may one day give birth to a monster. And, in fact, the tales of monsters concern precisely this. For mothers corrupt the lineage of the child, who descends not from the father but from her vivid imagination.

The definition of the monster as 'a living being with negative value' does not simply refer to its capacity to jolt us into awareness of life's vicissitudes. It is also formulated as a dismissal of Xavier Bichat's definition of life as 'the ensemble of forces that resist death'. What provoked Canguilhem's resistance is Bichat's dualism, his belief that the fundamental threat to life comes from outside life, from death. Is it not clear, however, that life is radically threated *immanently* – by life itself? This is so because life continuously delays, holds back, its own completion; it thus prevents subjects – living beings – from attaining any sort of harmony with themselves, with whom they once were or may become. *Life is constant de-completion as long as it is life*. We can never rest assured that life will continue in the same way. Is this not the point Miller, explicating Lacan, makes when he provocatively insists that the encounter with the gaze exposes the fact that 'monsters are us'? If the gaze disturbs our apprehension of ourselves, it is because it emerges from a place that is unlocatable, because experience is not foundation of knowledge. On this point Lacan agrees with Sartre, who argued that 'the look [gaze, in Lacan's terminology] cannot be looked at. As soon as I look in the direction of the look it disappears, and I no longer see anything but eyes.'[30] Because we cannot discern the point from which the gaze emanates, we cannot know what it sees in us. We are thus robbed of our placid understanding of ourselves and of what is on our horizon. Rejecting death as the primary threat to life, a threat that strikes only once and without offering any means of recovery, Canguilhem contends that the real threat is spawned by life itself. The term he uses to designate this peculiar threat – the *non-viable* – allows the threat to cling to the very thing it threatens.[31] One might also attribute to the term a temporal dimension, a prematurity, as in a 'non-viable fetus'. A life without a foundation. A life manifested without having undergone a process of ripening. The non-viable – the monster – refers to a life that teeters on the brink of destruction but also on the brink of reinvention. Canguilhem encourages this reading of the *non-viable* – when he reminds us that monsters have always, through the ages, provoked not only fear but also curiosity and fascination. 'The monstrous is the marvelous inverted, but it is marvelous nevertheless.' Canguilhem repeats a statement he made earlier in the essay, 'Life is poor in monsters', adding this time: 'The fantastic is a world.'[32]

In other words: life itself would be poor without these fantastic creatures. How to justify such a claim? We have already noted their heuristic value. By disappointing our confidence in the fact that 'the same engenders the same', these morphological failures alert us to the precarity of reality, even as they stir in us a horror of the unborn or unknown, of all that we cannot see coming. This look of horror is the very one we find in the open-mouthed, screaming figures in Bacon's paintings. Bacon's gaping mouths respond, as we claimed earlier, to Lacan's gaze, which does not see us as we are wont to see ourselves. I would thus agree, up to a point, with Deleuze's contention that Bacon's open mouths scream not at anything actual, but at 'the diabolical powers of the future knocking at the door'. (p. 51) I part ways with Deleuze, however, when he designates that future as death. Although, as he himself admits: 'This is all very curious.' (p. 51) Indeed! What is curious is the way Deleuze attempts to redefine death not as the all-too-predictable end of life we know it to be, but as an 'invisible force that life detects, flushes out, and makes visible through the scream'. (p. 40) This reformulation leads him – while speaking of artists such as Kafka and Beckett, as well as Bacon – wretched creatures all – to adopt the vocabulary of Canguilhem. For, Deleuze notes that these artists represent 'horror, mutilation, prosthesis [sic], fall, or failure [by erecting] indomitable Figures.' (p. 52) Are the latter not direct kin to Canguilhem's stubbornly *non-viable* monsters – seemingly without origin, a threat to the species – or, better, to the idea of the species as uniform? The second reason for the praise he heaps on these monsters follows directly from this. It concerns the importance Canguilhem attributes, as did Bachelard before him, to imagination. The place of imagination in the work of these thinkers merits a long discussion; all we can say here is that as a staunch enemy of positivists, Canguilhem was loath to dismiss the fantastic inventions of monsters throughout the centuries as wrought by naïve thinking as yet unschooled by rational science.

While we began by distinguishing monstrosity from the monstrous as a difference between irregular physical attributes and culpable acts, our analysis has shown that there is more to this distinction. After crediting the fantastic with the capacity to constitute a world, Canguilhem has this to say: 'It is here that the thorny question of the relation between monstrosity and the monstrous arises. They are two concepts from the same etymological stock… in the service of two forms of normative judgment – the medical and the juridical.'[33] Monstrosity is a matter of *medical* judgment. How so? If Canguilhem considers the monsters whose history he recounts to be a fitting topic for those engaged in medical practice and the science of biology it is for reasons similar to Freud's decision to abandon his belief in the tales of seduction reported to him by his hysterical patients, in order to take them *seriously as reminiscences*. The latter term refers to a different order of truth than that which is susceptible to verification or denial. Again, the importance of imagination for Canguilhem and for psychoanalysis is clear. It is not necessary that things exist for them to have consequences in the actual world. But Canguilhem is adding here a further point. He is claiming that for medical science to proceed properly – as a science of life – it must divest itself of the belief in '*medical* monsters'.

To understand his claim, we turn again to Bichat, who diagnosed the cause of disease as the result of a loss of harmony with the world outside the self. Canguilhem rejects this diagnosis on the grounds that it assumes the outside to be an objective exteriority to which a living being must conform. Bichat was only able to view diseased individuals as 'medical monsters' – that is: as objectively categorisable as monsters – because he used something situated outside life as a measure against which the individual struggles and is judged as healthy or sick. Here Canguilhem, never one to miss an opportunity to remind us that the science of biology is the science of life, insists that disease is not entirely reducible to physical-chemical mechanisms. The sick – like the well – must respond to their circumstances by inventing 'vital norms', that is to say: ways, or *techniques,* of living – in the face of life's uncertainties. While positivists hold all subjects to the same statistically calculated norm and hold out for a scientific eradication of life's uncertainties – a preposterous goal – the patients who walk into medical and psychoanalytic offices and clinics present themselves not as objects or generalities, but as unique living beings.

In one of his best-known essays, 'The Living and Its Milieu', Canguilhem develops an argument he made earlier against Bichat's conception of the world beyond the self.[34] I will highlight a few points crucial for my argument. The point made above – it is not medical judgment, relying *exclusively* on physiological data, that determines the patient's health, but the patient herself, who invents or fails to invent a viable relation to her milieu – is supported by a larger argument: if biologists must not lose sight of the fact that biology studies living beings, they must also keep in mind the fundamental distinction between facts and values.

In *The Normal and the Pathological*, Canguilhem cautions biologists that an inability to draw this distinction is tantamount to being 'unable to distinguish food from excrement. Certainly, a living being's excrement can be food for another living being but not for him. What distinguishes food from excrement is no physico-chemical reality but a biological value.'[35] The terms of this warning are meant to assure that it will not be forgotten. In 'The Living and Its Milieu', however, Canguilhem reverts to a milder phrasing, insisting that living beings are 'not indifferent' to the conditions in which life is possible for them. And yet, in the history he details of numerous contributions made in the debates regarding the relation between the living and their milieux, he pauses to underscore a crucial argument formulated by the French biologist, Jean-Baptiste Lamarck: if the environment acts on living beings it is only 'via the intermediary of need, a subjective notion implying a reference to a positive pole of vital values.'[36] *Need,* in this context, has the force of what we might call a judgment of taste, formulated this time, however, not in literal, visceral terms, yet bearing all the non-negotiable power it had not only for Lamarck but also for Freud. Lacan drew attention to this under-appreciated concept in his *Ethics* seminar:

> If Freud speaks of the reality principle, it is in order to reveal to us that from a certain point of view it is always defeated; it only manages to affirm itself at the margin. And this is so by reason of a kind of pressure...Freud calls [it] not 'vital needs'...*but die Not des Lebens*... An infinitely stronger phrase...Pressure, urgency... the state of emergency in life.[37]

Freud and Lacan line up, along with Canguilhem, on the side of Lamarck. Elsewhere, Canguilhem returns to this concept of need in order to clarify a crucial, and quite complex, definition of what it means to live: 'To live is to radiate; it is to organize the milieu from and around a central reference point that cannot be referred to without losing its original meaning.'[38] It is commonplace to imagine a milieu as a territory that wraps or curves around living beings. This holds true here: a central reference point commands the centre of the milieu it organises. Yet *from* and *radiates* add a lateral dimension as well; living beings extend themselves, step beyond themselves in order to enter into a milieu. In order to forestall an ego psychological reading of the relations he is attempting to sketch out, Canguilhem throws in a caveat against referring to the central point. Why? It can only be because to do so would imply that the living being – the central reference point – were 'pulling all the strings', which we know is untrue. For, this central point – a living being – does not act willingly, but on the urging of its 'vital values'. This reading is, in fact, confirmed at the end of the essay: If 'a center does not resolve into its environment... [if it] is not reducible to a crossroads of influences.... [it is because it is] an appreciation of values in relation to a need. And...a need is an irreducible, and thereby absolute, system of reference.'[39]

I have obviously embarked on this discussion of the milieu as a means of challenging Deleuze's characterisation of Bacon's Figures as isolated from any background. Between the Figures and the space that surrounds them there is, by Deleuze's account, no relation of any kind. According to this thesis – one might say – the space around the Figures 'does not map the space of a room or a landscape or a group of figures onto the space of a painting [...] if it maps anything, it maps the surface of the painting itself.' These spaces 'explicitly reject a narrative or sequential reading of any kind.'[40] While these words sound like they might have been lifted from *The Logic of Sensation,* they are actually taken from Rosalind Krauss's influential essay, 'Grids'. Deleuze wrote *The Logic of Sensation* at a time when art critics had begun to pay closer attention to the grid in order to respond to its ubiquitous appearance in the work of prominent artists. Among these were those artists cited earlier for their avid interest in Muybridge, whose photographs of galloping horses and striding men and women were shot against a gridded or black background. The various moving figures in the photographs were not shown to inhabit or traverse an actual terrain. The early and still dominant explanation for this curious deletion of backgrounds is that it introduced an abstract element, which permitted Muybridge and later artists to distance themselves from the derided ideology of artistic realism. The element of abstraction was associated with the camera itself, with this new technology that intervened in the real world and deposited there something foreign and abstract.

While neither Bacon nor Muybridge was interested in recording reality, my point is that this is not really the point. They both pushed the question of reality to the margins and focused instead on the question of life. Once this question is opened, the question of values, and thus of the milieu, begins knocking at the door, as many prominent biologists will tell you. Among these we have thus far mentioned only Lamarck; but another key figure, the German biologist Jakob von Uexküll, whose influence on French and German philosophers is considerable, must also be mentioned. Uexküll carefully distinguished between *Welt* (the universe of science), *Umgebung* (the banal geographical environment), and *Umwelt* (the milieu of behaviour proper to the living). It is the latter – and not the banal *Umgebung* – that is of interest for understanding what is at stake in Muybridge's photographs and Bacon's paintings. Here is how Canguilhem describes the relation between the *Umwelt* and living beings:

> The milieu of behavior proper to the living (*Umwelt*) is an ensemble of excitations...[but to] act on a living being, a physical excitation has not only to occur but also be noticed. Consequently, insofar as the excitation acts on the living being, it presupposes the orientation of the living being's interest; the excitation comes not from the object but from the living. [...] A living being is not a machine, which responds to excitations with movements, it is a machinist who responds to signals with operations.[41]

The robust theorisations of the milieu, that territory into which the living extend themselves and thereby become social beings, allow us to see beyond Deleuze's reading of Bacon's paintings. I am not implying that Deleuze is unaware of or disinterested in this question of the milieu, only that he overlooks it in *The Logic of Sensation*.[42] The assumption embedded in his argument is that the bare backgrounds in Bacon's paintings merely block or *displace banal geographical* settings. What it fails to contemplate, however, is that the empty or black backgrounds suggest an *Umwelt* or, in Canguilhem's terms, a milieu. My reading of the paintings is that Bacon's Figures, his monsters, are *not isolated*. In fact, it is through their fraught habitation in a milieu that they become monsters.

The central theme of the Figure's isolation is introduced on the first page of *The Logic of Sensation*. Deleuze points out that there is a round area or ring, a contour, that surrounds the Figures and isolates them from all else. He refers to these areas as 'places' or '*lieux*', almost as if to fend off the possibility of their being *milieux*. (p. 5) The round, oval, or curved areas often appear as furniture, chairs or beds, for example, that surround the Figures and yet, Deleuze adds, 'they do not consign the Figure to immobility... [but constitute] an operative field.' (pp. 5-6) What he does not say, nor even hint at, is that these contoured spaces take the shape of Muybridge's zoopraxiscope often visible in its original form in Bacon's paintings. Of course they do not consign the Figures to immobility; they are borrowed from that famous 'philosophical toy', that pioneering apparatus of motion studies, the zoopraxiscope. Two questions arise from this: 1) How does Muybridge's invention relate to the problematic of the milieu?; and 2) What is there to suggest that this problematic has any relevance to Bacon's 'operative field'?

I will address both questions while recalling upon earlier arguments. Canguilhem opposes the vitalist assumption that life and abstraction are at odds with each other. It is life itself that 'pulls all the strings', including those that produce technologies and abstract ideas. Knowledge is a *form* of life, not something that inevitably lags behind it. Abstract thought enables us to perceive possibilities we cannot see with our own eyes and to realise these possibilities in gadgets that function as new organs of perception. It is apparent from this that inventions are *not constrained by laws of adaptation*. Everything thus happens as if the relation between the individual and its milieu emerged as a theoretical concern as a result of the elimination of the contradiction between the empirical and the abstract.

As noted earlier, Crary argues that the black backgrounds and grids against which Muybridge's figures were photographed, interrupted their continuous movement and *severed the relations between foregrounds*. This promoted an automation of perception and a mechanisation of movement. That is, Muybridge's invention contributed to Taylorism.[43] Yet he confesses at one point that it is possible that these disruptive elements – black backgrounds and abstract grids – produced a 'flashing up' of novel intuitions. It is easy to detect in this another echo, this time of Walter Benjamin's reference to the 'dynamite of a split second' in his famous essay, 'The Work of Art in the Age of its Technological Reproducibility'. Rather than a deadening of life, these interruptions enabled possibilities unimaginable without them. Recently, film theorists have begun to uncover the connections between early cinematic apparatuses and biological conceptions of the milieu. As it turns out, Uexküll, whose work was known to Benjamin, was actively interested in the chronographic apparatuses of Muybridge and Marey which he used as research tools for the development of his theory of the *Umwelt*.[44]

We leave these investigations to others, but hold them in mind as we return to the artistic pursuits of Bacon. In response to a question posed to him by Sylvester, 'What do you think are the essential things that go to make an artist?' Bacon responds not in general terms, but with a list of his own peculiar passions, including a book he purchased which contained images of filters. Just filters, nothing else. What was it about them that fascinated Bacon? His answer: 'The way they were formed suggested all sorts of ways in which I could use the human body [which is] after all...a filter.'[45] Now, one of the concepts we associate with Benjamin is that of the stimulus shield which protected the psyche from the onslaught of stimuli produced by modern life. This concept not only evidences the rise in importance of the living/milieu conflict, it also makes room for the unconscious amid the smog of factories and the miles of assembly lines. Yet one should not confuse Benjamin's filtering operation with the one to which Bacon gestures. For, although both propose that individual beings do not respond to all stimuli coming from their milieu, Benjamin's filter *protects*, while Bacon's s*elects*.

To understand Bacon's answer to Sylvester's (rephrased) query – 'what is essential to you as an artist?' – one has to return to the crucial Lamarckian/Freudian concept of *die Not des Lebens* (vital need) and Canguilhem's gloss of it: it is not enough that stimuli occur, they have to be noticed. This insight did not have to be imparted to Bacon. He had it on his own. Throughout the interviews he states over and over in various ways that 'It's really a question in my case of being able to set a trap with which one would be able to catch the fact at its most living point. [...] suddenly there comes something which your instinct seizes on as being for a moment the thing you could begin to develop.'[46] When Canguilhem asserts that a living being is situated at the *absolute* centre of *its* milieu, the term *absolute* does not serve to pinpoint the position, but to qualify the nature of the centre, which is absolute, a vital need, as distinguished from needs. Needs are universal; they are the brute necessities required for sustaining the life of the species. Need, on the other hand, is an irreducible value that *compels* individual living beings to *select* or *seize* those facts that comport with their need. Need does not reveal itself as something other than an urgency; it has to be found, encountered in the world by chance. In other words, the milieu can only be conceptualised by acting in it, by setting up, as Bacon does, small experiments, some of which will turn out to be generative.

In *The Normal and the Pathological*, Canguilhem writes, 'a living species is viable only if it shows itself to be fecund'.[47] By this he means to say that the individuals of a species should not be assumed to be interchangeable, but recognised as distinct *de jure*, each driven by an urgent need. To put it in terms appropriate to the work of both Bacon and Canguilhem, a fecund world is one that is not poor in monsters.

1   The phrase 'running like a girl' is meant to evoke Iris Marion Young's essay, 'Throwing Like a Girl: A Phenomenology of Feminine Body Comportment, Motility, and Spatiality', *Human Studies*, vol. 3 (1980) pp. 137–56. The essay deals with Merleau-Ponty's conception of the flesh.

2   Jean Paul Sartre, *Being and Nothingness*, (New York: Philosophical Library, Inc, 1992) p. 521.

3   Ibid., p. 519.

4   Ibid., p. 520.

5   Linda Williams, 'Film Body: An Implantation of Perversions', *Cine-Tracts,* vol. 3, no. 4 (Winter 1981), p. 24.

6   Gilles Deleuze, *Francis Bacon: The Logic of Sensation*, trans., Daniel W. Smith (Minneapolis: University of Minnesota Press, 2003) p. 40. Hereafter, page numbers will be given in parentheses in the text.

7   Jacques Lacan, *The Four Fundamental Concepts of Psycho-Analysis*, ed. Jacques-Alain Miller, trans. Alan Sheridan (London: The Hogarth Press and the Institute of Psycho-Analysis, 1966), p.84; my italics.

8   Ibid., p. 83.

9   Jacques-Alain Miller, 'Of a Gaze, The Strangeness', *Lacanian Review*, issue 16, Winter 2025, p. 29.

10   Ibid.

11   Jonathan Crary, *Suspensions of Perception* (Cambridge, Mass. and London: MIT Press, 1999), p. 140, my italics.

12   See Marta Braun, *Eadweard Muybridge* (London: Reaktion Books, 2010).

13   David Sylvester, *Interviews with Francis Bacon: The Brutality of Fact* (New York: Thames & Hudson, 2016), p. 37.

14   Ibid.

15   Noël Burch, *Life to Those Shadows, ed. Ben Brewster* (Berkeley and Los Angeles: University of California Press, 1990).

16   Jacques Lacan, *The Ethics of Psychoanalysis; Book VII*, ed. Jacques-Alain Miller, trans. Dennis Porter (London, New York: Tavistock / Routledge, 1992), *p. 46.*

17   Sylvester, op. cit., p. 14.

18   Gaston Bachelard, *The New Scientific Spirit*, trans. Arthur Goldhammer (Boston: Beacon Press, 1984), p. 13.

19   Mary Tiles, 'What does Bachelard mean by rationalisme appliqué?', Radical Philosophy, no. 173 (May/June 2012), p. 25.

20   The work of Alain Badiou – which focuses on questions of mathematics, ethics, art, and love – is a clear and exemplary instantiation of this philosophy.

21   Georges Canguilhem, 'Introduction: Thought and the Living', *Knowledge of Life*, ed. Paola Marrati and Todd Meyers, trans. Stefanos Geroulanos and Daniela Ginsburg (New York: Fordham University Press, 2008), p. xx.

22   Canguilhem, 'Monstrosity and the Monstrous', in *Knowledge of Life*, ibid., pp. 137, 145.

23   Ibid., p. 135.

24   Ibid.

25   Georges Canguilhem, 'Epistemology of Biology', *A Vital Rationalist: Selected Writings from Georges Canguilhem,* ed. Francois Delaporte, trans. Arthur Goldhammer (New York: Zone Books, 2000), p. 72.

26   Canguilhem, 'Monstrosity and the Monstrous', op. cit., p. 135.

27   Ibid. See Robert Antelme, *The Human Race*, trans. Jeffrey Haight and Annie Mahler (Evanston: Marlboro Press, 1992), p. 220.

28   See Fethi Benslama, 'Man's Property / Propriety', *Robert Antelme's The Human Race: Essays and Commentaries,* ed. Daniel Dobbels, trans. Jeffrey Haight (Evanston: Marlboro Press, 2003), pp. 71–82. Benslama offers a compelling account of the paradoxical attempt to 'de-specify' members of one's own species.

29   Canguilhem, *Knowledge of Life*, op cit., 134.

30   Sartre, op. cit., p. 494.

31   Canguilhem, 'Monstrosity and the Monstrous', op. cit., p. 136.

32   Ibid., p. 145.

33   Ibid., p. 137. See also Samuel Talcott's thorough account of the entanglements, as well as the differences, between Canguilhem's terms, 'monstrous' and 'monstrosity', in *Georges Canguilhem and the Problem of Error* (Springer Nature, 2019), pp. 275–89. Talcott's reading of Canguilhem's oeuvre is one of the few to focus on the philosopher's political background.

34   Canguilhem, 'The Living and Its Milieu', *Knowledge of Life*, op. cit., pp. 98–120.

35   Canguilhem, *The Normal and the Pathological*, (New York: Zone Books, 1991), p. 220.

36   Canguilhem, 'The Living and Its Milieu', op. cit., p. 104.

37   Jacques Lacan, The Ethics of Psychoanalysis, op. cit., p. 46.

38   Canguilhem, 'The Living and Its Milieu', op. cit., pp. 113-14.

39   Ibid.

40   Rosalind Krauss, 'Grids', *October* 9 (Summer 1979), pp. 52 and 55. Krauss sees the grid as a structural element that admits both materialist and mystic readings.

41   Canguilhem, 'The Living and Its Milieu', op. cit., p. 111.

42   See, for example, the short essay 'Instincts and Institutions', in Gilles Deleuze, *Desert Island and Other Texts* (New York: Semiotexte, 2004), pp. 9 – 14.

43   Frederick Winslow Taylor (1856–1915), was a pioneer in scientific management.

44   See 'The Stock Image (Muybridge)', in Antoine Traisnel, *Capture: American Pursuits and the Making of a New Animal Condition* (Minneapolis: University of Minnesota Press, 2020).

45   Sylvester, op. cit., p. 223.

46   Ibid., p. 60.

47   Canguilhem, 'The Normal and the Pathological', in *Knowledge of Life*, op. cit., p. 125.

Creative Mutilation: Of Monsters and Milieux

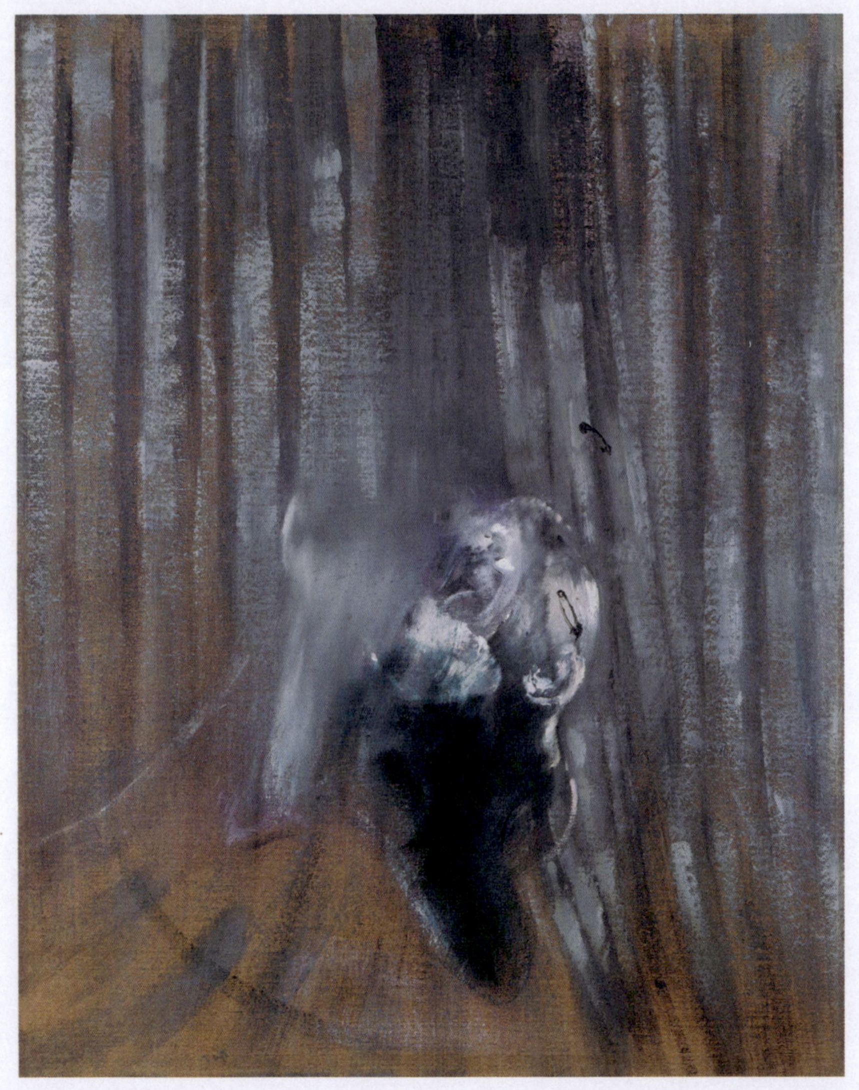

fig. 6 *Head V*, 1949

'FRANCIS BACON: DECADENT?'

Sacha Golob

Francis Bacon: decadent? A provocative question. An important one, too, I argue: one that sheds new light on Bacon's relationship to form, to pessimism and to existentialism.

Decadence is a vague, shifting concept.[1] It is often a condemnation: the accusation is sometimes of a drift from traditional certainties, sometimes of a lack of originality.[2] These condemnations are frequently combined with a historical story: a diagnosis of when, where and why decline set in. The archetype for such histories is the vast literature, piling up in every century since Sallust, on the fall of Rome.[3]

Neither dimension helps in understanding Bacon. Crudely accusatory uses of the term are ill-fitted for art criticism. To equate decadence with cultural staleness obscures the fact that canonically 'decadent' authors, such as Baudelaire or Huysmans, are paradigm cases of innovation. To equate decadence with a loss of tradition makes nonsense of canonically 'decadent' conservatives such as Lionel Johnson. And Bacon shows little interest in historical time, insisting on reading its signifiers in purely formal terms: a Nazi armband becomes a non-semantic compositional device to 'break the continuity of the arm and to add the colour of this red round the arm'.[4]

The concept of decadence in which I am interested is very different. It is visible in figures such as Walter Pater and Paul Bourget and received its most sophisticated articulation in Friedrich Nietzsche's later work. It implies a distinctive relation to form, to content and, through both, to life.

Formally, Bourget defined decadence in mereological terms: it occurs insofar as the parts take priority over the whole.[5] Otherwise put, decadence undermines what philosophers from Plato onwards have identified as an 'organic unity', unities in which the whole is prior to its components. The underlying idea is that in organisms, the components, for example a bird's wings, can be only understood in terms of how they serve the larger entity: as Breitenbach summarises, discussing the great Enlightenment thinker Immanuel Kant, 'the form and functioning of the organism's parts depend on the form and functioning of the organism as a whole'.[6]

Bourget defines such 'decadence' across both a literary context, his discussion focused on Baudelaire, and a political one: society 'must be assimilated to an organism', becoming decadent when its parts, for example the various individuals, no longer subordinate their energy to the whole.[7]

Nietzsche follows Bourget in this broad usage: 'freedom of the individual'...'*equal* rights for all' exhibit the telltale mereology of political decadence, of parts uncoordinated with the whole. [8] But more important for current purposes is Nietzsche's mereological definition of stylistic decadence:

> For the moment I am only going to look at the question of style. – What is the hallmark of all literary decadence? The fact that life does not reside in the totality any more. The word becomes sovereign and jumps out of the sentence, the sentence reaches out and blots out the meaning of the page, the page comes to life at the expense of the whole - the whole is not whole any more. But this is the image of every decadent style: there is always an anarchy of the atom, disintegration of the will.[9]

As is clear from the context, an attack on Wagner, Nietzsche intends this as a diagnosis of artistic decadence more broadly, rather than for literature alone: Wagner is thus a 'typical decadent',[10] insofar as he allows 'too much liveliness in the smallest parts'.[11]

This formal model of decadence is visible across nineteenth and early twentieth-century philosophy: von Hofmannsthal's Lord Chandos sums up the situation as one in which 'everything disintegrated into parts, those parts again into parts'.[12] At times, this is embraced; at other times, it prompts a reactionary lurch back to Classicism. Pater, for example, presents Plato as confronting an Athens 'sickly with off-cast speculative atoms,' the product of a centrifugal 'inorganic' tendency destroying Greek culture.[13] Pater's Plato seeks to counter this by reinforcing the priority of the whole through 'the life-giving principle of cohesion'.[14]

This gives a formal definition of decadence, but what of the question of content? Are there images or conceptions of the world symptomatic of decadence on this model?

Again, the crude accusatory definitions with which I began are no use. For example, given Nietzsche's own avowed 'immoralism', he could not simply identify decadence with a loss of traditional ethical certainties, something that he regards as positive. Nietzsche's achievement instead was to elaborate the mereological idea he inherited from Bourget with a certain psychological structure, a specific model of how the self might come undone.

For Nietzsche, the decadent is marked above all by *psychological conflict*, the child of an age which lacks the resources to mediate and balance its competing drives. The result is psychic fragmentation as the various parts of the self resist any attempt to order them into a coherent whole: an internal 'chaos and anarchy' reigns.[15] Bourget's original model is thus re-applied to the decadent's internal economy, now defined by 'an anarchy of the atom'.[16] With the 'loss of a centre of gravity', competing dimensions of the self spin free and disordered, smashing into one another.[17] Such conflict often centres around drives viewed as 'animalistic', drives towards cruelty or aggression for example, which Nietzsche fears moderns can neither accommodate nor control nor be reconciled with, leaving them 'wild dogs' in the 'cellar' of the mind.[18]

Such a split psychology has two main consequences in Nietzsche's eyes. On the one hand, it exhausts, as the decadent is thrown one way then the next by competing pressures, unable to find any position from which all can be reconciled or stabilised. In extreme cases, this results in a breakdown in the capacity for agency: 'disintegration of the will', as the self becomes merely a battlefield in which opposed psychological and cultural forces play out.[19] On the other hand, such conflict may give rise to a repressive fanaticism as individuals desperately stamp an order onto themselves, trying to overcome their internal conflicts by brute force. Nietzsche sees this, exemplified in Christian asceticism, as an extension of the internalisation of cruelty demanded by any social order:

> Lacking external enemies and obstacles, and forced into the oppressive narrowness and conformity of custom, man impatiently ripped himself apart, persecuted himself, gnawed at himself, gave himself no peace and abused himself, this animal who battered himself raw on the bars of his cage and who is supposed to be 'tamed'; man.[20]

These two very different responses, exhausted collapse on the one hand and compulsive self-persecution on the other, nevertheless bear a common fruit, a dissatisfaction with life: a distinctive 'feeling of... inhibition', 'deep depression...and black melancholy'.[21] Unable to reconcile their instincts and unable to assert their will except through vindictive self-torture, the decadent is marked by 'paralysis, distress, and numbness' and in the fanatic's case by 'a form of violence that undermines life'.[22]

Nietzsche thus translates Bourget's formal definition into a decadence of content and from that into a diagnosis, a diagnosis of 'man, the sick animal'.[23] Decadence, for Nietzsche, 'the loss of all the forces of organization, which is to say separation, division, subordination, and domination', thus constitutes a form of 'declining life'.[24]

My suggestion is that we read Bacon's work as a sophisticated response to decadence in the sense outlined. The claim is not, of course, that Bacon was focused on Bourget or Nietzsche's writings, but, rather, that his work explores and is symptomatic of the social and psychological forces they identified, in both formal composition and thematic content.[25]

To begin, the question of form and the mereological relationship. The pieces of the Baconian figure constantly break and buckle through the lines that should delimit its whole. A nose or a cheek bone or an eye socket swells to contort the face; likewise, Bacon admired Degas's ability to show how 'the very top of the spine...almost comes out of the skin altogether...this thing seems to protrude from the flesh'.[26] [fig. 15]

At other points, the body's integrity and organisation fail entirely, leaving a kind of slumped, viscous liquid or a slowly leaking sack. Such images embody what Nietzsche called the 'disintegration' of the individual: the face, the locus of agency, or the skeleton, the structure which marshals the body, break down. 'The whole is not whole any more', as Nietzsche put it in his anti-Wagner writings.[27]

Indeed, Bacon's overwhelming focus on living beings, animals or people, constitutes an ironic rejoinder to the philosophical tradition's talk of 'organic unities' as that in which the whole determines the behaviour of the parts: in Bacon, it is precisely in flesh that this principle fails.

Next, the content dimension of decadence. Bacon's avowed aim is to break beyond mere likeness to expose the 'pulsations' or 'emanation' of the depicted, an 'emanation which has to do with personality and everything else', effectively the counterparts of Nietzsche's talk of 'drives' and 'desires'.[28] At times, these pulsations or emanations tear apart the figure; at others, they leave it supine and exhausted. Frequently, a new unity, that of the cage, is superimposed, replacing the face or the skeleton as the dominant organisational principle.

As in Nietzsche, the struggle with our animality is central to this: the Baconian figure is so often marked by a simian curve of the jaw or a canine bend of the back.

Bacon is here tracing, I suggest, the very same psychological and social landscape that Nietzsche mapped: the same internal breakdown of the subject, the same oscillation between frenzy and exhaustion, the same constraints and the same recourse to the bloody, ersatz order of the cage. The same 'animal who battered himself raw on the bars of' his enclosure, the same decadence of form and of content.[29]

Yet, there are important differences between these approaches, Nietzsche's and Bacon's. To understand them, I need to say something about the relationship between diagnostic and valuational uses of 'decadence'.

Nietzsche's stance on decadence is never simply negative: he admires, in some complex sense, some of its exemplars and he sees its traits even in himself, 'I am a decadent, I am the opposite as well'.[30] Nevertheless, he clearly connects decadence with pessimism, with a distaste for life, that he fundamentally opposes to his own vision of life affirmation.[31]

For Nietzsche, such pessimism arises from the decadent's exhausting internal conflicts, magnified when the agent, seeking some semblance of order, beats their instincts into line or drifts in to escapist fantasies of another, better world. This is how he reads Wagner: a 'decaying, despairing decadent, who suddenly [sinks] down helpless and shattered before the Christian cross', desperate for 'metaphysical comfort'.[32] Nietzsche's use of 'decadence' is thus at once diagnostic and valuational: it explains the distinctive interplay between Wagner's psychology and his work, and it warns against their influence.

This brings me to two fundamental differences between Nietzsche and Bacon. Again, when I speak of such 'differences' I do not mean that Bacon held some kind of systematic theory. But he does have a distinctive, indeed instantly recognisable, perspective, visible both on the canvas and in his interviews, and that perspective diverges from Nietzsche's in important ways.

First, Bacon places enormous emphasis on accuracy, on mapping the phenomenon. The aim of art is 'recording', 'reporting', analogous to a crime scene photo and occasionally even marked up like one. Like many phenomenologists, Bacon believed that the price of such accuracy was doing violence to ossified representational conventions.[33] In focusing on depiction, Bacon thus avoids any claim to offer a solution to decadence. Such solutions are not his task, any more than the crime scene photographer is meant to restore law and order. Nietzsche in contrast, seeks a new form of life, an escape from decadence, an escape that leaves behind both ape and human as 'a laughing stock or a painful embarrassment'.[34] Bacon, in contrast, aims only to depict where we stand, showing those two creatures as inseparably bound. [fig. 20]

Second, Bacon does not draw the pessimistic verdict which Nietzsche assumes follows from decadence: Nietzsche had expected to find 'nausea, this weariness, this fatigue, this disgust' with oneself and with life, a 'deep sadness'.[35] This is the basis for his verdict that decadence marks a form of 'declining life', where his duty is to offer some alternative such as the *Übermensch*. But Bacon's own experience is very different: he describes it as an 'exhilarated despair'.[36]

One clear way to see the difference is to focus on chance. For Nietzsche, life is ultimately affirmable only insofar as I view all of it as willable: every tragedy, every accident, transfigured by re-imagining it a product of my own agency and placing it within my own narrative. Life is 'a fragment and riddle and grisly accident' until I 'recreate all 'it was' into 'thus I willed it!' '.[37] Nietzsche's idea is that:

> [M]any horrifying and brutal acts, traits, persons, and events can be made to appear beautiful and admirable under the right conditions of genuine organic unity.[38]

Such willing thus allows Nietzsche to restore, through narrative, precisely that self-control and the organic unity that decadence threatens.

This drive to recreate such unity, to find life 'admirable', is never visible on Bacon's canvas. Yet, in a way that Nietzsche did not foresee, Bacon nevertheless avoids pessimism by a gambler's pleasure in riding life's risks: rather than trying to subject chance to the will, to claim 'But thus I willed it', Bacon simply waits for the coin to land. Consider his famous remark on the butcher's carcasses:

> If I go into a butcher's shop, I always think it's surprising that I wasn't there instead of the animal.[39]

There is no sense for Bacon in imagining a scenario in which I 'willed this': rather, it is precisely the brute chance that is important, for 'if life excites you, its opposite, like a shadow, death, must excite you'.[40]

The result is a situation in which 'one's basic nature is totally without hope', the unredeemed decadence which Nietzsche so feared, 'yet one's nervous system is made out of optimistic stuff', so escaping the pessimism Nietzsche thought must follow from that.[41]

In sum, Bacon's work articulates and tracks the very same decadence of form and content found in Nietzsche. Yet Bacon rejects the pessimism, the wearying sense of decline which Nietzsche thought must follow from it. Bacon also rejects the tendency to condemn and the desperation to offer some alternative on which Nietzsche prided himself.

One way to express the point is that whilst Nietzsche recognises the possibility of a 'pessimism of strength', supposedly found in the Pre-Socratic Greeks, i.e. a pessimism without decadence sustained by the distinctive resources of Attic tragedy, Bacon is closer to something of which Nietzsche did not conceive, a *decadence without pessimism*.[42]

I want now to show how this reading plays out with respect to two of Bacon's most powerful works, the triptychs from 1972 and 1973 showing the death of George Dyer. [fig. 38], [fig. 39]

In both, formal decadence is immediately visible. In the 1972 triptych, the body leaks and pools, some parts are missing or in the process of vaporisation; others swell and bulge with disproportionate force, particularly in the first panel, or are overdrawn by lines which blur their identity and function, particularly in the third panel. In the 1973 triptych, the left panel shows the body twisted by its own parts, as Bacon's white strokes of pain suggest the hip or the shoulder as pivots turning the rest of the mass. The centre panel shows the same leakage as in 1972, but now more malevolently cast, with a winged pattern to the stain.

In both cases, there is decadence of content too. The images are of an irresolvable conflict, a conflict from which the scene allows no exit, the only doorway leading into darkness. The figure, Dyer himself, is racked by those tensions, entirely beset. He is a battlefield, a canvas, on which they play out, rather than any kind of autonomous subject disposing of them as he will. There is no sense of control nor of agency: this is precisely what Nietzsche called the 'disintegration of the will'.[43]

I stressed two crucial points at which Bacon and Nietzsche diverge, however, and these are likewise visible in the images.

First, Bacon's aim is simply to report. Indeed, the 1973 triptych includes arrows to direct the viewer, an artistic intervention showing a concern to ensure his document is read closely and accurately. [fig. 39] It also suggests a certain detachment. Decadence in Bacon's work is not a biographical matter; there is no confessional outpouring of emotion from the artist. Rather, the painting serves to delineate and articulate a precise set of psychological circumstances. In this, Bacon's 'reporter' or 'recorder' is quite different from figures such as the 'witness', so central to the twentieth-century work on genocide. The witness is defined by the impossibility of their report: as Primo Levi, put it, 'we, the survivors, are not the true witnesses' precisely because the survivors did not 'touch bottom', were not 'drowned'.[44] The result is a set of paradoxes, familiar from writers such as Agamben: attempts to bear witness speak only to 'the impossibility of bearing witness', since having survived implies that the report cannot but be inadequate.[45] In Bacon, in contrast, distortion is not a sign of an unachievable project; rather, it is required precisely because, in breaching representational conventions, it alone allows an adequate testimony.[46]

Second, there is no condemnation of Dyer nor moralising of his situation nor contempt for it: Nietzsche, in contrast, worried that decadence would inevitably breed 'despisers of life'.[47] By extension, without the threat of pessimism to drive a counter-reaction, Bacon feels no need to offer a positive alternative of the kind Nietzsche sought, on which 'mankind is a rope fastened between animal and overman'.[48]

One way to see this is in the role of narrative. Nietzsche, as noted above, saw self-narrativisation as key to overcoming the disgust that might trigger pessimism: by seeing every aspect of life as a necessary chapter, willed by him, in an act of his own self-creation, he became able to embrace that which had repulsed him:

> To recreate all 'it was' into a 'thus I willed it'—that alone I should call redemption.[49]

It is a mistake to claim that narrativity is entirely absent from Bacon's work: the 1973 triptych clearly suggests some order of sequence among the panels. [fig. 39] But there is no sense of an authorial hand stitching back together what decadence has torn apart - and no sense that the absence of such unity or such 'redemption' impoverishes us.

Where Nietzsche saw decadence in comparative terms, a form of 'declining life', that needed a replacement, Bacon's approach is closer to a text such as Bataille's *Blue of Noon*. Bataille's protagonists, like Dyer, lie sprawled in luxury hotel rooms, sick, drenched in sweat, somewhere between corpse and animal, 'gasping for breath, panting'. [50] This is the same 'gilded squalor' which Bacon himself said he liked to inhabit.[51] He and Bataille find it powerful for a similar reason: the productive tension between gold and dirt, the unresolved and unresolvable conflict between the refined and the animal. Bacon's work does not locate decadence in a 'decline and fall' narrative of the type offered by *Dorian Gray*, nor does it judge it in comparison to some other form of life, be it that of upstanding citizen or possible *Übermensch*. Instead, it offers an articulation of the condition, at once detached and exhilarated, channelling the intensified sense of a life that feels its own mortality, its carcass but thinly veiled.

The Contrast with Existentialism: Deleuze and Kuspit

In closing, it may help to show why my approach differs from others used to understand Bacon's work.

Existentialism is a classic point of reference for Bacon studies. Yet as soon as one moves beyond pablum about the 'human condition', what is most striking is the difference between Bacon's vision and the existentialist one. Most importantly, Bacon's painting lacks the 'heroic moment', the moment through which the existentialist transfigures their surroundings and their life: in grasping our authentic selves, both Sartre and Heidegger allow what is effectively an escape from decadence, a life radically changed by courage.

The difference is most evident when it comes to death. Heidegger, for example, thinks of death in terms of two attitudes. One is inauthentic and seeks to cover up our own mortality through busywork and feigned insouciance, as if to say 'one of these days we'll die too, in the end; but right now it has nothing to do with us'.[52] The other is authentic: authentic confrontation with death leaves Dasein 'resolute' in 'its own superior power, the power of its finite freedom'.[53] Neither model, the bold resolution of the authentic or the glib chatter of the inauthentic, matches the bare disintegration of Dyer, propped up in his chair or racked and twisted on the lavatory. [fig. 38], [fig. 39]

My point here meshes naturally with the language of decadence and mereology I introduced above. The inauthentic Heideggerian agent is 'dispersed' [*zerstreut*] or 'fragmentary'.[54] He 'loses himself in trivial matters, desperately seeking "distraction" [*Zerstreuung*] in "things of little significance".[55] The authentic agent, in contrast, manages to re-forge some genuine unity by finding a narrative that binds together their choices. This is Guignon's influential summary:

> Martin Heidegger's conception of authentic resoluteness gives us a picture of life as an unfolding story aimed at a fulfilment of a specific sort. Such resoluteness provides a focus and continuity to a life that can help an individual find meaning and order during times of personal difficulties.[56]

This is precisely the kind of organic unity that might repair decadence, a unity in which some overarching focus productively binds up the days and hours. But there is no such transfiguration, no such fulfilment and no such narrative available in Bacon: his images are images of decadence.

Of course, there is much more that could be said as to the details of the existentialist picture here but, whilst that yields a more complex story, it does not bring it any closer to Bacon's worldview. For example, Sartre's *Being and Nothingness* is silent on our relationship to animality whilst Heidegger explicitly imposes an 'abyss' between ourselves and any ape or dog: both are at odds with Bacon's worldview.[57]

Consider next Deleuze's vitalism. This has some affinities with my reading: both stress forces prior to the 'face' or to the 'subject', prior to the powers of rational agency and recognition. Yet Deleuze projects a metaphysical optimism onto Bacon that is quite alien to him. Here is Deleuze on those forces, previously unseen, and now made visible through Bacon's work:

It is within this visibility that the body actively struggles, affirming the possibility of triumphing, which was beyond its reach as long as these powers remained invisible, hidden in a spectacle that sapped our strength and diverted us. It is as if combat had now become possible. The struggle with the shadow is the only real struggle. When the visual sensation confronts the invisible force that conditions it, it releases a force that is capable of vanquishing the invisible force, or even befriending it. His is indeed a figurative miserabilisme, but one that serves an increasingly powerful Figure of life.[58]

This possibility of triumph supposedly unites Bacon and Beckett:

In the very act of 'representing' horror, mutilation, prosthesis, fall or failure, they have erected indomitable Figures, indomitable through both their insistence and their presence. They have given life a new and extremely direct power of laughter.[59]

What Deleuze offers here is salvation: an unseen world that promises an irrepressible joy and triumph, a 'new life', 'indominable' through every pain. Yet Bacon's images never testify to such a resurrection: Deleuze has simply swept away the decadence on which Bacon set out to report, replacing it with a vitalist reworking of a familiar theology.[60]

Finally, consider Donald Kuspit's critique of Bacon. Uniquely, Kuspit recognises the importance of decadence in the Nietzschean sense for Bacon, and he deserves recognition for that. His error is to assume, as Nietzsche typically did, that such decadence implies pessimism:

[S]ustained, compulsive attention to the inevitability of death is a symptom of decadence, for eventually it leads to skepticism about – the deprecation and detriment of – life. Bacon, who has been called an existentialist – in our sense the most decadent contemporary philosophy – is simultaneously a decadent, in the sense of cultivating a nihilistic perception of and attitude to life. While he carries this cultivation to eloquent heights, making it the stance of a dandy, its nihilistic core remains articulate as more than a posture.[61]

Much is wrong here. I have already noted the deep gap between Bacon and existentialism. The accusation of dandyism is equally misguided since the dandy is marked by insisting on a gap between his behaviour and that of the animal: 'To the dandy the self is not an animal, but a gentleman'.[62] It is hard to think of any less Baconian sentiment. I leave aside Kuspit's more bizarre accusations, on which 'A neo-Cartesian, Bacon's solitary asserts "I masturbate, therefore I am" '.[63]

What is most important are two errors. First, Kuspit alleges that Bacon himself 'is...a decadent'. Maybe – but it is a mistake to put matters in such crude biographical terms, as if art criticism could be done by totting up champagne corks. A regular and orderly existence might produce violent and original work; years of dissolute living might yield nothing but kitsch and banality. As an artist, Bacon is a reporter on a precise set of psychological and cultural conditions, conditions of decadence: that is what his work articulates. We know something of Bacon's own stance on those conditions from his interviews and other remarks. But it is a mistake to think the works give a transparent index to the artist or to infer from depictions of decadence to the psychology behind it – just as it would be with Nietzsche, who having diagnosed and railed against decadence, admitted that he himself was personally implicated in it.[64]

Second, Kuspit claims that decadence renders Bacon guilty of the 'deprecation and detriment of life'.[65] Kuspit's assumption, one Nietzsche made too, is that decadence implies pessimism. As I showed, this is false: decadence is compatible with what Bacon called an 'exhilarated despair'. This is driven by an intense sense of life's fragility. Not fragility in the sense that any of us might get cancer or be hit by a bus: does anyone seriously think the phenomena Bacon treats would be alleviated by more hospitals or pedestrian crossings? Rather, it is an intense sense of how easily and forcefully the modern self, as decadent, as a site of drives that it can neither easily reconcile or control, decomposes long before death – that is the fragility in question.

The Baconian image is a report on such decadence, on such fragility, on such de-composition. It is not a complete report by any means. As I noted in the opening to this essay, Bacon is largely uninterested in the question of historical time. He remarks in passing that 'even when Velásquez was painting, even when Rembrandt was painting' they were conditioned by a religious framework that has now been 'completely cancelled out'.[66] [fig. 16] But he makes no sustained inquiry into how universal the situation he depicts is: to take the question that obsessed Nietzsche and Heidegger, was there ever a time before decadence?

Rather, what Bacon offers is a uniquely visceral recording of decadence as he saw it around him, a recording which dispenses with both the existentialist belief in a heroic turning point and the reassurances of Deleuzian vitalism. It is a report made possible by a commitment to brutal accuracy and by a gambler's hope that evades the pessimism Nietzsche thought inevitable: even 'if I was in hell I would always feel I had a chance of escaping'.[67]

1 There is a huge, scattered literature on decadence, with the term carrying different implications in different disciplines. For recent overviews see David Weir, *Decadence* (Oxford University Press, 2018), Julien Freund, *La Décadence* (Paris: Broché, 2023). On the term's etymology, see Richard Gilman, *Decadence: The Strange Life of an Epithet* (New York: Farrar, Straus and Giroux, 1979).

2 Douthat's recent work, for example, defines it in terms of 'institutional decay, cultural and intellectual exhaustion…in which repetition is more the norm than innovation'. Ross Douthat, *The Decadent Society* (London: Simon & Schuster, 2020), p. 9.

3 On the discourse's Roman origins, see Georgios Vassiliades, *La 'res publica' et sa décadence* (Bordeaux: Ausonius, 2021).

4 David Sylvester, *The Brutality of Fact* (London: Thames & Hudson, 1987), p. 65.

5 Paul Bourget, *Essais de psychologie contemporaine* (Paris: Lemerre, 1883), pp. 19-20.

6 Angela Breitenbach, 'Laws in Biology and the Unity of Nature' in Breitenbach and Massimi (eds.), *Kant and the Laws of Nature* (Cambridge University Press, 2017), p. 241.

7 Ibid, p. 20.

8 Friedrich Nietzsche, *The Case of Wagner* in *The Anti-Christ, Ecce Homo, Twilight of the Idols, and Other Writings*, trans. Judith Norman (Cambridge University Press, 2010), p. 7.

9 Ibid.

10 Ibid, p. 5.

11 Ibid, 'Second Postscript'; Ibid p. 5.

12 Hugo von Hofmannsthal, *The Lord Chandos Letter and Other Writings* (New York: New York Review Books, 2005), p. 122.

13 Walter Pater, *Plato and Platonism* (London: Macmillan, 1910), p. 6.

14 Ibid, p. 6.

15 Friedrich Nietzsche, *Twilight of the Idols* in *The Anti-Christ, Ecce Homo, Twilight of the Idols, and Other Writings*, op. cit., 'Socrates', p. 4.

16 Nietzsche, *The Case of Wagner*, op. cit., p. 7.

17 Friedrich Nietzsche, *Ecce Homo* in *The Anti-Christ, Ecce Homo, Twilight of the Idols, and Other Writings*, op. cit., 'Books'.

18 Friedrich Nietzsche, *Thus Spoke Zarathustra*, trans. Adrian del Caro, (Cambridge University Press, 2006), p. 30.

19 Nietzsche, *Twilight of the Idols*, op. cit., 'Errors' p. 2.

20 Friedrich Nietzsche, *On the Genealogy of Morality*, trans. Carol Diethe (Cambridge University Press, 2007), II, p. 16. For the sake of a clear overview, I suppress exegetical complexities around the transition from 'bad conscience' to decadence and the degree to which Nietzsche sees decadence as amplified in particular historical periods.

21 Nietzsche, *Twilight of the Idols*, op. cit., 'Germans' p. 6; *On the Genealogy of Morality*, op. cit., III, p. 17.

22 Friedrich Nietzsche, *Ecce Homo*, op. cit., 'Books'.

23 Nietzsche, *On the Genealogy of Morality*, op. cit., III, p. 14.

24 Nietzsche, *Twilight of the Idols*, op. cit., 'Skirmishes', p. 37.

25 Bacon in fact knew Nietzsche well, memorably praising him as having 'forecast our future for us… the Cassandra of the 19th century' ('Francis Bacon: Remarks from an Interview with Peter Beard' in *Francis Bacon's Recent Paintings 1968-1974* (New York: Metropolitan Museum of Art, 1975), p. 20). Passing remarks in his letters credit Nietzsche's emphasis on self-creation and his suspicion of 'people who back the helpless in their search for power without really knowing what the powerless want' ('Letter to Sonia Orwell' in *Francis Bacon: A Self-Portrait in Words*, ed. Michael Peppiatt (London: Thames & Hudson, 2024), p. 145). Nothing in what follows hangs on any specific claim regarding Bacon's knowledge of Nietzsche's texts.

26 Sylvester, op. cit., p. 47.

27 Friedrich Nietzsche, *Nietzsche Contra Wagner* in *The Anti-Christ, Ecce Homo, Twilight of the Idols, and Other Writings*, op. cit., p. 7.

28 Sylvester, op. cit., p.174, p. 82.

29 Nietzsche, *On the Genealogy of Morality*, op. cit., II, p. 16.

30 Nietzsche, *Ecce Homo*, op. cit., 'Why I am So Wise', p. 2. For Nietzsche's admiration for certain decadents, see the paean to the ascetic priest in the *Genealogy*, III, p. 15.

31 On Nietzsche's positive story, see Bernard Reginster, *The Affirmation of Life* (London: Harvard University Press, 2006). I suppress complications regarding the difference between affirmation and 'optimism', which Nietzsche typically associates with deluded Socratic rationalism.

32 Nietzsche, *Nietzsche Contra Wagner*, op. cit., 'Broke Away', p. 1.; Friedrich Nietzsche, *The Birth of Tragedy*, trans. Ronald Speirs (Cambridge University Press, 1999), 'Self-Criticism' p. 7.

33 Sylvester, op. cit., p. 60.

34 Nietzsche, *Thus Spoke Zarathustra*, op. cit., p. 6.

35 Nietzsche, *On the Genealogy of Morality*, op. cit., III, pp. 13-4.

36 Sylvester, op. cit., p. 83.

37 Nietzsche, *Thus Spoke Zarathustra*, op. cit., p. 112.

38 Patrick Hassan, *Nietzsche's Struggle Against Pessimism* (Cambridge University Press, 2023), p. 221.

39 Sylvester, op. cit., p. 46.

40 Ibid., p. 78.

41 Ibid., p. 80.

42 By extension, there is no attempt in Bacon's work to recreate either the beautiful illusion of pre-Socratic Apollonian art or the communal deindividuation of the Dionysian chorus (Bacon's figures are individuals at the point of failure, but individuals nevertheless, remaining separate even in sexual coupling – for example, 1953's *Two Figures*).

43 Friedrich Nietzsche, *The Case of Wagner*, op. cit., p. 7.

44 Primo Levi, *The Drowned and the Saved*, trans. by Raymond Rosenthal (London: Abacus, 1989), p. 64.

45 Giorgio Agamben, *Remnants of Auschwitz: The Witness and the Archive* (London: Zone Books, 2002), p. 34.

46 Sylvester, op. cit., p. 40.

47 Nietzsche, *Thus Spoke Zarathustra*, op. cit., p. 52.

48 Ibid., p. 53.

49 Ibid., p. 110.

50 Georges Bataille, *Blue of Noon*, trans. Harry Mathews (London: Grafton Books), p. 14; Sylvester, op. cit., p. 52.

51 Sylvester, op. cit., p. 78.

52 Martin Heidegger, *Being and Time*, trans. Macquarrie and Robinson (Oxford, Blackwell: 2001), p. 297.

53 Ibid., p. 436.

54 Ibid., p. 167, p. 276.

55 Ibid., p. 441, p. 216.

56 Charles Guignon, *On Being Authentic* (London: Routledge, 2004), p. 204.

57 Martin Heidegger, *Pathmarks*, trans. William McNeill (Cambridge University Press, 1998), p. 157.

58 Gilles Deleuze, *Francis Bacon: The Logic of Sensation*, trans. Daniel W. Smith (London: Continuum, 1990), p. 62.

59 Ibid.

60 One further reason to be wary is the supposed analogy with Beckett, one often made and one which Bacon himself tended to mock: 'the artist 'rejected any comparison between Beckett's work ('all those ghastly dustbins') and his own' (Michael Peppiatt, *Francis Bacon* (London: Phoenix., 1996), p. 341 n1).

61 Donald Kuspit, 'Francis Bacon: The Authority of Flesh', *Artforum*, Vol. 13, 1975, p. 55.

62 Ellen Moers, *The Dandy*, (Lincoln, Nebraska, University of Nebraska Press, 1978), p. 18.

63 Donald Kuspit, op, cit., p. 56.

64 As he puts it, 'I am a decadent, I am the opposite as well' Nietzsche, *Ecce Homo*, op. cit., 'Why I am So Wise', p. 2.

65 Kuspit, op. cit., p. 55.

66 Sylvester, op. cit., p. 29.

67 Ibid., p. 200. I am hugely grateful to Ben Ware and to the audience at the 2023 conference organised by the Estate of Francis Bacon and King's College London for their many helpful comments and suggestions.

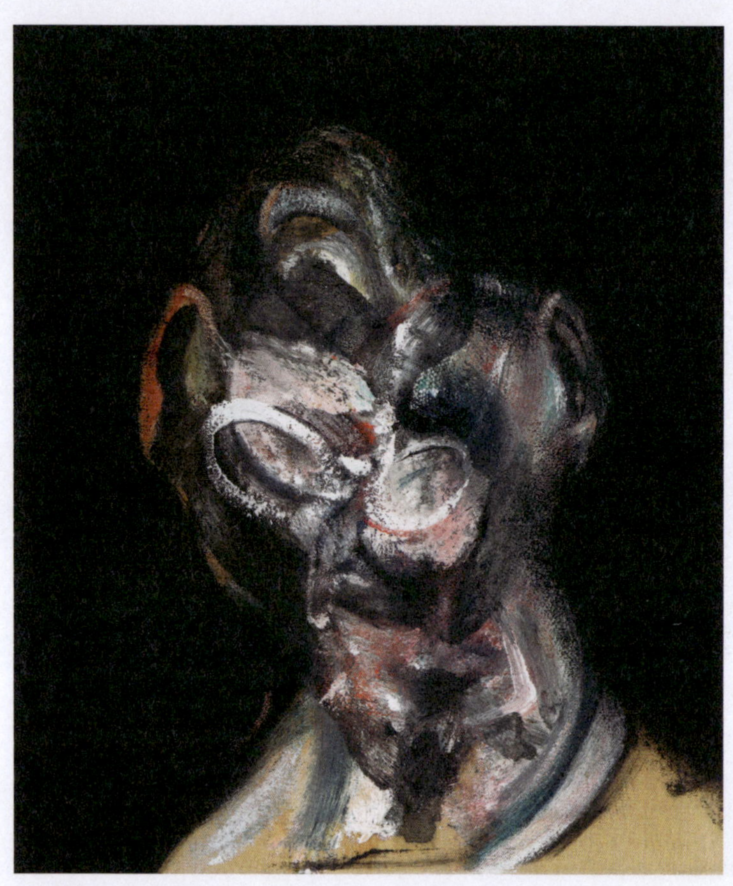

fig. 7   *Portrait of Man with Glasses I*, 1963

FRANCIS BACON'S EYES: BLINDNESS, PORTRAITURE, AND THE DISORDERING OF THE SENSES

Dany Nobus

Introduction

In a conversation with the French journalist Franck Maubert from the early 1980s, Francis Bacon pondered the possibility that his work might very well constitute a long, permanent analysis on himself. When considering this aspect of his art, Bacon went on to paraphrase the words of Arthur Rimbaud in two famous letters from May 1871, which are generally known as the 'letters of the seer' ('lettres du voyant'). In the first letter, which was addressed to Georges Izambard, a teacher at Rimbaud's school in his hometown of Charleville, the young man wrote: 'I want to be a poet and I'm working to make myself a *seer* [je travaille à me rendre *Voyant*]: you won't begin to understand, and I almost can't explain to you. The thing is to arrive at the unknown by a disordering of *all the senses*. The suffering is enormous, but you have to be strong, to be born a poet, and I've recognized I'm a poet'.[1] In the second letter, which was written two days later to the poet Paul Demeny, Rimbaud repeated his conviction in almost exactly the same terms: 'I say you must be a *seer*, make yourself a *seer*. The Poet makes himself a *seer* by a long, immense and reasoned *disordering* of *all the senses*. All the forms of love, of suffering, of madness; he seeks himself, he drains all the poisons in himself, so as to keep only the quintessences'.[2]

In being reminded of Rimbaud, Bacon only recalled a few words from these illustrious sentences, notably those that capture the means, the instrument, the technique, or even the condition for turning oneself into a seer. Speaking to Maubert (in French), Bacon opined: 'Perhaps when all is said and done I'm performing a long, permanent analysis on myself. (He's laughing.) It invokes Arthur Rimbaud's "disordering of the senses". Yes, maybe that's what I'm putting into practice. I'm working on myself'.[3] It is worth noting, here, that Bacon did not repeat the all-embracing operation upon which Rimbaud insisted – in Bacon's paraphrase, Rimbaud's 'le dérèglement de tous les sens' became just 'le dérèglement des sens' – yet he still intimated that the object of the process of disordering should not be restricted to one or the other sensory quality, but should involve a multiplicity of derangements, or at least a form of disturbance that is sufficiently powerful to serve more than a single purpose.

Whereas Rimbaud's letters to Izambard and Demeny have elicited a large body of scholarship, this small passage from Bacon's conversations with Maubert, including the reference to Rimbaud, has received little or no attention in the enormous body of literature on Bacon's life and works, perhaps because the remark tends to be considered as rather frivolous and otiose.[4] In addition, the persistent lack of scholarly engagement with Bacon's curious reflection upon the nature of his artistic practice is compounded by the fact that he himself did not elaborate on his own comparison.[5] Nor did Maubert invite his interlocutor to explain the connection in greater depth. He did not ask Bacon what exactly he had in mind with his mention of Rimbaud, as if he (Maubert) immediately understood, or as if the invocation was not worth pursuing.[6] But what exactly is the relation between performing a permanent analysis on oneself, notably through the act of painting, and a disordering of the senses? How does a disordering of the senses facilitate the analysis of oneself in the act of painting?

To complicate matters further, in French, the word 'sens' does not just mean 'sense', i.e. the physiological faculties of hearing, tasting, smelling, touching, and seeing, because it may also refer to 'meaning' (sense-making) and to 'direction', 'orientation', and 'viewpoint'. There is little doubt that when Rimbaud endeavoured to explain to his correspondents the fundamental condition for being confirmed in one's status as a poet, the meaning of 'sens' he had in mind was that of human perception, if only because this is the meaning that accords with his project of becoming a seer. Yet we should not be so sure that the same is true when Bacon rehearsed the words in the presence of Maubert, given the painter's visceral aversion to story-telling and the meaning that flows from it.[7] Hence, what we are left with when reading this passage is a series of questions that are as thought-provoking as they are puzzling, especially when it comes to developing an understanding of the nature of Bacon's artistic activity. Assuming that Bacon was referring to *psycho*analysis when he employed the term 'analysis', how does this experience require a disordering of (all) the senses? How do (all) the senses – in one, two, or all the meanings of the word – become disordered when analysis is taking place? Given that Rimbaud was primarily a poet and Bacon a painter, how does this disordering of (all) the senses play out in the different artistic practices to which they had committed themselves? What does it mean to enact a disordering of (all) the senses in the visual arts and how would this act (or the long, permanent process associated with it) take place? Also, neither Rimbaud nor Bacon had a psychoanalyst at their disposal to facilitate or expedite the operation – although Bacon could have had if he had wanted to – which in turn raises the question to what extent the artistic activity itself may come to bypass and occupy the role that is conventionally reserved for the psychoanalyst.[8]

In what follows, I shall attempt to situate the place and unpack the importance of Rimbaud's statement within Bacon's lifelong artistic journey. In doing so, I shall to some extent draw on Lacan's reflections on the split (*le schize*) between the eye and the gaze in his Seminar of 1964, which are in themselves an extension of *Le visible et l'invisible*, the unfinished, posthumously published work by Maurice Merleau-Ponty.[9] However, I shall also endeavour to open two dimensions that neither Lacan nor Merleau-Ponty fully addressed in their analyses of visual perception. The first dimension is that of the phenomenological status of blindness, which is not to be interpreted here as the powerlessness of the eye, even less as the absence of an optical system, but rather as the destruction, impairment, distortion, derangement, or disappearance of vision as the full, clear and direct optical access to an external object.[10] The second dimension, which I shall only touch upon in the conclusion of my text, is that of the relation between the (subject of the) painter, the (object of the) painting, and the creative act that mediates between both. This is a dimension that Lacan did consider, at least tangentially, during his discussion of Velázquez's *Meninas* in three sessions of May 1966 of his Seminar 'The Object of Psychoanalysis', but which he did not as such reconnect with his earlier considerations of the split between the eye and the gaze.[11] As I shall try to show, these two dimensions remain intertwined throughout Bacon's work and can effectively be ascertained both in Bacon's approach to painting, i.e. in his artistic practice, and in how he captured the reality of his figures on the canvas.

Painting (the) Blind

If we return to Rimbaud's visionary letters to Izambard and Demeny of May 1871, with which Bacon was clearly familiar, the first thing to note is that the absolute, overarching disordering of the senses – which I propose to restrict, here, to the human faculties of perception – does not by definition accord equal value to each of the five sense organs: the eyes, the ears, the nose, the tongue, and the skin. In other words, just because Rimbaud advocates a disordering of *all* the senses does not imply that each of these is to be disordered in the same way, or to the same degree.

The overall aim of the operation, as described by Rimbaud, was to allow the poet to become a seer (*un voyant*). However, quite paradoxically, in Rimbaud's portrayal of the poet *qua* seer, the disordering of smell, hearing, taste, and touch does not matter nearly as much as the disordering of vision, which is expected to be exhaustive, comprehensive, complete. Blindness is the necessary precondition for attaining the hallowed status of the seer. The archetypal figure of 'the blind poet' Rimbaud had in mind, here, is unlikely to have been John Milton or William Wordsworth – even though both experienced severe disturbances of vision at some point during their life – but rather the first poet in Western cultural history who was fully deserving of this name, and which would have encouraged Rimbaud to indeed refer to him as 'the Poet'. The man in question – although it is by no means certain that he is more than just a name – is the poet whose blindness at one point even became synonymous with his name: Homeros, or Homer.[12]

Being blind would have prevented Homer from passing down his poetry in writing, leaving the act of recording and transcribing the verses to others. But it would have also compelled him to pay more attention to the musicality, the rhythm and the metre of his words, irrespective of their being sung or merely declaimed. More importantly though, it would have forced him to put all his faith in another human faculty. This mental process does not belong to the realm of the senses, but draws upon the cognitive function that makes the Poet turn inwards, while simultaneously introducing the dimension of time. Homer's blindness redirects him to Mnemosyne, the Greek goddess of memory, which was also revered as the mother of the nine Muses.[13] In effect, one might argue that it is the Poet's blindness which, in the opening verses of the *Iliad* and the *Odyssey*, makes him appeal to the Muse, who does not just represent a source of inspiration, but constitutes the offspring of recall, memory, remembrance, historical reflection – exactly those functions which the analyst too is attempting to invoke when patients are invited to say anything that comes to mind in the foundational psychoanalytic principle of free association.[14]

But there is more to Rimbaud's words than the implicit invocation of Homer as the blind first Poet. For Homer is never acknowledged in Greek mythology as a prophet, seer, or soothsayer. Upon inviting the Muse to sing in the opening lines of both the *Iliad* and the *Odyssey*, Homer acts as her mouthpiece, allowing himself to become the receptive vessel through which her stories come to life. When it comes to acts of premonition, the role is generally accorded to other figures. The most famous is undoubtedly Teiresias – the blind Theban prophet who also makes an appearance in the *Odyssey*, but whose claim to fame is primarily based upon his dramatic interventions in Sophocles's *Oedipus Rex* and *Antigone*.[15] On each occasion, it is Teiresias who steers the narrative towards its tragic climax by unveiling the truth to those who have thus far been blind – in the metaphorical sense of failing to acknowledge the true nature of the affairs in which they are embroiled. In *Oedipus Rex*, Teiresias's revelation of the truth is perhaps the most poignant, because although it allows Oedipus to see – for the very first time – how he himself has unwittingly thrown Thebes into ruin, he famously reacts to the disclosure of the truth with an act of self-blinding.[16] As long as Oedipus has the capacity to see, he remains totally blind; it is only when he finally starts to see clearly that blindness becomes his fate.

If the disordering of all the senses that Rimbaud presents to Izambard and Demeny as the precondition for the emergence of the Poet as a seer were indeed to accord pre-eminent status to the field of vision, then Bacon's recollection of Rimbaud's principle in his conversations with Maubert would make this field of vision even more prominent than any of the other senses, purely by virtue of the artistic practice to which the principle is applied. In poetry, the poet (blind as he or she may be) makes the words appeal to a multiplicity of senses – vision and hearing, sight and sound no doubt being the most common ones, but by no means to the detriment of all the others. This is especially true if the poet aims at creating a unique experience of synaesthesia – spoken words suddenly acquiring a sense of vision, taste, smell, and even touch.[17] Painting, however, is the quintessential *visual* art. It may not entirely exclude the other senses, especially for the painter who is going through the act of painting, but the painting itself fixates its audience in the strict position of viewers, spectators of what is being presented to them on the canvas that offers itself to the curious, hungry eye. Unlike the poem, the painting is not meant to be read and heard. The painting is not meant to be touched, smelled, or tasted. This does not by definition mean that the painting cannot speak and that it exists entirely outside the structure of language, regardless as to whether it contains fragments of text within the framework of its appearance, or by way of a title that the artist has given to it. Both a painting (or a sculpture or a film) and the spectator who watches it exist as what John Berger called a 'way of seeing', i.e. as historically determined forms that are invariably embedded in discursive, ideological assumptions about beauty, taste, class, truth, etc.[18]

When Bacon invoked Rimbaud's disordering of the senses as the primary factor facilitating the process of analysis that he may have been conducting on himself through his act of painting, it is therefore safe to say that the disordering in question would have been almost entirely restricted to the field of vision. And indeed, if blindness is to be conceived as I did earlier, notably as the destruction, impairment, distortion, or disappearance of vision as the full, clear and direct optical access to an external object, it is quite extraordinary to see that, of all the twentieth-century figurative painters, Bacon is the painter of blindness par excellence. Again, blindness is not to be interpreted here in a narrow sense, as the powerlessness of the eye, but rather as the destruction, impairment, redirection, distortion, or disappearance of vision as the full, unclouded, and direct optical access to an external object.

The conventional psychoanalytic interpreter of art would probably argue, in this respect, that for some repressed unconscious reason Bacon suffered throughout his life from a severe type of what Freud, in his celebrated essay on 'The "Uncanny"', called 'Augenangst', which James Strachey has translated alternatively as 'fears about the eye', 'anxiety about the eyes', and 'anxiety about eyes', but which simply means 'eye anxiety'.[19] Tempting as it may be, I would prefer not to diagnose Bacon as suffering from 'Augenangst', not least because the label carries the risk of pathologising a unique creative process. That being said, for an artist who spent his entire life working in the field of vision, it is truly remarkable how much Bacon seemed to have struggled with the physiological faculty of seeing, watching, or observing, both within the figurative framework of his paintings and in the very act that brought them into being and shaped them into their final, finished form. Bacon could not tolerate anyone watching him paint. Even those who were closest to him did not have access to his studio when he was painting. In his final working space at 7 Reece Mews he never painted from life, i.e. from 'sitters' or 'models' who were present when he was given over to the creative act. When sitting for a portrait some time during the 1950s, Lucian Freud disclosed that when he first arrived at Bacon's studio the painting looked already completed. Of the eight paintings for which Lisa Sainsbury sat for Bacon, he destroyed five, whereas the three others were painted after she had already left. A portrait of Cecil Beaton, for which the photographer also sat, was equally destroyed.[20] The only existing photograph of Bacon painting is a pre-arranged snapshot taken by John Edwards in 1984 of the artist revising the centre panel of *Three Studies for a Portrait of John Edwards*, 1984, at the Marlborough Fine Art gallery.[21] [fig. 49] Apart from the fact that the image has been staged, it hardly shows the painter at work, because he is completely outside his creative space and only seems to add a little revision to an already existing work.

Much like the Poet, Bacon painted his characters blind, i.e. without having direct visual access to their features, but appealing to memory. Speaking to David Sylvester, Bacon conceded that the process of painting is synonymous with recalling, whereby the resulting distortion of the appearance then paradoxically allows the figure to be recorded more accurately in its truthful appearance.[22] At the same time, the numerous pairs of spectacles that were found in Bacon's studio after his death confirm that he routinely wore glasses whilst painting, evidently not to have a better, clearer view of his sitters, but in all likelihood to have a closer contact with the brushstrokes and the material substance of the paint.[23] What mattered to Bacon more than anything else, including in the works of other painters he admired, was the way in which they had employed their palette, used their tools, and applied their strokes onto the canvas. Talking to Maubert about his favourite Rembrandt painting – the unfinished *Self-Portrait with Beret* at the Musée Granet in Aix-en-Provence – he did not reflect upon the composition as a whole, but singled out the elementary traits of the work: 'If one approaches, if one examines very closely every detail, the only thing one sees is brushstrokes, as if they were due to chance'.[24]

Emphasising the importance of solitude and memory, Bacon did not want any witnesses to his artistic process. He did not want to be visually followed by anyone other than himself, which in practice meant that it was the paint, its texture and colours that became endowed with agency.[25] Yet Bacon did not only paint blind in the sense that he preferred memory over optical access. He also performed a disordering of the sense of vision on the painted figures themselves, as if he also could not allow the emerging appearance to see himself in the act of painting. If we take Lacan's conceptual distinction between the eye and the gaze, in his 1964 Seminar *The Four Fundamental Concepts of Psycho-Analysis*, as an index of the phenomenological disjunction between the empirical function of seeing and the transcendental occurrence of the look, then Bacon's disordering of vision in the painted figures on the canvas does not by definition imply that he somehow tried to ensure that the product of his creative act would not look back.[26] Instead, the functioning optical system of the appearances was consistently replaced with (and displaced to) a much less readily identifiable representation of the objectifying and potentially intimidating glance which, to paraphrase Lacan, looks at the painter in his existence as an artist in the act of creation from all sides.[27] Both throughout the process of painting and in the finished product, the canvas invariably looks back at the painter, much like it does at the spectator, but from a site, point, or constellation that is both everywhere and nowhere, precisely because the sense of vision in the painted appearances is fundamentally disordered.

The Ten Ratios of Disordered Vision

Looking through the massive body of work that has now been collected and annotated in Bacon's *Catalogue Raisonné*, there are but eight pictures in the colossal amount of paintings, drawings and sketches that have survived the artist's own, forever eager hands of destruction in which the sensory system of vision of the figures on the canvas remains fully intact.[28] There are but eight pictures in which the sense of vision is not, in one way or another, disordered and where – following Bacon's own association in his conversation with Maubert – the work of analysis that he was carrying out on himself seems to have stuttered, stagnated, or even failed.

The first is a portrait from the late 1920s or early 1930s, in which Bacon still seems to be in search of his own style and which most spectators are unlikely to even recognise as a signature 'Bacon'. [fig. 12] As Martin Harrison states in his commentary on it: 'Slightly awkward, if engaging in its naïveté, it is evident that Bacon was at an exploratory stage regarding technique, and experimenting with media ... [T]here are no comparators in Bacon's extent oeuvre for the drawing style'.[29] What makes the picture stand out, however, from other early works, is that the eyes of the young man have been painted in full and almost identically. If they give the impression that they are ever so slightly directed to his left side, it is merely because the sclera of his right eye is more prominently visible than that of his left eye. But there is no doubt that his sense of vision is undisturbed.

The second is the 1951 *Portrait of Lucian Freud*, which is widely considered to be Bacon's first portrait of a named sitter, and which is therefore the primary result of 'the process of painting from a live model [that Bacon always found] awkward and embarrassing'.[30] In this case, the painting displays the prototypical Baconian frame, yet again it does not stand out as a classic Bacon, let alone a Baconian masterpiece. The third was most likely painted shortly after the Freud portrait and was Bacon's first attempt at capturing the reality of Pope Innocent X, after Velázquez, [fig. 17] even though Bacon himself occasionally intimated that he had been equally inspired by a photograph of Pope Pius XII who was carried above a crowd of admirers in his emblematic *sedia gestatoria*.[31] The fourth and fifth are 1953 variations on the series of eight Popes that Bacon painted in quick succession during that year and which were reportedly begun as a portrait of David Sylvester that gradually acquired the image of a Pope.[32] The sixth and seventh are again paintings of a Pope, which are part of a series of six that Bacon produced in 1961 and which he effectively conceived as a double triptych, or one might even say a single hexatych, although it was never displayed as such.

Finally, the eighth painting in which the figure's sense of vision is not somehow disordered is perhaps the most interesting one, because it concerns a picture within a picture, which is itself part of a triptych of three different, named figures. The work in question is called *Three Portraits – Posthumous Portrait of George Dyer; Self-Portrait; Portrait of Lucian Freud*, 1973. It is remarkable not only because Bacon moved away, here, from his common practice of employing the triptych as a formal tool for creating three variations on the same theme, but also because on the left and right panels the figures (of George Dyer and Lucian Freud respectively) are duplicated, while the three mirrors reflect nothing.

By contrast with these extremely limited representations of non-disordered eyes, no less than ten ratios of visual disordering can be identified which run through Bacon's entire oeuvre.[33] In the interest of space, I shall just summarily name and illustrate them. In each case, however, it concerns an operation on the sense of vision of the representational figures by means of a specific act of painting that, in itself, may take various forms, insofar as it can sometimes be achieved through a simple brushstroke, or a small intervention on the technical equipment that enables seeing to happen, but at other times is being accomplished with equal effectiveness by the absence of paint – the sense of vision disappearing as a result of the figure's gradual absorption into the blank canvas. In no particular order, the ten ratios of blindness in Bacon's work can be designated as omission, obfuscation, closing, cutting, deformation, squinting, looking awry, fading, shuttering, and breaking. These are by no means the only techniques to which the artist could have had recourse to effectuate a disordering of vision, yet I have found no evidence of other ratios, such as enucleation, or slicing.

Of these ten ratios of blindness, the general public is no doubt most familiar with the practice of omission, if only because it is a key feature of the 1944 triptych with which Bacon sealed his fame as the greatest figurative painter of the twentieth century: *Three Studies for Figures at the Base of a Crucifixion*, 1944. [fig. 1] Whatever the nature of the life-form that Bacon represented in this triptych—and they are commonly referred to as biomorphs—one of the most striking characteristics of these three figures is that their eyes are missing, which crucially contributes to the semantic ambiguity of the distended mouths in the centre and right panels. And if the figure in the centre panel belongs to the same species as its two companions, one would feel hard pressed to see the piece of cloth that is wrapped around its head as a blindfold, for the simple reason that there is no visual sense organ in the first place—the cloth serving, therefore, perhaps more appositely as a headscarf, a hairband, or even a serviette. The second technique of obfuscation is easily recognisable in *Painting 1946*, [fig. 13] which created quite a stir when it was first exhibited at the Redfern Gallery in London, and which Bacon considered to be a defining moment in his career. Here, the spectator is quite literally left in the dark about the central figure's eyes, because the top half of its head is concealed by the pitch black internal space of the umbrella above its head. The cadmium orange droplets on the figure's upper lip may suggest that, much like the chunks of flesh surrounding and containing it, this proto-human life-form has also been exposed to an act of butchery during which his eyes were removed, yet the shadow that is cast by the umbrella, and which contrasts sharply with the strikingly white exposure of its chin, collar, and teeth, makes every inference purely speculative.

The technique of closing runs through Bacon's entire pictorial output and is not restricted to one type of figure or one specific format. It occurs in the self-portraits as much as it is being used in the portraits of others, and it may feature in stand-alone paintings as much as it can be part of one or more panels of a triptych. In this case, the figure's eyes are represented, yet the sense of sight is removed because the eyelids are closed. Two examples of this technique are the *Study for Portrait III (after the Life Mask of William Blake)*, 1955, and the centre panel of the triptych *Three Studies for Self-Portrait*, 1983. Unlike closing, cutting involves the partial removal of one or more parts of a figure's sense of vision, either through the application of a simple brush stroke, which is the case for the vast majority of this type of blinding—see, for instance, *Head II*, 1961, and the right panel of *Three Studies for Self-Portrait*, 1972—or through the mere absence of paint, which results in the figure remaining partially blind because half of its eyes becomes absorbed by the (unprimed) canvas in 'Seated Figure', c. 1978. Cutting differs from omission, because in the ratio of cutting the viewer knows that the figure is endowed with a sense of vision, since enough of the sensory organs is left intact. Cutting may coincide with a closure of the other part(s) of the sensory organs, but it may also allow the uncut part of the eyes to remain open.

The fifth ratio, of deformation, may adopt various modalities of expression and is also not restricted to one or the other figure or format. It differs from cutting, because here the viewer can still identify the presence of two eyes, or a supposedly complete sensory organ of vision, yet one or both parts of the optical system are misshapen, contorted, disfigured. Much like the previous techniques, deformation can be part of one panel in a triptych or feature in a stand-alone picture. Two examples include the centre panel of *Three Studies for Portrait of Henrietta Moraes*, 1963, [fig. 27] and *Portrait of Lucian Freud*, 1965. By contrast with deformation, squinting constitutes a subtler ratio, which either represents the eyes of the figure as pointing in different directions, or (as is perhaps more common in Bacon's later work) captures the eyes as narrowed or partly closed, suggesting that the figures have difficulty seeing what they are exposed to, or are exposed to an unusually intense source of light, which makes them involuntarily adjust their eyes. Examples include *Study for Figure VI*, 1956-57, *Study for Self-Portrait*, 1980, [fig. 44] and the centre panel of *Three Studies for a Portrait (Peter Beard)*, 1980.

The seventh ratio, of looking awry, represents the figures on the canvas as looking in an unexpected, strange, or 'wrong' direction. It is especially prominent in Bacon's self-portraits of the late 1970s and early 80s, yet it can also be detected in other paintings, such as *Portrait of a Man Walking Down Steps*, 1972. In the self-portraits, the figures generally avert their eyes, looking downwards or sideways, thus making them blind to the eye of the painter who attempts to bring their appearance to life on the canvas (see, for instance, *Three Studies for Self-Portrait*, 1980). In *Portrait of a Man Walking Down Steps*, 1972, which is considered to be a portrait of George Dyer painted shortly after his death, the vulnerability of the character is overdetermined and multifaceted. With one hand holding on to the window frame and the other hand seemingly attached to the strangely curved banister, the figure's feet are positioned awkwardly and incongruously, as if he has already lost his balance and is desperately trying to cushion the impact of the fall. Yet perhaps the most striking feature of the painting is that the character's eyes are not fixated on any material aspect of the situation he is finding himself in, but peering in the distance, towards someone or something that lies outside the canvas. The figure is blind to the circumstances of his fall and blind to whatever it is that may help him maintain his balance.

Fading and shuttering, the eight and the ninth ratios of blindness, are similar insofar as they both involve pictorial representations of the disordering of vision that are the result of a process of decomposition—in the literal sense of the word as the sense of vision being barred from the actual composition of the painting. However, fading differs from shuttering, because it involves a technique that allows the sensory organs to merge with the background, whereas shuttering always involves the presence and power of additional, clearly identifiable brushstrokes, which often stand out through their colour-scheme or the repetition of the strokes. Two typical examples of fading are the painting *Head*, 1948, and *Head VI*, 1949, [fig. 14] which remains one of Bacon's best loved and most disturbing pictures.[34] Shuttering tends to make a later appearance in Bacon's output, even though it is not completely absent from the earlier work. Much like many of the other ratios, it is not restricted to a singular figure, nor to a certain form or framing. Good examples of the process of shuttering include *Study for Portrait of Isabel Rawsthorne*, 1982 and the three panels of the Mick Jagger triptych, 1982. [fig. 46] Bacon himself reflected upon the technique of shuttering in his interviews with Sylvester, in which he conceded that he had derived it from Degas:

[I]n his pastels he [Degas] always striates the form with these lines which are drawn through the image and in a certain sense both intensify and diversify its reality. I always think that the interesting thing about Degas is the way he made lines through the body: you could say that he shuttered the body, in a way, shuttered the image and then he put an enormous amount of colour through these lines. And having shuttered the form, he created intensity by putting his colour through the flesh.[35]

Finally, the tenth ratio of blindness, which I have decided to call 'breaking', is probably as familiar as the omission with which I started my enumeration, partly because it features conspicuously in Bacon's most famous Pope-portrait, *Study after Velázquez's Portrait of Pope Innocent X*, 1953, [fig. 8] partly because its source and origin – the silent scream of the woman in the Odessa steps scene in Eisenstein's *Battleship Potemkin* – have lodged themselves in our collective memory as one of the most dramatic figurations of anguish and despair. It is important to note, however, that the representational figuration of 'breaking', here, does not apply to the sensory organ of vision as such, but rather to the 'artificial eyes', i.e. the spectacles, that allow vision to be maintained. Another, less well-known example of this ratio features in Bacon's *Portrait of Man with Glasses I*, 1963. [fig. 7] Hence, in the tenth ratio of blindness, Bacon does not break the physiological organ of the eye, but only its prosthetic extension – the specially constructed lenses that we refer to as glasses. But the effect is the same: in having their spectacles taken away – broken, damaged, or destroyed – the figures lose their ability to see.

Conclusion

At this point, it is tempting to examine how this recurrent, seemingly obsessive representation of disordered vision in Bacon's work should be interpreted. Where does it stem from? How can it be explained? What does it mean, over and above Bacon's own oblique reference to Rimbaud's disordering of the senses, as the precondition for conducting a process of analysis on oneself via the act of artistic creation, or what could perhaps also be called a 'painting cure'? Might we go so far as to claim that in rendering his figures blind, or in disordering their vision, the painter would effectively enhance their capacity to set his own creative experiments free? The disordering of the figures' sense of vision would then make space for chance and accident, and allow the painter to be purely guided by the materiality of brush and paint – simultaneously allowing the figures to acquire an appearance that is neither abstract nor illustrational, but representative of the truth of their innermost being.

Interesting as these observations might be, they unfortunately reduce the question of Francis Bacon's eyes to a semantic issue, to the search for a plausible story-line, which could not be further removed from what Bacon intended to achieve, as he himself relayed in his first interview with David Sylvester.[36] If blindness is to be taken as a central, puzzling characteristic of Bacon's work, it is thus perhaps not the meaning of it that matters, but rather the place it occupies in his artistic labour. To elaborate this point would require an in-depth study of (1) the relation between seeing, blindness and the gaze, (2) the status of the painting, as what is being seen by the painter without it looking back from the point – the organ(s) of vision – that is commonly identified as the principal source of seeing, (3) the relation between the act of painting, the visible absence of the model's physical reality, and the memory of what the painter is trying to capture on the canvas, and (4) the relation between the visual act of the painter, the blindness of the figure(s) on the canvas, and the eye of the spectator. Each of these four interrelated areas of investigation would warrant close examination, yet to address them I shall restrict myself to a mere three statements, which will probably generate more questions than answers, but which may nonetheless elicit a fresh approach to an aspect of Bacon's work that remains largely unexplored. I shall leave the fourth issue untouched, because it brings into play the eye of the spectator and would necessitate a detailed consideration of the historical and contemporary reception of Bacon's works, which falls beyond the scope of this text.

As far as the relation between seeing, blindness, and the gaze is concerned, it is difficult to avoid the conclusion that, in rendering his figures blind, Bacon merely wanted to stay in control of his work. The painter, as initiator and agency of the act, looks at the painting as the object and eventual outcome of the artistic process, but the painting is prevented from looking back. Even the self-portrait is not allowed to reflect the painter's eye, unless – and perhaps this is the only exception in Bacon's immense series of self-portraits – the painter's eye is already (partially) closed. I am referring, here, to *Self-Portrait with Injured Eye*, 1972, [fig. 37], which was painted shortly after the death of George Dyer and captured the painter with a swollen, deformed eye after a drunken brawl in London's West End—a prototypical case, one might say, of life imitating art. Yet in relying on Lacan's lectures on the split between the eye and the gaze from 1964, one might counter-argue that, in rendering his figures blind, the painter abdicates rather than consolidates control, because in depriving his figures of the physiological sense of vision and inducing a form of blindness, the location of the seeing eye is replaced with the ubiquity of the gaze, which transforms the subject-object relation and turns the painter into the recipient of a source of power that is always already situated elsewhere, somewhere in the space of the canvas, but outside his hands.

Perhaps this is why the 1953 painting of David Sylvester gradually turned itself into a Pope, with the caveat that his Holiness was eventually allowed to see, but maybe only for David Sylvester to speak through his avatar's eyes with an unequivocal reprimand or a harrowing question: 'Look what you've done to me!', 'How on earth could you allow me to become a Pope?'. Be that as it may, the statement that I would like to adduce with regard to the first issue is that the imposition of blindness, in the broad sense of a disordering of vision, makes space for the emergence of the gaze as an object of desire, i.e. as an object to which the painter can only respond with the rhetorical question 'What do you want?', which is in this case as much addressed to the canvas as it is to himself.

These succinct remarks immediately conjure up the question concerning the status of the painting, again not in the sense of what it means or what it represents, but in the sense of what place it occupies in the painter's own world of perception. Lacan devoted an entire lecture to this question on 11 March 1964, yet here I merely wish to repeat a highly evocative phrase by Merleau-Ponty, from the last text that he saw published during his lifetime, and with which Lacan would have been more than familiar: 'Ultimately the painting relates to nothing at all among experienced things unless it is first of all "autofigurative". It is a spectacle of something only by being a "spectacle of nothing", by breaking the "skin of things" to show how the things become things, how the world becomes world'.[37] What Merleau-Ponty had in mind, here, is that a painting is less created than it is endowed with the power to shape itself, but (one may add) also with the power to shape and reshape its alleged creator.

Of the four issues that I identified above, the third would deserve the most extensive elaboration, because it probes deeper than any of the others into the nature of Bacon's artistic practice. At this point, it is worth recalling that, by contrast with most of his contemporary figurative painters, such as Lucian Freud, Bacon stopped painting from 'sitters' or 'live models' when he moved to 7 Reece Mews in November 1961. In fact, anyone who has seen the 'arrangement' of Francis Bacon's studio – whether in the reconstruction of Dublin's Hugh Lane Gallery, or in the photographs of Perry Ogden – will have rapidly arrived at the conclusion that the chaos and disorder would have made the presence of a sitter next to impossible.[38] However, the upshot of Bacon's persistent refusal to paint from live models is that the blindness of the figures in his paintings appears to reflect the disordering of the painter's own sense of vision. In the absence of a live model, or merely relying on flat, two-dimensional photographs, Francis Bacon's eyes are forced to turn inwards, looking for images of appearances that have been recorded in his memory, searching for memory traces of the figures that captured his imagination, or trying to capture the impact on his own mind of what the eyes of other painters (and often photographers) had registered in the living world.

To develop this point, we might return to Derrida's reflections on vision and self-representation in *Memoirs of the Blind*, in which he paid detailed attention to Charles Baudelaire's 1863 essay 'The Painter of Modern Life' ('Le peintre de la vie moderne').[39] The fifth section of this essay, which is no more than five relatively short paragraphs in length, is entitled 'The Art of Memory (Mnemonic Art)'. By way of conclusion, a small extract from Baudelaire's text should suffice to convey the essence of Bacon's own existence as a figurative painter:

> [A]ll good and true draughtsmen draw from the image imprinted on their brains, and not from nature. To the admirable sketches of Raphael, Watteau and many others, I would reply that these are notes – very scrupulous notes, to be sure, but mere notes none the less. When a true artist has come to the point of the final execution of his work, the model would be more of an embarrassment than a help to him . . . In this way a struggle is launched between the will to see all and forget nothing and the faculty of memory, which has formed the habit of a lively absorption of general colour and of silhouette, the arabesque of contour. An artist with a perfect sense of form but one accustomed to relying above all on his memory and his imagination will find himself at the mercy of a riot of details all clamouring for justice with the fury of a mob in love with absolute equality. All justice is trampled under foot; all harmony sacrificed and destroyed; many a trifle assumes vast proportions; many a triviality usurps the attention. The more our artist turns an impartial eye on detail, the greater is the state of anarchy. Whether he be long-sighted or short-sighted, all hierarchy and all subordination vanishes.[40]

I do not know whether Francis Bacon ever read these lines, but if he did I cannot resist the feeling that, after having read them, he may have closed his eyes and started a new painting.

1 Arthur Rimbaud, 'To Georges Izambard', in *Selected Poems and Letters*, trans. Jeremy Harding, notes John Sturrock (London: Penguin Books, 2004), p. 236.

2 Ibid., pp. 238-39. The two 'letters of the seer' also contain Rimbaud's famous dictum 'I is somebody else' ('Je est un autre').

3 Franck Maubert, *L'odeur du sang humain ne me quitte pas des yeux. Conversations avec Francis Bacon* (Paris: Mille et une nuits, 2009), p. 41. My translation.

4 An excellent essay by James Wishart on Bacon's reliance on French poetry makes no mention of Rimbaud at all. In fact, the only serious consideration of Bacon's indebtedness to Rimbaud is to be found in a monograph by Miguel de Beistegui, who argues that 'Bacon achieves in painting the task that Rimbaud . . . had ascribed to poetry'. Ironically though, de Beistegui remained unaware of Bacon's own invocation of Rimbaud, probably because the text of his conversation with Maubert was only published just prior to the release of de Beistegui's book. See James Wishart, 'Francis Bacon and French Poetry: Towards a Genealogy of Image as Process', in Martin Harrison (ed.), *Francis Bacon: La France et Monaco/France and Monaco* (Paris: Albin Michel, 2016), pp. 169-82; Miguel de Beistegui, *Immanence: Deleuze and Philosophy* (Edinburgh: Edinburgh University Press, 2010), p. 174.

5 I am grateful to Martin Harrison for drawing my attention to the fact that Bacon also referred to Rimbaud in his third conversation with Michel Archimbaud, from April 1992, just a few weeks before his death. However, in this exchange, Bacon merely mentioned that he had read Rimbaud, alongside Racine, Baudelaire and Proust, in the original French. See Michel Archimbaud, *Francis Bacon: In Conversation with Michel Archimbaud* (London: Phaidon Press, 1993), p. 113. Bacon's books at the Hugh Lane Gallery in Dublin do not include a French edition of Rimbaud's works, but only a 1988 copy of Paul Schmidt's English translation of the poet's complete poetry, prose, and letters. See Arthur Rimbaud, *Complete Works*, trans. Paul Schmidt (London: Pan Books, 1988), reference number BB3.25.

6 Almost forty years after first meeting Bacon, Maubert revisited the times he spent with the artist in a short memoir, which also reproduces some of the episodes and fragments of conversation that he supposedly found most memorable, but the Rimbaud citation is not included in it. See Franck Maubert, *Avec Bacon* (Paris: Gallimard, 2019).

7 See, for example, David Sylvester, *The Brutality of Fact: Interviews with Francis Bacon*, third enlarged edition (London: Thames & Hudson, 1987), p. 25.

8 For a more detailed exploration of Bacon's creative activity as a psychoanalytic painting cure, see Dany Nobus, 'From Sense to Sensation: Bacon, Pasting Paint and the Futility of Lacanian Psychoanalysis', in *Francis Bacon: Painting, Philosophy, Psychoanalysis*, ed. Ben Ware (London: Thames & Hudson, 2019), pp. 95-116.

9 See Jacques Lacan, *The Four Fundamental Concepts of Psycho-Analysis* (1964), ed. Jacques-Alain Miller, trans. Alan Sheridan (London: The Hogarth Press and the Institute of Psycho-Analysis, 1977), pp. 67-119; Maurice Merleau-Ponty, *The Visible and the Invisible* (1960-1961), ed. Claude Lefort, trans. Alphonso Lingis (Evanston IL: Northwestern University Press, 1968).

10 My broad definition of blindness, here, may also serve as a counterweight to the pre-eminent status accorded to vision in the history of Western philosophy, which was only dislodged by an emerging anti-ocularcentric current in the thought of early twentieth century French philosophers, such as Bergson. For the classic, critical historical survey of the sovereignty of sight in the Western philosophical tradition, see Hans Jonas, 'The Nobility of Sight: A Study in the Phenomenology of the Senses', *Philosophy and Phenomenological Research*, 1954, 14(4), pp. 507-19. For the decentring of visuality in twentieth-century French philosophy, see Martin Jay, *Downcast Eyes: The Denigration of Vision in Twentieth-Century French Thought* (Berkeley/Los Angeles CA-London: University of California Press, 1993).

11 See Jacques Lacan, *Le Séminaire XIII, L'objet de la psychanalyse* (1965-1966), sessions of 11, 18 and 25 May 1966, unpublished.

12 The etymology of the Ancient Greek Homeros (Ὅμηρος) was only associated with blindness *after* the poet had been described and depicted as blind, possibly following the model of the blind bard Demodocus in *The Odyssey*. Much like everything else about Homer, his blindness remains an open question. See, for instance, James I. Porter, *Homer: The Very Idea* (Chicago IL-London: The University of Chicago Press, 2021), pp. 135-46; Jonas Grethlein, *Reading the Odyssey: A Guide to Homer's Narrative*, trans. Sabrina Stolfa (Princeton NJ-Oxford: Princeton University Press, 2024), pp. 77-78.

13 On Mnemosyne as the mother of the nine Muses, see Hesiod, Theogony, in *Theogony and Works and Days*, trans. M. L. West (Oxford: Oxford University Press, 1988), p. 30, where Mnemosyne is simply rendered as Memory.

14 Freud glosses free association in various places throughout his works. See, for example, Sigmund Freud, Freud's Psycho-analytic Procedure (1904a), in *The Standard Edition of the Complete Psychological Works of Sigmund Freud, Vol. 7* (London: The Hogarth Press and the Institute of Psycho-Analysis, 1953), p. 251.

15 See Homer, *The Odyssey*, trans. Emily Wilson (New York NY-London: W. W. Norton & Company, 2018), pp. 282-84; Sophocles, *The Three Theban Plays: Antigone, Oedipus the King, Oedipus at Colonus*, trans. Robert Fagles (London: Allen Lane, 1982), pp. 183-185 & pp. 110-15.

16 Sophocles, *The Three Theban Plays*, p. 237.

17 Poetry has drawn on synaesthesia since time out of mind. In the third part of Aeschylus's *Oresteia* trilogy, the Leader of the Furies incites his companions with the words 'ὀσμὴ βροτείων αἱμάτων με προσγελᾷ', which have been rendered in English as varied as 'the reek of human blood – it's laughter to my heart' and 'the whiff of human blood is smiling out at me'. See Aeschylus, *The Oresteia*, trans. Robert Fagles (London: Penguin Books, 1979), p. 242; Aeschylus, *The Oresteia*, trans. Oliver Taplin (New York NY-London: Liveright, 2018), p. 133. As he disclosed to Sylvester, Archimbaud, Maubert, and countless others, Aeschylus's trilogy and especially its third part occupied a special place

in Bacon's literary sources of inspiration, including for the 1944 *Three Studies for Figures at the Base of a Crucifixion* [44-01] which emboldened Maubert to employ a synaesthetic paraphrase of the aforementioned words as the title for his book of conversations: 'The smell of human blood doesn't leave my eyes'. See, for instance David Sylvester, *The Brutality of Fact: Interviews with Francis Bacon*, op. cit., pp. 49 & 130; David Sylvester, *Looking Back at Francis Bacon* (London: Thames & Hudson, 2000), p. 21; Michel Archimbaud, *Francis Bacon: In Conversation with Michel Archimbaud*, op. cit., p. 112; Franck Maubert, *L'odeur du sang humain ne me quitte pas des yeux*, op.cit., p. 34.

18 John Berger, *Ways of Seeing* (London: BBC and Penguin Books, 1972).

19 See Sigmund Freud, The 'Uncanny' (1919*h*), in *The Standard Edition of the Complete Psychological Works of Sigmund Freud*, Vol. 17 (London: The Hogarth Press and the Institute of Psycho-Analysis, 1955), pp. 217-56 and pp. 231-32 in particular.

20 See Martin Harrison, 'The Act of Painting', in Martin Harrison and Sophie Pretorius (eds.), *Revisions: Francis Bacon in the Act of Painting* (London: Thames & Hudson, 2024), pp. 9-26 and p. 9 in particular.

21 The photograph is reproduced in Martin Harrison, *In Camera: Francis Bacon – Photography, Film and the Practice of Painting* (London: Thames & Hudson, 2005), p. 195 and on the front free endpages of Martin Harrison and Sophie Pretorius (eds.), *Revisions: Francis Bacon in the Act of Painting*, op.cit..

22 David Sylvester, *The Brutality of Fact: Interviews with Francis Bacon*, op.cit., p. 46.

23 I am grateful to Martin Harrison for confirming this point.

24 Franck Maubert, *Avec Bacon*, op. cit., p. 30, my translation.

25 This emphasis on the quality of the paint – its texture and colour scheme – in Bacon's relation to art is what Deleuze at one point designated as 'haptic vision'. See Gilles Deleuze, *Francis Bacon: The Logic of Sensation (1981)*, trans. Daniel W. Smith (London-New York NY: 2017), pp. 91-92 & 106; Gilles Deleuze, *Sur la peinture* (1981) (Paris: Minuit, 2023), pp. 250-251. See also Franck Maubert, *Avec Bacon*, op. cit., p. 64.

26 Jacques Lacan, *The Four Fundamental Concepts of Psycho-Analysis*, op. cit., pp. 67-78.

27 Ibid., p. 72.

28 My tally is based on a careful examination of the pictures reproduced in the *Catalogue Raisonné*, but that does not mean it is exhaustive. Any additional suggestions of paintings by Bacon in which one or more of the figures' sense of vision is not disordered will be gratefully received. There is one triptych [77-05] that I deliberately omitted from my list of paintings with figures whose sense of vision remains undistorted, because in its final version Bacon made a radical change to its centre panel. In the first version of *Triptych 1974-77*, which was shown at New York's Metropolitan Museum of Art in 1975 for its Bacon retrospective, the centre panel includes a reclining figure holding binoculars whose external lenses display the figure's peering eyes. In 1977, Bacon painted the entire figure out and it is without it that the triptych now appears in the *Catalogue Raisonné*. See Martin Harrison (ed.), *Francis Bacon: Catalogue Raisonné*, Volume IV: 1971-92 (London: The Estate of Francis Bacon, 2016), pp. 1130-33; Martin Harrison & Sophie Pretorius (eds.), *Revisions: Francis Bacon in the Act of Painting*, pp. 38-41.

29 Martin Harrison (ed.), *Francis Bacon: Catalogue Raisonné*, Volume II: 1929-57 (London: The Estate of Francis Bacon, 2016), p. 116.

30 Ibid., p. 238.

31 See, for instance David Sylvester, *The Brutality of Fact: Interviews with Francis Bacon*, op. cit., pp. 25-26.

32 Martin Harrison (ed.), *Francis Bacon: Catalogue Raisonné*, Volume II: 1929-57, op. cit., p. 324.

33 The term 'ratio' should be understood here in the same way as Harold Bloom employed it in his acclaimed book *The Anxiety of Influence*: a device or movement that allows the artist to perform an operation on a work of art. See Harold Bloom, *The Anxiety of Influence: A Theory of Poetry*, 2nd edition (New York NY-Oxford: Oxford University Press, 1997).

34 This aspect of fading was also picked up by Bacon in his examination of the Rembrandt portrait at Aix-en-Provence. As he said to Sylvester: '[I]f you think of the great Rembrandt self-portrait in Aix-en-Provence, for instance, and you analyse it, you will see that there are hardly any sockets to the eyes, that it is almost completely anti-illustrational. I think that the mystery of fact is conveyed by an image being made out of non-rational marks'. See David Sylvester, *The Brutality of Fact: Interviews with Francis Bacon*, op. cit., p. 58. See also Martin Harrison, 'Irrational Marks: Bacon and Rembrandt', in Pilar Ordovas (ed.), *Irrational Marks: Bacon and Rembrandt* (London: Ordovas, 2011), pp. 26-49; Martin Harrison, *In Camera: Francis Bacon—Photography, Film and the Practice of Painting*, op. cit., pp. 212-13.

35 David Sylvester, *The Brutality of Fact: Interviews with Francis Bacon*, op. cit., p. 176. See also David Sylvester, *Looking Back at Francis Bacon*, op. cit., pp. 49-50.

36 Ibid., p. 25.

37 Maurice Merleau-Ponty, 'Eye and Mind' (1961), trans. Michael B. Smith, in Galen A. Johnson & Michael B. Smith (eds.), *The Merleau-Ponty Aesthetics Reader: Philosophy and Painting* (Evanston IL: Northwestern University Press, 1993), p. 141.

38 See Perry Ogden, *7 Reece Mews: Francis Bacon's Studio* (London: Thames & Hudson, 2001).

39 Jacques Derrida, *Memoirs of the Blind: The Self-Portrait and Other Ruins (1990)*, trans. Pascale-Anne Brault & Michael Naas (Chicago IL-London: The University of Chicago Press, 1993).

40 Charles Baudelaire, 'The Painter of Modern Life' (1863), in *The Painter of Modern Life and Other Essays*, ed. and trans. Jonathan Mayne (London-New York NY: Phaidon, 1965), p. 16.

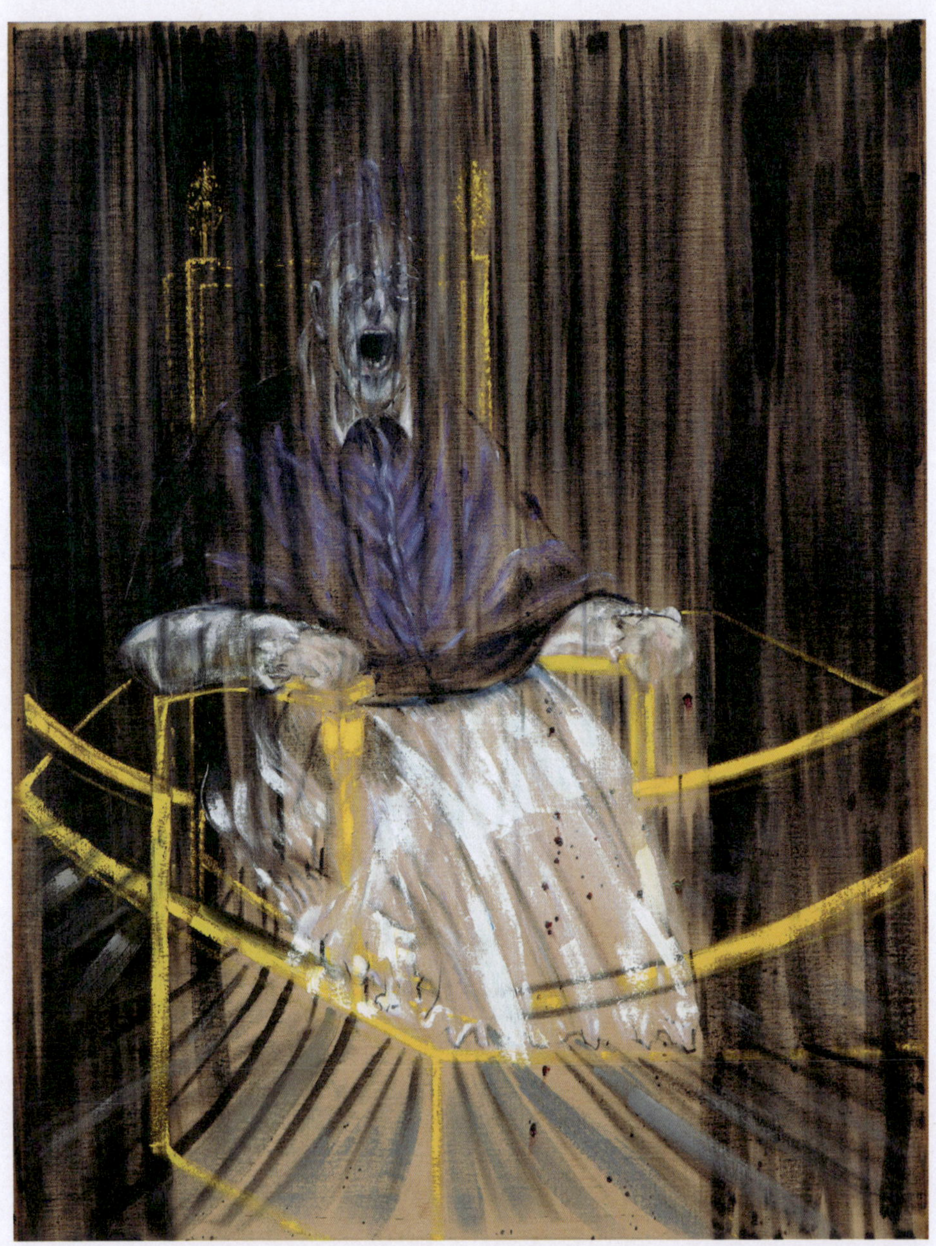

fig. 8   *Study after Velázquez's Portrait of Pope Innocent X, 1953*   **78**

'A NOTHING COULD REPRESENT ME BEST': THE POPE IN JEAN GENET AND FRANCIS BACON

Aaron Schuster

The Two Popes

In 1953 Francis Bacon paints one of his most celebrated artworks, *Study after Velázquez's Portrait of Pope Innocent X*, [fig. 8] working from photographic reproductions of Diego Velázquez's masterpiece. Although he visited Rome the next year, he declined to see the original, hanging in the Galleria Doria Pamphilj. In 1955 Jean Genet writes *"Elle"*, a short, one-act play about a photographic session with the pope. In 1953, Jacques Lacan pronounces his groundbreaking Rome discourse, about language and psychoanalysis; a few months earlier in Rome, on the occasion of a congress on 'The basic attitude of the Christian psychotherapist', Pope Pius XII himself remarked that 'Nobody will deny that there can be, and not seldom is, an irrational feeling of guilt, even a sick one.'[1] Around this time, Lacan tried, and failed, to get a private audience with the pope. Genet also expressed his fascination with winning a papal audience: 'Genet told Laurent Boyer that if the Pope invited him to the Vatican he would go without a second's hesitation, so fascinated was he by ecclesiastical pomp.'[2] Bacon, in contrast, had zero interest in seeing the pontiff, although in a way he came the closest: one of his papal portraits sits today in the Vatican museum.

To follow this confluence of dates a little further: in 1955, Lacan comments on Genet's play *The Balcony*, to which *"Elle"* is closely connected. Some years later, in his 1961-1962 seminar, Lacan gives an extended interpretation of French Catholic playwright Paul Claudel's Coûfontaine trilogy, whose first part, set in Restoration-era France, involves a drama about a kidnapped pope. The heroine of this play, Sygne de Coûfontaine, is persuaded to save the pope by marrying his kidnapper, who was also the butcher of her family during the Terror. In the final scene, Claudel conjures a truly Baconian image: the figure of the dying Sygne, refusing her last rites, her face contorted by a spasm into what Lacan calls a *signe-que-non*, a sign of no. Genet's theatre is also one of radical refusal. Ironically, due to his great lyricism, Genet was called by some critics a Claudelian playwright, but a Claudel of farts and turds. At one point in *"Elle"*, the pope suggests that the photographer take a picture of him while shitting: 'At that moment that I rid myself of all that reeking matter, I become closer to God, and I enjoy it. [...] But, without a doubt—you are right. We cannot offer the world the image of a Pope on his pot.'[3]

What about a screaming pope? Art critic Robert Hughes called Bacon 'the Genet of painting', a phrase that's sometimes repeated, no doubt referring to their criminality, homosexuality, and dissolute life-styles. Hughes wrote of the 'lavishness' with which Bacon, like Genet, 'uses his own psyche as experimental material', something which might be said of many artists.[4] Biographical details aside, nowhere are the two artists closer than in their shared fascination for the pope, this towering and iconographically rich symbol of authority and religiosity, whom they submit to a number of transformations: blasphemous, tortuous, violent, comedic, formal, and also, maybe, strangely pious. In what follows I will explore the connections between the papal artworks of Francis Bacon and Jean Genet, avowed atheists whose radical aesthetics were, in different ways, bound up with a Christian imagination. This will allow us to address the broader philosophical question of the relationship between art and religion in modernity, and the problem of the image and its beyond.

The Sugar Pope

Let us begin with Genet. The play is titled, with quotation marks, *"Elle"*, "She" or "Her", the genderbending title referring to the feminine gender of the word 'holiness' in French: *Sa Saintété* means His Holiness, but the noun 'holiness' is itself female. (This is taken literally in the 2024 film *Conclave*, based on the novel by Robert Harris, where a secretly inter-sex cardinal ends up getting elected to the papal office; Genet already anticipated this twist.) It was written in the autumn of 1955, around the same time as the composition of *The Balcony*, but it was not published in his lifetime. The play was first published in 1989, and had its theatrical premier in Parma, Italy at the Teatro Due on April 24, 1990, where, confirming the genderbending, Genet regular and acclaimed actress María Casares played the pope.

The short play is in one act. We are on the set of a photo shoot: a photographer is meant to be making publicity photos of the pope, which will be sent out in five sets of three million copies to spread his glorious image across the world. While awaiting the pope's arrival, the photographer converses with the usher, and there is also a brief visit from a cardinal. The pope finally arrives, gliding across the floor on roller skates, as if – he explains later – he were being carried by angels, light as a pure mirage. There follows some rather colourful metaphysical discussions about images and identity, but, despite all the exalted talk, the photographer doesn't get his photo. Instead, the pope delivers a series of five songs called 'The Laments of the Pope' (The second one is missing, and last two are actually recited by the photographer and the usher, in the pope's absence). In the end, a second photographer shows up, in order to photograph the papal photography session, which in fact never takes place. The cardinal briefly reappears and the curtain falls.

As Albert Dichy notes in his introduction to the play, "*Elle*" presents a reversal of the setup in *The Balcony*: instead of imposters becoming the roles they were only playacting and seizing actual power (the bishop, the judge, and the general), it's the real pope who complains of being an imposter, a mere actor, even a 'ham actor.'[5] 'I am a mannequin,' he declares.[6] The pope is on a quest to find his image, the image that would make him into the holy figure that he is. The photographer is meant to provide this image, but ultimately he cannot. Meanwhile, the pope, who has a philosophical sensibility, lucidly articulates the paradox he finds himself in: 'It's a strange state though, to be the one waiting to be conceived.'[7] The pope's relation to his identity is an *anticipatory* one, and much of the play consists in the pope's theoretical self-reflections on what it means to be, and not to be, an image.

The paradox he keeps returning to is that the papal image is both him and not him, since it is external to himself, and even seems to lead an autonomous life beyond him. In an uncanny reversal, it's the image that makes use of the person to realise itself: 'I was becoming a prop for gestures destined to define the most unattainable image ever.'[8] He thus experiences his identity as total alienation, as an 'absence from all representation.'[9] The pope felt so little connected to his image that he once engaged in a mischievous act of pre-digital manipulation: on the photographic negative he replaced his body parts with fragments from other people, including 'the hand of a Belgian high bishop', leaving only his ear, and ear hairs, 'to authenticate this image'.[10] The image is total fakery, a manufactured artifice. The pope therefore questions whether the exalted papal clichés, all his 'imaginary' images, are not the wrong ones to understand what the pope truly is. Despite the contrived setting of the photo shoot, the pope expresses an aesthetic indifference: 'My image could be anything.'[11] Furthermore, he suggests that the best image might be not an image at all, but an object, even a most ordinary, humble thing. 'I was trying to figure out what object would best represent me and my noble absence. I thought at first of a thimble, of a stuffed giraffe, of a lint brush – my humility could not disregard this: I thought of a spat-out cigarette butt – yes, I had the idea that as soon as a cigarette butt is flicked through the air, it becomes the Pope and has a right to all pontifical respects.'[12]

This deconstruction of the image mirrors modern art's overturning of classical representation. From the retinal pope we arrive at a ready-made pope – his incarnation in a lowly, everyday object, like a thimble, stuffed animal, brush, or flying cigarette butt. This link to theology is not so far-fetched: Boris Groys made the connection between the mystery of incarnation and avant-garde art, calling Christ a readymade god.[13] To paraphrase Lacan's definition of sublimation, which itself derives from the readymade, Christ is a miserable, ordinary man who is elevated to the dignity of the Son of God.[14] In fact, this theological resonance was already explicit from the early days of the readymade: in 1917, the same year that Duchamp made *Fountain*, the upturned urinal signed R. Mutt, another piece of plumbing, this time an upside down cast iron plumbing trap, was presented as a sculpture titled *God*.[15]

Genet proposes his own comedic version of this readymade the-ology, which is foreshadowed near the start of the play. While waiting for the pope, the usher offers a photographer a cup of coffee and then, holding out a sugar bowl, asks 'One pope? Or two?'[16] The photographer is at first taken aback, but then plays along: 'Excuse me, and thank you for the pope. Another, if you please.'[17] When the pope later makes his appearance, it is revealed that not only is he in on the joke, it was his invention. In the third song of 'The Laments of the Pope', named 'The Song of the Sugar Cube', the pope recounts his quest to find the perfect image for himself, ending with his saccharine solution: 'Fortunately though, in my anguished quest, the idea of using an object from everyday conversation came to me… and then the idea of a sugar cube came to me! I was delighted! I released a famous secret bull – establishing, reg-ulating and codifying, the representative powers of little bits of sugar.'[18]

At an earlier point in the play, this problem of incarnation is posed from a different angle. The pope asks the photographer about his per-sonal life, whether he has kids, if he is married. The photographer takes out a photo of his two children, and hands it to the pope. After briefly remarking on it, he expresses his frustration with images – 'Images, always images! I have had enough!' – and then tears the photo into little pieces. When the photographer protests, saying 'You've gone too far!', the pope replies: 'What have I done? I tore up a piece of paper. But as for your adored creatures, I did not touch them. My word, you idolise them!'[19]

The irony of this exchange is that the pope behaves in a completely modern, secular manner, as if symbols had no intrinsic or incarnate value but only an informational one. A photo is not a person, so why get angry if it's destroyed? According to the pope's rationalist stance, a photograph is only an efficient vehicle for referring to the persons who are pictured in it, and is, as such, replaceable and disposable. The spontaneous reaction of the photographer, however, betrays a more enchanted or magical attitude. By taking offence, he treats the photo not merely as sign that refers to his children, but as a 'sacred' object that contains or crystallises their presence. Thus the pope does indeed touch his children by ripping apart their photograph. Or, as Paul Moyaert explains, 'I no longer need to hurt you physically; cutting up your picture is sufficient as this gesture is symbolically equivalent to physically hurting you. The symbolic action has the power to satisfy the desire.'[20]

Genet's sugar cube pope is a continuation of this spontaneous fetishism of everyday life, or human sensibility for strongly embodied symbols. His theological provocation is that the sweetener pope is no less ridiculous than Christ's presence in little disks of bread, or God's incarnation in a miserable human being. But he goes further: the 'Song of the Sugar Cube' ends by detailing the fantastical consequences of the symbolic equation pope = sugar. 'Thus, in all places in the world, and during every second, millions of followers consume incredible amounts of my image. Instead of receiving thousands of pictures of an old man, the convents, the presbyteries, the bistros, the barracks, the reform schools, the parliaments, the train stations, the airports, receive tons of white sugar, ideal images of Our Gullibility. They put me in a hot cup of coffee, of milk, of chamomile, phooie!! I melt. A kid, an old woman, munches me. More Pope?'[21] Millions worldwide eat and drink the pope; thus, reality becomes suffused with his pontifical presence. This is the pope's goal: not only to become himself by acceding to an image, but to spread his popeliness across the globe, to be daily imbibed with the morning coffee. Instead of real presence, one might speak here of a surreal presence, a *praesentia surrealis*.[22]

A short story by Guillaume Apollinaire, one of the forefathers of surrealism, prefigures Genet's surreal Christianism. In 'The Sacrilege' a Catholic priest, Father Seraphim, who is lamenting the sad state of the world, sanctifies a bakery so that the oven will produce loads of eucharist bread to bless the whole population:

> Here and there, the vent-hole of a bakery glowed. Father Seraphim went over to one of them and, stretching out his hands, pronounced the sacramental words:
> 'This is my Body, this is my Blood,' thus consecrating the entire oven. By dawn he was weary, but knew that he had consecrated enough bread to give communion to a million men. On this very day, he thought to himself, the multitude will be satiated with the Eucharist. Thanks to it, men will once more become good, and from noon onwards the reign of God will begin on earth. What a miracle, and what jubilation there will be![23]

Father Seraphim blesses the bakery oven, so that everyone eating its bread ingests the body of Christ, unwittingly taking the divine presence into their bodies. Soon after, the priest is embarrassed by what he's done and begs forgiveness from the Archbishop, who absolves him and bursts into laughter. But Genet's pope is not embarrassed; his sugary form seems the best solution to the insoluble problem of finding an image. In fact, the photographer never gets his photo. But the usher reassures him: 'Don't worry about it, my poor friend. You're wasting your time. In place of a photo, you'll have a sugar cube.'[24] There is another, perhaps unwitting, reference here to the history of the readymade: sugar cubes, or marble blocks in the form of sugar cubes, feature in Duchamp's assisted readymade *Why Not Sneeze, Rose Sélavy?* The made-up name – Rose Sélavy was Marcel Duchamp's female alter-ego, his "Elle," as it were – is a play on desire: *Éros c'est la vie*, ('Eros is life').

The Real Presence

Bacon was obsessed by Velázquez's *Portrait of Pope Innocent X* (c. 1650), which is widely considered one of the greatest portraits ever made, if not the greatest.[25] (Similarly, *Las Meninas* is often considered to be the ultimate painting, the pinnacle achievement of the art form, the so-called 'theology of painting'). As the story goes, the shock of seeing the papal portrait was such that Innocent X exclaimed: '*È troppo vero! È troppo vero!*' ('It's too true! It's too true!') – the soul of the politically savvy and calculating pope, ironically called 'Innocent', laid bare by the artist. Bacon says: 'I've always thought that this was one of the greatest paintings in the world, and I've used it through obsession.'[26] And: 'In Velázquez it's a very, very extraordinary thing that he has been able to keep it so near to what we call illustration and at the same time so deeply unlock the greatest and deepest things that man can feel.'[27]

Did Velázquez fabricate the truest image of the pope? A humanist portrait revealing the man behind the ideal image, the mortal beneath the papal cloak? Not exactly: there is something else at stake than simply providing a realistic illustration of the person of Innocent X, Giovanni Battista Pamphilj. There is something shocking in the portait, a dangerous truth that points to a dehiscence in the image, the revelation of his living 'soul'. Bacon aspired to achieve such a truth-effect in painting, and to also unlock the deepest feelings, but he cannot paint in the same way as Velázquez. In his time, flooded with technologically produced images of reality, the only way to attain a similarly powerful effect is to do violence to the image, to distort or warp it in a non-realistic manner. He must break with the verisimilitude of Velázquez, whose genius lay in keeping extremely close to illustration – 'one really does believe that

Velázquez recorded the court at that time and, when one looks at his pictures, one is possibly looking at something which is very, very near to how things looked' – while allowing another dimension to come through.[28] For Bacon, on the other hand, it's only the stain or distortion that can unlock something in the image, thus revealing the 'brutality of fact' and returning 'the onlooker to life more violently'.[29] This violence is why Bacon didn't like his models to be present while painting: 'They inhibit me because, if I like them, I don't want to practise before them the injury that I do to them in my work.'[30] One might imagine a similar inhibition had Bacon been painting in the presence of the Velázquez, not wanting to violate the master's living portrait.

Study after Velázquez's Portrait of Pope Innocent X [fig. 8] was preceded by several other pope paintings, and then succeeded by several more, till the last one, *Study of Red Pope, 1962, Second Version*, 1971. [fig. 34] Moreover, Bacon painted several depictions of the crucifixion, including his breakout work *Three Studies for Figures at the Base of a Crucifixion*, from 1944. [fig. 1] It's difficult not to view this painting through the lens of the sci-fi aesthetics of H.R. Giger, in the films *Dune* and *Alien*; and indeed, Ridley Scott had proposed to Giger the demonic creatures of Bacon's *Crucifixion* as a source for the alien xenomorph. (This retroactive effect in which Bacon's originals come to resemble the images they inspired is another example of the autonomous life of images). Here, however, I will limit myself to this sole painting, due to its iconic status in Bacon's oeuvre.

Like in Velázquez, the pope is seated in his chair, but it is no longer a papal throne: the robust wood and gilded seat has been transformed into a kind of garish yellow contraption, with slats vaguely reminiscent of playground monkey bars. He is wearing a purple cloak, in contrast to the red in Velázquez, thus reversing the 1464 decree of Pope Paul II that 'his cardinals were to wear robes of rich scarlet instead of purple, the poor Tyrian-purple mollusks being all but extinct by this time.'[31] (Portraits of earlier popes sometimes have them clad in purple; the photographs that Bacon worked from were black and white). The whole painting is covered by white striations, which gives the feeling of viewing it through a tattered veil, sometimes connected by commentators to the veil in Titian's portrait of Cardinal Filippo. The hands grip the chair arms more tightly than in Velázquez. Is the pope sitting in an electric chair? The pope is screaming, his face gripped by a terrible agony. The black void of the open mouth is ringed by the 'enclosure of the teeth', to use the Homeric phrase, little white teeth.[32] Bacon said he wanted to paint the ultimate scream: 'I did hope one day to make the best painting of the human cry.'[33] Bacon drew on Poussin's *The Massacre of the Innocents* and the scene of the murder of civilians by Tsarist soldiers in

Eisenstein's *Battleship Potemkin*, where a woman, having been shot, cries out on the Odessa steps. The pope who was contemporary with Bacon was Pius XII, a controversial figure because of his refusal to speak out against the Nazis and the Holocaust. Unlike Velázquez's portrait with its highly expressive eyes of Innocent X, Bacon's pope has no eyes. But he does wear glasses. The wispy glasses hanging on the pope's visage are like an unholy combination of the wireframe spectacles seen in photos of Pius XII – the same pope who made the Kafkaesque pronouncement about irrational guilt before the congress on Christian psychotherapy – and the shattered pince-nez on the bloodstained woman's face in *Battleship Potemkin*.

Not only is the subject matter Catholic, but one might interpret the effect of the painting using a religious conceptuality. This is how one of the leading interpreters of Bacon's work, his close friend Michel Leiris, who was raised a Catholic, writes about his art. Leiris, uses the term 'real presence' to describe the effect of Bacon's painting. In Catholic doctrine, real presence refers to the 'true, real, and substantial' presence of the flesh and blood of Christ in the bread and wine of the Eucharist (according to the formula of the Council of Trent) – a mystery whose exact nature and status was the subject of much theological controversy and sometimes strange speculation. For Leiris what is important is the doubleness of incarnation, the presence of the invisible within the visible, the intangible within the tangible, the infinite within the finite. Bacon's paintings strike the viewer with a vivid, carnal reality, a 'presence that feels alive'. Bacon's contorted bodies are wracked, as it were, by another dimension but this is located nowhere else than in the body itself, in its torsion or division. His canvases possess a non-religious sacrality, whose horror and ecstasy is akin to that exuded by sexuality:

> As if the picture had its own life, and constituted a new reality instead of being a mere simulacrum... that feature in a Bacon canvas which is immediately apprehended and asserts itself unequivocally and independently of any sense of agreement or disagreement... is the kind of *real presence* to which his figures attain, even though this presence has no connection at all with any kind of theology. Through the agency of the figures, the spectator who approaches them with no preconceived ideas, gains direct access to an order of flesh-and-blood reality not unlike the paroxysmal experience provided in everyday life by the physical act of love. And this presence is graced with a wild ambiguity, an alluring iridescence, which makes it a sensuous delight, but one so intense that, despite the attractiveness of its painterly vehicle, to some people, repelled perhaps by its searing impact, it can appear wholly abhorrent.[34]

To shift registers: It is striking that Lacan also appeals to the Christian notion of real presence in relation to the psychoanalytic clinic, specifically the phenomenology of obsessional neurosis where what is at stake is a defence against this presence, or an 'insult to real presence'.[35] This presence also has a 'wild ambiguity', alluring yet horrifying and destructive. In this neurotic Catholicism, the Eucharist plays a double role. On the one hand, Lacan observes that the sacrament is a fertile source of sexual fantasies. He cites the case of a woman who 'imagined to herself that there were male genitalia in the place of the communion wafer'.[36] He also makes a rare reference to his own clinical practice: one of his patients fantasised that he would place a communion wafer in the woman's vagina, so that 'the host would wind up serving as a hat atop the subject's penis at the moment of penetration'.[37] But it's not only that neurotics are able to make use of the Eucharist to elaborate their erotic fantasies, like some X-rated Buñuel picture. Lacan also finds in the Christian notion of real presence something telling for psychoanalytic theory, something deeply true.

Desire is never simply about the pain of unfulfillment and the pleasure of satisfaction. There is a real presence of desire, that gives it a dramatic character. The neurotic insult to the sacred object of Christian devotion is a symbolic means for keeping at bay this presence: not God's but the Other's desire. This desire underlies psychic reality, giving it a direction and guidepost, yet also threatens to destabilise and destroy it, for one can never know what the Other wants or how to represent it. The obsessional desires above all to keep desire under control, to reduce the enigma of desire to concrete demands that can be conformed to or complained about, so as to prevent any of its real presence from breaking through.[38] Yet this presence inevitably ends up manifesting itself in the bizarreness and elaborateness of the very defences meant to contain it. Ironically, the neurotic lives life as a defence against living presence, dramatically trying to de-dramatise the drama of living.

Art, as opposed to neurosis, can do something else with this presence. It can, as Bacon says, return us to life more violently. Art can render the real presence of desire in a non-destructive way, through an aesthetic veil, without recourse to pathological defence mechanisms. (Or it can reveal the truth of these defences, without defending against them). In the case of Bacon's painting, the 'searing impact' of a lacerating presence is manifested in the pope's abyssal scream.

The Screaming Pope

In contrast to Genet's playfully ambiguous and surrealistic attitude to religious ceremony, Bacon's interest in religion is more anthropological.

Christianity is understood as a tremendous nerve meter, a world-historical dramaturgical apparatus for generating what Nietzsche famously called an 'orgy of feeling'.[39] Therein lies Bacon's attraction to the imposing iconography of the pope and the violent scene of the crucifixion. But Bacon paints these traditional religious figures as subject to another 'passion'. Bacon describes the decline of religion in this way: 'Man now realizes that he is an accident, that he is a completely futile being, that he has to play out the game without reason.'[40] Instead of illustrating a divine transcendence, and the world as the plan of a demiurgic creator, art is now 'entirely a game'; more precisely, a game of chance.[41] And if there is a chance for art after religion, it lies in its ability to do something with the accidental and drifting character of existence, to integrate it into its very practice and make something of it – this practice of the accident is Bacon's realism. The fabricator of religious icons was sometimes conceived as a medium through which the image of Christ would appear; the Baconian artist is a vehicle through whom the accident happens.

In an interview with Marguerite Duras, Bacon explains how chance is central to his process. He starts by making marks on the canvas and waiting for the accident, which he also calls the 'stain', to occur. The stain resists comprehension. If one understands or recognises what has been produced then it enters into a narrative and becomes representational. But the stain is a chance to break with familiar forms and patterns, with the domain of figuration. In order to do so, however, the accidental mark needs to be elaborated. One must have both an innate sense for the stain, and the technique to develop it, a discipline to follow its intrinsic force, and this is what Bacon calls the 'technical imagination'. 'The technical imagination is the instinct that works outside the law to turn the subject on its head with the force of nature.'[42] With his disfigured figures, Bacon seeks to avoid both illustrative painting and abstraction, where tension is dissipated in a wash of colour and shape. At the same time, he also opposes the readymade due to its all too static character. Artists are 'ripping out a piece of dirt and putting it on a pedestal', but 'what's needed is for the "force" with which they rip out the earth to "turn".' To merely select and arrange given objects is to remain within the orbit of one's 'personal system', the order of the 'imaginary imagination' which inevitably spins around itself. The technical imagination forces one outside one's personal system; it works beyond the law (of identity), turning the subject 'on its head'. But the discipline of the accident is something hard won and risky. The unruliness of the force it unlocks can sweep away the tableau. Hence so many overworked, botched, and ruined paintings. The technical imagination fails and the insurgent power of the accident is lost.[43]

Bacon's description of his artistic process is not unlike the procedure of psychoanalytic therapy. Psychoanalysis creates an artificial speech situation – via its central rule: say anything that comes to mind – with the aim of fostering a setting where something unexpected can happen. You can't plan surprise, but you can create conditions that are more conducive to it. Not to confess one's sins or to tell one's life story, but to produce a break in narrativisation, a rupture in the ego's monologue, a stain, a deviation, a slip – that is the point of the analytic procedure. And the art of analysis is to gamble on the break, to follow its logic and see where it leads, to have the 'technical imagination' to articulate its unforeseen pathways and errant connections, its torsion of the person. Instead of a psychoanalysis of Bacon, Bacon's artistic method can help to illuminate what is at stake in psychoanalysis.

Ironically, Bacon and Duras never speak about the scream in their conversation, but if there is one subject that brings them together, it is this. Duras once defined writing as the art of 'screaming without sound'.[44] Bacon says that his aim is 'to paint the scream more than the horror'.[45] What does this mean? The horror is what ties the scream to a scene, relates it to its cause: to scream at or in the face of something terrifying, like a monster, or an assailant, or the death of God. To paint the scream more than the horror means to separate the factum of the scream from the meaningful context in which its embedded, to isolate it from narrative explanation. (This isolation is effected even more explicitly in other paintings, like *Head VI*, [fig. 14] where the head and torso of the screaming pope are encased inside a cube). Bacon says 'the moment the story enters, the boredom comes upon you'.[46] Stories, with their psychological descriptions and cause-and-effect relations, are inherently boring. Or rather, they are all too interesting, but in a soporific way that dulls the senses. The scream, for both Bacon and Duras, marks a radical rupture with storytelling. One can tell a story about a scream, but the scream is a break in the story: it cries out a silence. Lacan says *le cri fait le gouffre où le silence se rue*, 'the scream makes the abyss where silence rushes'.[47] Writing of Duras's fiction, Alexi Kukuljevic explains that the silence of the scream constitutes 'a break-down in cohesion, in synchrony, a collapse of "the correlation between cause and effect" that makes one question the story as such and as a whole. In all of Duras's writing, the story turns around a resistant kernel.'[48] It is this resistant kernel, this silence produced in and by the scream, that Bacon renders viscerally present through the stain of painting. Indeed, to call *Study after Velázquez's Portrait of Pope Innocent X* [fig. 8] the portrait of a 'screaming pope' is already to grant the figure too much ownership over the scream, too much agency, and to turn the painting into a minimal story: the pope screams. But the pope is not the agent of the scream. He is rather the vehicle for a scream that traverses him, undoing his identity as the authoritative figure par excellence that is the 'pope'.

Here we may return to *"Elle"*. Bacon's scream, emitted from the pitch blackness of the gaping maw of the mouth, is the materialisation of the *nothing pope* that, even beyond the cigarette butt pope and the sugar cube pope, Genet's sacred pontiff secretly aspires to: 'Then I took this even further, to the idea that a nothing could represent me best. A nothing? That's hard to grasp!'[49]

The Pope on a Pot

In fact, Genet's aesthetics are closer to the aristocratic universe of Velázquez than Bacon's, despite Bacon's avowed obsession with the painter. Recall Velázquez's goal of achieving official status in the court of Philip IV: in *Las Meninas* he (rather mischievously) painted himself with the red cross of the Order of Santiago, which he didn't receive till three years after completing the painting. Genet is fascinated by such official symbols and signifiers of power. For him, what man fundamentally wants is 'to feel himself trapped inside a ceremonious jelly [*une gelée cérémonieuse*]' – a fabulous metaphor for the enjoyment secreted by the codes, rituals, and insignia of the symbolic order.[50] In its philosophical rigour, Genet's theatre provides a phenomenology of this ceremonious jelly, detailing its four essential characteristics: detachability, immobility, solitude, and fatality.[51]

Like Brecht, Pirandello, and Beckett, Genet is one of the great masters of modernist metatheatre. Starting with *The Maids*, his characters are always playing actors playing other characters, and reflecting on the resulting paradoxes of identity: I is the image in which it is alienated; the double constitutes the originality of the original (whose origin is thus displaced from itself). In *"Elle"* this metatheatrical dimension is underlined by the doubling of the figure of the photographer at the very end of the play, the arrival of the second photographer. The photographer doesn't get his snapshot, and instead another photographer comes to document the (failed) papal photo session. In lieu of a conclusion, *"Elle"* ends in a mise-en-abyme of images, photography of photography, spinning around a fundamental absence:

> *Second Photographer*. So I'm here, as agreed.
> *The Usher*. But who told you to come in?
> *First Photographer*. Don't insult him, please, he's me...
> *The Usher*. I can see that he resembles you, but he can't be you, since you are here and he is there.
> *First Photographer*. This is my official photographer. He's the one

who's in charge of setting up the unforgettable scene, and preserving the image [....] The scene in which I'd be in the act of photographing the Pope.

Enter the Cardinal.

The Cardinal. So is the pose finished yet? Hey, two photographers?[52]

The perversity of Genet's theatre is that his characters are always playing (theatrical) games, his theatre is always and necessarily a metatheatre. At the same time, Genet's plays are also passionately in search of a real beyond the theatre – even while ironically condemning any such 'real' or 'beyond' as but another illusion of the theatrical charade. In *The Balcony* this *fake* real is the revolution happening outside the walls of the luxury brothel named 'The Balcony'.[53] In *"Elle"* it is represented by the pope's nostalgic dreams of his early days as shepherd, and his questions about the photographer's family life: his children, if his girlfriend loves him, whether he makes enough money to support his 'little family', and so on—things which signify the opposite of divine glory and alienation in the image.[54] There is always an outside to the theatre, or a reference to such an outside, that is fully inside the theatre, and part of its illusion: the fake real.

The *real* real, as it were, can only be one thing: a pure nothing. And this nothing can only act in a negative way, as the wounding of the charade, the puncturing of appearances, and the voidance of the cere-monial. But then the artistic question becomes: how to positively picture this voiding, what phenomenal, and bodily, form can it take? Genet's pope provides a remarkable answer to this. *There is one posture which is not an imposture*, he says: squatting to shit. In the middle of the play, the pope delivers an extended ode to shitting, which I will quote in full:

My son, it is on the pot, when I am tranquil, when I relax myself, where I have been visited by the most fecund thoughts, but the highest thoughts, those which leave a trace of fire – from wild game and ice cream – in Christianity. My son, listen: when softly, heavily, but tenderly, my tissues relax, when my organs loosen, an angelic sweetness descends upon me. All of a sudden, I am good. And pious. Charity halos me in the pose of an old Turk. We do not know how to shit on our knees. Thus, I conclude that the only posture which is not an imposture is the squatting posture. And at the moment that I rid myself of all that reeking matter, I become closer to God, and I enjoy it. An angel then – visible, my dear fellow, visible – puts his finger, gloved with white snow, to my temple. Then I have the desire to spread an infinite goodness across the world. My heart opens to the mystery of lepers, of Arabs, of heretics, and High Society ladies.

Oh how many bulls were divinely inspired within me there! Suddenly everything becomes accessible to me: the beauty of rubies and satin brocades – which I discreetly equate that strange matter my entrails have been making for twenty-four hours – leaves me when this goodness visits. But, without a doubt – you are right. We cannot offer the world the image of a Pope on his pot. The world would not believe it. This would not be the image of the Pope! Yet, does this mean the Pope would be a series of poses? Hence, my young friend, offer pontifical postures to this mannequin. Go to it![55]

If anal erotism was regarded by Freud as key to obsessional neurosis – the control over one's bowel movements as the paradigmatic instance of that passion for self-control which itself takes over and then controls the neurotic's life – Genet's innovation is the invention of an anti-authoritarian anality. In shitting, what one shits out is the hierarchy and authority of the symbolic order.[56] One cannot crap kneeling, as the pope says: 'We do not know how to shit on our knees.'[57] Squatting is the antithesis of the model gesture of obedience. Although this passage would seem to be the pinnacle of blasphemy and irreverence, it should be emphasised that the pope expresses himself in a totally pious, Christian way: when he craps he is closest to God. Specifically, the God of 'an infinite goodness spread throughout the world', one who embraces all of creation in its wretchedness, contortions, agonies, and wounds – what Genet calls in his essay on Giacometti the tramps and the garbage, the refuse of the world.[58] Eschatology is transformed into scatology. Incidentally, the question of what remains of the eucharist after ingestion was a matter of some controversy in the ninth century, under the heading of 'stercoranism', the heretical belief that Christ's body is transformed into *stercus* (dung). Origen, one of the early Church fathers, readily admitted that the eucharist was crapped out like any food.[59]

But the pope shrinks away from his own elegy to defecation. He is, after all, an eminently theatrical personage, and 'We cannot offer the world the image of a Pope on his pot. The world would not believe it.' And so he returns to the theatrical charade, represented by the photographer, whom he asks to provide him with the correct 'pontifical postures'. *"Elle"* thus moves in a tension between two extremes: on the one hand, a hyper-theatricality, the whirligig of representations, culminating in a photographer photographing a photographer photographing; and, on the other, an abyssal nothingness, a beatific anal expulsiveness. The totalising closure of the symbolic order versus its fundamental groundlessness or disorder.

The Nothing Pope

This double dynamic helps to reveal what is at stake in the modernity of art. Genet's pope is searching for his identity – the image that would constitute the ground of his popeliness – but what he finds is a non-identity, a non-identity that's nevertheless caught up in the theatre of identity, the mirror world of images and representations. A nothing would represent me best, says the pope. But what is the image of nothing?

If Bacon is the 'Genet of painting', this should be understood in a specific sense. Bacon also takes up, in an original way, the problem of the nothing or the unrepresentable. *Study after Velázquez's Portrait of Pope Innocent X* [fig. 8] provides, in effect, the visual representation that Genet's pope complains is lacking, an image of the 'nothing pope'. Bacon paints the nothing as a stain: the scream that tears through the figure. Through the disfiguration of representational figures their non-identity gains a visual tangibility, a real presence. Bacon's pope becomes the vehicle for the scream that undoes him. Genet's pope, on the other hand, while aware of his nothingness, is first and foremost a mediatic figure, a celebrity product of the society of the spectacle. His peculiarity is that he is a celebrity endowed with a deconstructive intelligence about his own 'ontological' status, as a nothing whose identity will have been constituted – the moment of becoming-pope is always an anticipated one – through his identification with an externally produced image. *Bacon, the artist of forces that rip through the image; Genet, of the impasses of identity inherent to the image.* Strictly speaking, Bacon is not the Genet of painting, but that makes the encounter between the two artists, and their popes, all the more interesting. They meet at a crucial point, the point of negativity, and this zero-point is what is stake, in different ways, in art, philosophy, psychoanalysis, and also, if I may put it this way, life.

From the highly publicised trips of John Paul II to the social media of Francis ('The Virgin Mary was the first influencer, the influencer of God' read one post), the contemporary papacy has moved in the direction of a mediatic pontiff, and Genet's play was (as usual) highly prescient. The real presence of a surreal Catholicism meets the mediatic powers of spectacular society (defined as capital accumulated to the point it becomes image). The Church uses digital capitalism to spread the Word of God, yet for the spectacle God is but another content to extend its beguiling techno-presence – where is religion in this? Both Genet and Bacon stake out artistic positions in opposition to the society of the spectacle, represented for them by the ubiquity of photography. But for Genet, a quasi-religious presence already suffuses the mediatic world of images, after the so-called death of God.

It is tempting to associate Bacon's pope with Nietzsche's last pope from *Thus Spoke Zarathustra*: 'But now he himself is dead, this most pious human being, this saint in the woods who constantly praised his god with singing and growling.'[60] But we need to be careful here about what we mean by the death of God, together with his faithful earthly servant, the 'most pious human being'. This event does not simply designate the demise of the other world and the loss of transcendence, whether viewed negatively (nihilism) or positively (de-alienation). The loss of transcendence does not yield immanence. Rather, what rebounds on the human being from the collapse of the distinction between immanence and transcendence, this world and the next, is the split itself. The loss of transcendence goes together with a splitting of this world, a crack or a fracture within immanence. (One of the best names for this, but not the only one, is the Freudian unconscious). Art inhabits this split. It no longer represents the other world, like in religious art, but finds itself in a permanent state of crisis with regard to this one. Its vanguards are the always-beyond-themselves agents of this crisis. Despite all the strategies to legitimise and defend art, to define its role and value, its place in society can never be secure – for it exists only through its non-identity with the social and historical context in which it intervenes. If modern art continues to revive a religious, occult, or esoteric sensibility, starting from the early days of Dada and the readymade, it does so not so much out of nostalgic longing for transcendence but as a means of articulating its crisis vis-à-vis this world.

Theodor Adorno famously claimed that nothing about art is self-evident, 'not its inner life, not its relation to the world, not even its right to exist.'[61] This logic ought to be extended. For example, psychoanalysis is therapy that has lost its self-evidence, that is, the 'obvious' or 'unquestioned' task to find a cure. In psychoanalysis, what it means to be healthy or cured itself becomes a point of crisis, and this is what distinguishes it from other therapies that promote optimisation and social hygiene – and makes its own position in society, its 'right to exist', so tenuous. Lacan, in this sense, offered a psychoanalysis of psychoanalysis, troubling Freudianism's own adoption of a developmental and socially normative perspective. Like modern artists, he embraced provocation and flirted with fraudulence, imposture, and dandyism (recall his early dealings with surrealist circles – Lacan's dissertation was appreciated by Dalí, and he published it in the journal *Minotaure*). However successful or not these tactics were, the point was to keep the crisis alive, the idea that psychoanalysis does not represent or merge with the society that it belongs to, but speaks and intervenes from an ex-centric position, a nonplace. Psychoanalysis may certainly be historicised, and explained in terms of the social forces that conditioned its emergence and development – but this is to put psychoanalysis in its place, whereas what psychoanalysis theorises and stands for is a nonplace (the unconscious) that troubles whatever framework that would purport to seize it. Psychoanalysis introduces a kind of wild Baconian stain in the system of knowledge. In a way more akin to art than psychology or psychiatry, it persists in its break.

And – this is the point I want to make – this loss reaches down to life itself. Nothing about life is self-evident, including its liveliness. We are forced to affirm the paradoxical idea that life is not 'natural', there is something stunning and fundamentally non-intuitive about the fact of being alive, and this non-naturalness is what defines the specificity of human life. In the scream this astounding non-self-evidence 'speaks'. Life, which might seem to provide the ultimate ground of existence, in the immediacy of raw sensation, cannot serve as an anchor in being because it does not coincide with itself, or is displaced with respect to itself. And that is what is shocking and *lively* about it. In the scream, there gapes a silence that cannot be screamed, and yet can only be screamed. There is a beyond to sensation that is nowhere else than in sensation but cannot be felt or experienced as such. The forces of life are fractured by death; the drives are troubled by an internal impediment that contorts them. It is this tension in experience towards what is impossible to experience that constitutes the electric presence, the fatal liveliness, of experience. That is why there is a 'logic of sensation', and not simply a sensation of sensation: the logic of sensation studies the logical impasse within sensation.

Gilles Deleuze writes that Bacon's pope is not terrified of death but screams at it. 'Life screams *at* death, but death is no longer this all-too-visible thing that makes us faint; it is this invisible force that life detects, flushes out, and makes visible through the scream.'[62] Deleuze's philosophy is sometimes interpreted as turning life into an ultimate ground, albeit a vertiginous one, a chaos (or chaosmos) of impersonal drives and desiring machines. It depends on how one understands the zero-point: the invisible, the untouchable, the inexperienceable, the unplaceable, the unlivable (death, or the death drive). Deleuze refuses a pessimistic understanding of psychoanalysis which puts the emphasis on the wounded and traumatic character of human existence. From the perspective of the drives, what matters is what they *do* with trauma, how they positively make use of it and transform it. Bacon: 'You can be optimistic and totally without hope. One's basic nature is totally without hope, and yet one's nervous system is made out of optimistic stuff.'[63] The *conditio humana* may be lost and hopeless, but the drives are indomitable – *life persists*. The drives make something out of broken, hopeless, and damaged life, and cannot help but do so. The cruelty of the nervous system is that it doesn't give up, it can persist in hell forever (or until the organism capitulates); its exhilaration is that life is not enclosed by its prescribed possibilities and forms, its stories and histories, but breaks out of itself, is torn from itself, is impossible for itself. When Bacon speaks of an 'exhilarated despair', he is close to (perhaps quoting) Duras's 'joyful despair'.[64]

Art brings us back to the zero-point, from where something new can emerge. This zero-point, however, is never merely nothing, but takes on different incarnate forms. If the vocal object (the scream) is pre-eminent for Bacon, for Genet it's the anal object that is decisive (farts and turds). In Bacon the pope's 'body escapes through the mouth'; in Genet it's through the ass.[65] Bacon and Genet propose an art that pierces through the 'ceremonious jelly', whose ultimate perfection is arguably represented by the glory of papal authority. But behind the pomp and ceremony of the office, what is revealed is not simply the naked human being, in all its fragility and contingency (or as a Christian would say, sinfulness). We are instead confronted with a void: the abyss of subjectivity, that which cleaves the 'naked human' from itself. This is the modernist passion. Art has the paradoxical task of rendering an image of a subject that cannot be imaged, without recourse to a beyond. In a remarkable historical coincidence, both Bacon and Genet do so by transforming the exalted figure of the pope into a divided subject for whom *I is an other* – whether it's the otherness of the abyssal scream 'where silence rushes' or the otherness of the beatific crap. Not writing as prayer, as Kafka thought, but shitting as prayer.

Postscript: Hoc est corpus capitalismi

The scandal of Genet's sugar pope is that 'her' holiness gets drunk up with the morning coffee. One imbibes the pope, like in Apollinaire's heretical story where one ingests the mass-sanctified bread loaves: what is at stake is an act of physical incorporation whereby a 'surreal presence' is spread throughout the population. Far from being a relic of the past, this act of holy ingestion may well describe the carnal relationship to our own contemporary beliefs and ideologies. On the other hand, Bacon's paintings, however much their reproduction has reduced their shock value, may still inspire a real bodily terror. On the Amazon.com webpage for the 1975 edition of Sylvester's *Interviews with Francis Bacon*, the 'top critical review' reads:

> This was recommended by a acting teacher and when I looked inside at the images It was like looking into a demonic nightmare. This man's inner vision of himself is represented in horrific imagery of

the human body and relationships with each other. The images are so twisted I can only believe that demons inspired his art. The suffering represented here is ghastly. Knowing what I know about the Universal laws of cause and effect and Law of vibration, attraction and action, It would be a great disservice for me to ingest this book further so I burned it and all its suffering to put it out of its misery. I suggest buying The Science of Getting Rich, Think and Grow Rich, The Dynamic Laws of Prosperity and The Answer. You will be well served by consuming and embodying this content. Thank you.[66]

1   Quoted in Patrick Vandermeersch, 'The Failure of Second Naiveté. Some Landmarks In the History of French Psychology of Religion', in *Aspects in Context. Studies in the History of Psychology of Religion*, ed. Jacob A. Belzen (Amsterdam/Atlanta: Rodopi, 2000), p. 242.

2   Edmund White, *Genet: A Biography* (New York: Alfred Knopf, 1993), p.a 503.

3   Jean Genet, *The Pope, in The Genet Translations: Poetry and Posthumous Plays,* trans. Mark Spitzer (Polemic Press, 2015), p. 144; translation modified.

4   Robert Hughes, 'Art: Out of the Black Hole,' *Time* (December 13, 1971): https://time.com/archive/6844030/art-out-of-the-black-hole/

5   Albert Dichy, 'Présentation', in Jean Genet, *Elle* (Décines: L'Arbalète, 1989), p. 13; Genet, *The Pope*, op. cit., p. 152.

6   Genet, *The Pope*, op. cit., p. 142.

7   Ibid., p. 142.

8   Ibid., p. 151.

9   Ibid., p. 151.

10   Ibid., p. 151.

11   Ibid., p. 156.

12   Ibid., p. 157.

13   'Accordingly, we can say that Duchamp's *Fountain* is a kind of Christ among things, and the art practice of the readymade a kind of Christianity in art. Christianity takes the figure of a human being and puts it, unchanged, in the context of religion, the pantheon of the traditional Gods.' Boris Groys, 'On the New', Res: *Anthropology and Aesthetics*, vol. 38 (Autumn 2000), 8. Didier Ottinger similarly argues, 'Comme les anciennes icônes, le readymade propose une épiphanie du vrai: la vérité de l'art rendu à son essence.' 'Libido et Saint-Esprit', in *Les Iconodules: La question de l'image* (Association des Conservateurs de Haute-Normandie; La Différence, 1992), p. 184.

14   Lacan's formula of sublimation, 'to elevate an object to the dignity of the Thing', echoes the definition of the readymade given in André Breton and Paul Éluard's *Dictionnaire abrégé du surréalisme*: 'an ordinary object elevated to the dignity of a work of art by the mere choice of an artist.' See Jacques Lacan, *The Seminar of Jacques Lacan, Book VII: The Ethics of Psychoanalysis*, ed. Jacques-Alain Miller, trans. Dennis Porter (New York: W.W. Norton, 1992), p. 112; André Breton and Paul Éluard, *Dictionnaire abrégé du surréalisme* (Paris: José Corti, 1969), p. 23.

15   Originally credited to Morton Schamberg, he now shares credit for *God* with Baroness Elsa von Freytag-Loringhoven, although some claim that she is the sculpture's sole artist, with Schamberg making documentary photographs of it; it has also been argued she was the artist behind *Fountain*.

16   Genet, *The Pope,* op. cit., p. 126.

17   Ibid., p. 127.

18   Ibid., p. 157.

19   Ibid., p. 146.

20   Paul Moyaert, 'Touching God in His Image', *The Heythrop Journal* (March 2015), p. 197.

21   Genet, *The Pope*, op. cit., p. 157.

22   I borrow this term from Stijn Van Den Bossche, who uses it in a review of Paul Moyaert's book *De mateloosheid van het christendom* (The Excess of Christianity): 'Geloven In Een Surrealistisch Perspectief? Een Theologisch Wederwoord Bij De Symbool-En Sacramententheorie Van Paul Moyaert', *Bijdragen: International Journal for Philosophy and Theology*, vol. 60 (1999): 324-45.

23   Guillaume Apollinaire, 'The Sacrilege', in *The Heresiarch and Co.*, trans. Rémy Inglis Hall (New York: Doubleday and Co., 1965 [1910]), p. 19.

24   Genet, *The Pope,* op. cit., p. 159.

25   'Baroque and realistic, dense and intense, this is one of the greatest portraits in the whole history of art. And it is impossible to give concrete, quantitative reasons for this opinion, which is shared by the vast majority of art historians and critics.' José Gudiol, *Velázquez 1599-1660,* trans. Kenneth Lyons (New York: Viking, 1974), p. 281.

26   David Sylvester, *The Brutality of Fact: Interviews with Francis Bacon* (New York: Thames and Hudson, 1987), p. 37.

27   Ibid., p. 28.

28   Ibid., p. 28.

29   Ibid., pp. 182, 17.

30   Ibid., p. 41.

31   Kassia St. Clair, *The Secret Lives of Colour* (London: Penguin, 2016), p. 139.

32   Lacan recalls this phrase, in *The Seminar of Jacques Lacan, Book XI: The Four Fundamental Concepts of Psychoanalysis,* ed. Jacques-Alain Miller, trans. Alan Sheridan (New York: Norton, 1981), p. 169.

33   Sylvester, *The Brutality of Fact,* op. cit., p. 34.

34   Michel Leiris, 'Francis Bacon, Full Face and in Profile', in *Francis Bacon,* trans. John Weightman (New York: Rizzoli International Publications, 1987), p. 6; emphasis added.

35   Jacques Lacan, *Transference. The Seminar of Jacques Lacan, Book VIII*, ed. Jacques-Alain Miller, trans. Bruce Fink (Cambridge: Polity, 2015), p. 257.

36   Ibid., p. 258. He is referring to a case of Maurice Bouvet; see Bouvet, 'Incidences thérapeutiques de la prise de conscience de l'envie du pénis dans la névrose obsessionnelle féminine', *Revue française de psychanalyse*, vol. XIV (1950), p. 217.

37   Lacan, ibid., p. 258.

38   Ibid., p. 259.

39   Friedrich Nietzsche, *On the Genealogy of Morals, trans.* Walter Kaufmann (New York: Vintage, 1989), p. 136.

40   Sylvester *The Brutality of Fact,* op cit., p. 28.

41   Ibid., p. 29.

42   Marguerite Duras, 'Entretien avec Francis Bacon', *La Quinzaine littéraire* (November 16-30, 1971): 16-17. All quotes in this paragraph are from this interview.

43   The recent volume *Revisions: Francis Bacon in the Act of Painting* (London: The Francis Bacon Estate and New York: Thames and Hudson, 2025), by Martin Harrison and Sophie Pretorius, provides valuable insight into Bacon's working process.

44   For a brilliant exploration of this, see Alexi Kukuljevic, 'Screaming Without Sound', *S: Journal of the Circle for Lacanian Ideology Critique*, vol, 12 (2019): 67-84.

45   Sylvester, *The Brutality of Fact,* op. cit., p. 48.

46   Ibid., p. 65.

47   Jacques Lacan, Seminar XII, *Problèmes cruciaux*, session of March 17, 1965, Staferla edition, http://staferla.free.fr/S12/S12.htm

48   Kukuljevic, 'Screaming Without Sound', op. cit., 72.

49   Genet, *The Pope*, op. cit., p. 157.

50   Ibid., p. 153.

51   See my 'Beyond Satire: The Political Comedy of the Present and the Paradoxes of Authority', in William Mazzarella, Eric Santner, and Aaron Schuster, *Sovereignty, Inc.: Three Inquiries in Politics and Enjoyment* (Chicago: University of Chicago Press, 2020), pp. 168-76.

52 Genet, *The Pope*, op. cit.,
    pp. 162-63.

53 The status of the revolution is
    strictly ambiguous within the play;
    it's suggested that it is but another
    scenario being played out in the
    brothel's studios, and the revolu-
    tionary leaders end up trapped
    inside 'The Balcony'.

54 Genet, *The Pope*, op. cit., p. 158.

55 Ibid., p. 144; translation modified.

56 This is a key theme that runs
    throughout Genet's entire political
    theatre. To give one other example:
    the French sergeant in Genet's
    anti-colonial masterpiece *The
    Screens*, who is the double of
    the play's hero (or antihero), the
    wretched Saïd, praises crapping as
    the ecstatic expulsion of symbolic
    hierarchy and officialdom: 'When
    you squeeze, you get glassy-eyed,
    something clouds over... and...
    what is it that clouds over and
    blots out? The world?... The sky?...
    No. Your rank of sergeant, and
    that of captain! And all that goes
    with it: the uniform, the stripes,
    the decorations and the officers'
    school diploma when you've got
    one!... And what's left? Emptiness.
    I'm telling you. (*Laughter*.) I've seen
    officers shitting – higher officers,
    general officers! – their eyes:
    emptied. Not empty; emptied,
    i-e-d, emptied. The stars on their
    képis, no longer stars when the
    eyes are emptied' (*The Screens*,
    trans. Bernard Frechtman (London:
    Faber & Faber, 2009), pp. 149-50).
    The salvific anality, or more simply
    fart jokes, in Genet's theatre would
    deserve a study of its own.

57 Genet, *The Pope*, op. cit, p. 144.

58 See Jean Genet, 'The Studio of
    Alberto Giacometti', in *Fragments
    of the Artwork*, trans. Charlotte
    Mandell (Stanford: Stanford Uni-
    versity, 2003).

59 'And if "everything that enters the
    mouth passes into the belly and
    is cast out into the toilet", also the
    bread that has been sanctified
    "by the word of God and prayer"
    being material in itself, "passes
    into the belly and is cast out into
    the toilet". And in accordance with
    the prayer that is added to it "in
    the analogy of faith" it becomes
    profitable and a cause of the clear
    vision of the mind which looks to
    what is profitable.' Origen, *The
    Commentary of Origen on the
    Gospel of St Matthew, Volume
    I*, ed. and trans. Ronald E. Heine
    (Oxford: Oxford University Press,
    2018), p. 79.

60 Friedrich Nietzsche, *Thus Spoke
    Zarathustra*, ed. Adrian Del
    Caro and Robert Pippin, trans.
    Adrian Del Caro (Cambridge:
    Cambridge University Press,
    2006), p. 210. Hugh Davies made
    this connection: 'Bacon's papal
    images support the Nietzschean
    declaration and may be viewed as
    visual equivalents of the pathetic
    figure of 'the last pope' featured in
    the section entitled 'Retired' in Ni-
    etzsche's *Thus Spoke Zarathustra*.'
    Hugh Davies, *Francis Bacon: The
    Early and Middle Years, 1928-1958*
    (New York: Garland Publishing,
    1978), p. 100. I first discovered this
    reference in Rina Arya's informative
    essay 'Assaying the Pope: Francis
    Bacon's Interrogation of Religion',
    *Implicit Religion: Journal for the
    Critical Study of Religion*, vol. 14,
    no. 3 (October 2011): 343-59.

61 Theodor Adorno, *Aesthetic Theory*,
    trans. Robert Hullot-Kentor (Lon-
    don: Continuum, 2002), 1.

62 Gilles Deleuze, *Francis Bacon: The
    Logic of Sensation*, trans. Daniel W.
    Smith (London: Continuum, 2003),
    p. 62.

63 Sylvester, *The Brutality of Fact*,
    op. cit., p. 80.

64 Ibid., p. 83; Marguerite Duras,
    'The Path of Joyful Despair: An
    interview with Marguerite Duras
    by Claire Devarrieux', in *Duras
    by Duras*, trans. Edith Cohen and
    Peter Connor (San Francisco: City
    Light Books, 1987), pp. 105-06.

65 Deleuze, *Francis Bacon: The Logic
    of Sensation*, op. cit., p. 16. As Ben
    Ware reminded me, anality also
    plays a crucial role in Bacon's
    aesthetics. To cite a couple of key
    instances: Bacon tells Sylvester 'I
    remember looking at a dog-shit
    on the pavement and I suddenly
    realized, there it is—this is what
    life is like. Strangely enough, it tor-
    mented me for months, till I came
    to, as it were, accept that here you
    are, existing for a second, brushed
    off like flies on the wall' (Sylvester,
    The Brutality of Fact, op. cit., p.
    133). And the first panel of *Triptych
    May-June 1973* shows Bacon's lov-
    er, George Dyer, seemingly taking
    a dump, before the life drains out
    of him in the centre panel.

66 I left the grammatical errors
    in the original, dated July 20,
    2018. See: https://www.amazon.
    com/Interviews-Francis-Ba-
    con-David-Sylvester/product-re-
    views/0500270570.

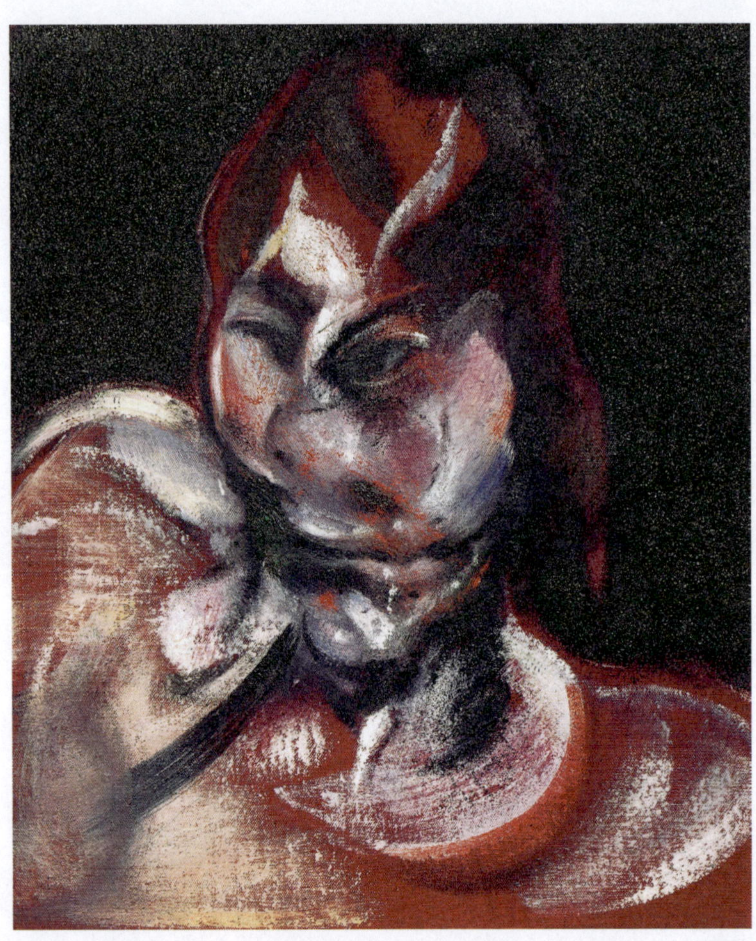

BACON IN THE COLD WORLD: ON WAGERS, WOUNDS AND REAL ABSTRACTION

Ben Ware

Take a chance on the artist—maybe you can realize a profit.
Marcel Duchamp

Born to Lose

Bacon's passion for gambling was seemingly inexhaustible. In the words of his close friend, the painter Michael Wishart, Bacon 'adored both cards and roulette, often playing several tables simultaneously, displaying the committed masochism of Dostoevsky, who claimed that the real thrill of involvement only began when he had pawned his wife's jewels and was staking the proceeds.'[1] In Blitz-era London – at a time when gambling was still illegal in the UK – Bacon hosted private roulette evenings at his studio in South Kensington, frequently taking elaborate measures to avoid detection by the police.[2] Years later, Monte Carlo, with its 'grandeur of futility' as Bacon described it, often provided the backdrop for the artist's high thrills, high stakes games. Here he came under the spell of 'the Belle Époque casino with its succession of large plush salons and magnificent views over the Mediterranean', not to mention the intoxicating 'atmosphere generated by fortunes being made and lost'.[3] Describing his passion, Bacon explained:

> I like the atmosphere of casinos, you talk to people at the bar and there is the excitement of whether they are winning or not winning and the despair of people who have lost everything and all that goes on in a very concentrated space. [...] I used to think that I heard the croupier calling out the winning numbers at roulette...the winning number, before the ball had fallen into the socket...and I used to go from table to table. [...] [In the end, though,] I'm a heavy loser. In fact, I think I must be the perfect compost for casinos because they must love somebody who comes in who is always losing.

In today's pathologising parlance, gambling is often spoken of in terms of 'compulsive' or 'problem' gambling, something 'damaging' to the individual and society as a whole. If one is to gamble, then the watchwords are moderation and self-control: set a strict spending limit, don't chase your losses, and be aware of any negative feelings that might cloud your judgment. But this demand for 'balance' or strict 'self-regulation' hardly does justice to the complexities of the human subject. Gambling might well be 'dangerous' and 'illogical', but this, as Walter Benjamin reminds us, citing the writer Anatole France, is precisely the source of its attraction: 'At its caprice [gambling] gives poverty and wretchedness and shame – that is why its votaries adore it. The fascination of danger is at the bottom of all great passions. There is no fullness of pleasure unless the precipice is near.'[4]

The allure of gambling, however, leads us into even murkier terrain. In an arresting scene in Karel Reisz's film *The Gambler* (1974), the ludopath Axel Freed (James Caan) tells his friend and money-lender Hips (Paul Sorvino), that all gamblers have one thing in common: 'they are all looking to lose!' Near the end of the film, when Axel hits upon a scheme that finally allows him to clear his debts, he takes himself to the bad part of town and engineers a fight with a local pimp – an encounter that results in him being slashed across the face with a knife. Bleeding profusely, Axel turns to observe his wound in a mirror before letting out a faint smile. The masochist, it would seem, always finds a way to lose and therefore to win.

The wager and the wound, as we shall see, turn out to be key to Bacon's modernism, though not in the way that we might expect.

There is quite clearly an intimate connection between Bacon's devotion to the roulette table and what we might call his *aleatory aesthetics*. According to Bacon himself, 'chance and accident are the most fertile things at any artist's disposal'.[5] As he puts it in his interviews with David Sylvester, 'if anything works for me, I feel it is nothing I have made myself, but something which chance has been able to give me.'[6] 'My ideal', he goes on, 'would really be just pick up a handful of paint and throw it at the canvas and hope that', with the intervention of chance, 'the portrait was there.'[7] If we ask why artistic practice comes to be defined for Bacon in terms of chance, the answer will be something like the following: it is only by making chance 'marks' on the canvas that the painter avoids cliché, succeeds in conveying the 'mystery of fact', and returns this fact more 'violently' onto the 'nervous system' of the spectator. But behind this aleatory method lies an intriguing ideological picture.

The world of chance does not itself appear by chance. Cutting a long story short, for most of the Enlightenment 'chance had been called the superstition of the vulgar.'[8] However, by the late nineteenth century, in the words of the philosopher Ian Hacking, 'chance had attained the respectability of a Victorian valet, ready to be the loyal servant of the natural, biological, and social sciences.'[9] How did such a transformation come about? Simply put: 'an avalanche of printed numbers' and the emergence of a new 'science' of statistics, with nation states classifying, counting, and tabulating their subjects anew.[10] An older determinism was thus eroded, but only for chance to come to the fore in a paradoxical sense. A new empire of chance opened up, but chance itself was rationalised, *tamed*, captured within a structure of new statistical and probabilistic laws. The world of chance thus became less, not more, chancy; and subjects themselves were more, not less, governed by what would later come to be known as 'big data'. As Hacking points out, the new statistical mania provoked a backlash, especially within the realms of art and ideas, which took the form of a demand for a restoration of the ancient and divine prerogatives of *pure chance*.[11]

It is in this context, then, that we can place such conflicting modernisms as Nietzsche's declaration that the 'lofty sky' above is a 'dance floor for divine chances... a gods' table for divine dice and dicers!'; Mallarmé's 1897 poem *A Throw of the Dice Will Never Abolish Chance*; Saussure's insistence on the 'arbitrary' or 'chance' nature of the linguistic sign; Duchamp's readymade *3 Standard Stoppages*; surrealism's employment of 'psychic automatism' and the 'divinity' of chance; Bataille's fascination with 'the giddy seductiveness of chance', its promise of a 'happiness beyond limits'; and, of course, Bacon himself. [12]

This recourse to chance, however, raises a number of intriguing questions regarding agency – some of which fall directly at Bacon's feet. While the artist occasionally speaks of chance and the unconscious in the same breath, this, quite clearly, is too hasty a move. In *The Psychopathology of Everyday Life* (1901), Freud famously writes that 'nothing in the mind is arbitrary or undetermined'.[13] While 'external' chance events do occur (beginning with our 'origin out of the meeting of spermatozoon and ovum'),[14] there are no accidents in the unconscious, no instances of 'internal' psychic chance.[15] Slips of the brush or the rag; botching up a painting so that it has to be re-done or destroyed; 'accidental' smears or colour splats on the canvas – these are all, at least by Freud's lights, interpretable, all grist to the analyst's mill. Think you are getting away with chance just because you're an artist? Well, think again.

The issue of agency also returns in a more explicitly political sense. Bacon frequently suggests that he is *employing chance*: he works, he says, hoping that chance is going to *work for him*. This sounds like a curious kind of outsourcing, where parts of the production process are delegated to a mysterious external agent or creative higher power. What should we make of such a move? First, we might see it as consistent with a certain subtractive element in Bacon. Not only does he wish to eliminate the 'storytelling aspect' of his paintings, he also seeks to remove, at least in part, any trace of direct artistic intention. But this economic dimension also leads in another direction. Despite his avowed atheism, Bacon's relationship to chance is clearly one of 'faith', and specifically faith in a quasi-divine force out of which he can artistically profit. This brings chance directly into the orbit of Friedrich Hayek's definition of 'the market' itself: that 'impersonal' and 'uncontrollable' force, whose 'nature' we cannot fathom, but to which we must all nevertheless submit.[16] Here, then, we are reminded of Adorno's observation that chance today is something of an impoverished concept: merely 'the form taken by freedom' under the 'spell' of capitalist unfreedom.[17]

Gambling on the Grotesque

Despite his remarks to the contrary, one might be forgiven for thinking that there is little in Bacon's painting that is actually left to chance. The artist compulsively repeats his highly specific pictorial formulas: monochromatic backgrounds, cut up with lines suggesting domestic interiors; the introduction of various staging devices – beds, sofas, cubicles, cages, chairs and tables – that foreground the famous bruised and bulging figures. Soap opera-like, Bacon also rolls out a familiar cast of characters – friends, lovers, popes, fellow artists, and, most importantly, himself – all of whom come in for similar aesthetic treatment. What is the overall effect?

In Edgar Allan Poe's remarkable short story 'The Facts in the Case of M. Valdemar' (1845), the titular character, who is terminally ill, is placed in a mesmeric trance immediately prior to taking his final breaths. With an appearance that is described as 'hideous beyond conception', Valdemar is presumed dead, until a 'broken and hollow' voice issues from his 'distended and motionless jaws', exclaiming 'I am dead…I say to you that I am dead'. The hypnotic process has arrested Valdemar's demise; he is alive, but now reduced to merely repeating the announcement of his own mortal passing: 'Dead! Dead!' When the attempt is made to re-awaken Valdemar, to lift him out of his hypnotic state, his whole frame crumbles, rots away upon the bed, leaving behind only a 'liquid mass of loathsome…detestable putridity.'[18]

Almost all of Bacon's figures are to be found in one of these two states: caught up in some kind of mesmeric undeadness, suspended between being and non-being; or else liquifying, like Bacon's late lover George Dyer in *Triptych August 1972*, [fig. 38] into a puddle of flesh coloured ooze, collecting on the carpet. Bacon clearly turns his back on the ideology of the beautiful, and he would no doubt have laughed at contemporary neo-Kantian theories which conceive of beauty as inciting us to moral 'fairness' and 'equality'.[19] But what of his great gamble with the grotesque?

In a footnote to his *Philosophy of Modern Music*, Adorno describes the grotesque as a form of aesthetic populism: 'From society's perspective the grotesque is generally the form employed to make alien and progressive factors acceptable. The bourgeoisie is willing to become involved in modern art if – by means of its form – it assures him that it is not meant to be taken seriously.'[20] The critic Clement Greenberg echoes Adorno when, referring specifically to Bacon, he speaks of the artist's grotesque productions as 'inspired safe taste' – a kind of pseudo-transgressive art that deliberately goes in search of 'rehearsed responses'.[21]

Both of these positions, however, come up short. In a series of virtuoso passages in his early work *Permanence and Change,* the theorist Kenneth Burke connects the grotesque and the revolutionary. The grotesque, he argues, is a higher stage of 'planned incongruity' (above humour) in which 'the perception of discordancies' is 'cultivated' to such a degree that inversions of the existing state of things suddenly become thinkable.[22] The grotesque merges what common sense divides; and divides what common sense merges. Like Marxist thought itself, then, the grotesque, according to Burke, 'realigns' consciousness, allowing for a radical reinvention of what counts as 'reason', 'logic', and indeed 'reality' itself.[23] From this perspective a Bacon work such as *Lying Figure with Hypodermic Syringe* (1963), [fig. 26] in which the human form is reduced to a heap of damaged and dis-organised matter, is less a populist aesthetic provocation and more a glimpse of a *different kind of human subject to come* – one whose precise identity remains to be determined.

But there *is* something in Greenberg's jibe regarding rehearsed responses. Bacon's great aesthetic wager – the one upon which he stakes almost everything – is that if the artworks succeed then they do so by making a violent impact upon the spectator's 'nervous system', 'unlocking' what he calls new 'areas of sensation'. But this sounds remarkably like a fixed formula: an attempt to elicit a specific kind of bodily or affective response from the viewer. In one sense, it is the oldest of all old modernist fantasies: the desire for pure aesthetic immediacy, which will return the spectator to a fuller sense of 'life'. Yet this fantasy has a philosophical hole in it: immediacy, as Adorno reminds us, is always already subjectively mediated, and therefore pure immediacy cannot be the basis for aesthetic experience.[24] What is required, then, is that artworks be mediated a *second time*: subject to a process of critical analysis and interpretation, which aims not at mastering them (crushing their immediacy under the weight of subjective mediation), but rather bringing to the fore their very enigmatic nature.[25]

Dialectics of Chance

This brings us directly back to chance. 'I always think of myself not so much as a painter', Bacon says, 'but as a medium for accident and chance.' At the same time, he insists that images should be 'deeply ordered', and that this ordering is essential to art's function of recording 'facts'. We might be tempted to call this Bacon's dualism. On the one hand, the repetition of a set of ordering rules and devices that hold the paintings together; and, on the other hand, the free play of chance. Except, of course, that the chance operation is already written into Bacon's aesthetic logic. Chance thus becomes necessity.

But here we might take a further dialectical step, one which goes by way of psychoanalysis. In his Seminar XI, Lacan returns to the idea of chance, borrowing two concepts from Aristotle's *Physics*: *tuchē* and *automaton*. In Aristotle, *automaton* refers to spontaneous events in nature, brought about by some external cause (the stone that rolls off a cliff and strikes the man on the head). *Tuchē* refers to chance events, relating specifically to purposive human action, that result in good or bad fortune (an unexpected encounter with an old acquaintance that turns out to be lucky or unlucky).[26] For Aristotle, when things happen by chance they happen accidentally or coincidentally, and 'chance is a *coincidental cause*. But in an unqualified sense chance causes nothing.'[27] In this respect, chance turns out to be something *uncanny*: both something and nothing; a cause and a lack of a cause; something that can only be apprehended through reason, but which, because fundamentally 'inexplicable', constitutes reason's own blind spot.[28]

Taking liberties, Lacan 'translates' *automaton* as *repetition* – the automatically functioning 'network of signifiers' that keep on returning, looping back – and *tuché* as *the chance encounter with the real*. If *automaton* is the repetitive mechanism of the symbolic (which is to say, language itself), the real is what 'lies behind' it, interrupting its smooth functioning.[29] But *automaton* and *tuché* should not be regarded as two separate spheres. Within the repetitive realm of the symbolic something gets produced that is beyond symbolisation; and this is precisely *tuché*, which, as Lacan says, first presented itself in the history of psychoanalysis in the form of the 'trauma'.[30] *Tuché* is therefore what erupts to disturb the symbolic, *out of* the symbolic itself. It is the surprise explosion of the real, which shakes up the subject's very reality; the reappearance of an originary trauma in the cracks of the *automaton*.[31] It is here, then, that we come across something like a Lacanian dialectics of chance and necessity. *Tuché* (as chance encounter) has a cause, and this cause is the necessity of the *automaton* (the symbolic *qua* repetition). But what lies behind the latter, driving it forward as an absent cause, is the *tuché* of the trauma that never stops insisting.

Bacon gives an indirect aesthetic twist to this crucial bit of Lacanian theory. While we might be tempted to think that in Bacon's paintings it is the repetitions (the seemingly endless return of familiar figures, faces, props and settings) that create the conditions for the eruption of chance events on the canvas, we should instead begin by turning this thought around. It is not that there is repetition and then, consequently, the appearance of chance. Rather, chance and accident are at the origin of Bacon's works.

How exactly to understand this? Following Lacan, we might say that what motivates repetition in Bacon is, at root, a trauma or *accident of being*. This is not something that we can locate simply by looking at Bacon's own colourful biography, it is not a particular 'experience'. It is instead an originary wound that inscribes itself in the psyche through the process of subjectification itself; one that, functioning as an *absent cause*, determines all that follows. By its very nature this trauma cannot be named or remembered, which is why it keeps on being repeated. Indeed, strictly speaking, it only materializes *retroactively* through its effects – which in Bacon's case are simply the pile-up of disturbances and distortions that we encounter in the paintings themselves. What therefore appears in Bacon *as if* by chance – the famous disfigured figures and frenzied colour marks – turns out in the end to be simply the *appearance of chance*. What we find in the works is in fact nothing other than the automatism of repetition – a repetition that, as Lacan would have it, is inseparable from *jouissance*. Far from reproducing sameness, however, it is the repetitions themselves that are the very source of the new (as variations on a theme), the singular, and the (occasionally) astonishing. It is only by repeating and repeating to excess, we might say, that Bacon is able to elevate the accident (of being) into something essential, to transform the wound into an unmistakeable artistic signature.

But this does not mean that chance gets completely sidelined. Instead, it is shifted to a different level: to the encounter between the work of art and the spectator, the object and the subject. The success of such an encounter is *necessarily contingent*: it might take place, or it might not – nothing can decide the matter in advance. Every work of art is, in one sense, a throw of the dice. The possibility of the work striking a particular spectator, throwing them temporarily out of joint, is always more or less a matter of fortune.

So what, at least in theory, would a *real* encounter with a Bacon painting actually entail? First and foremost, it would not be the purely affective encounter that the artist himself repeatedly insists upon, but rather the experience of finding oneself caught in the work's trap, feeling its enigmatic character making a claim upon us, a call for interpretation. But also something more specific.

Bacon makes good on Adorno's request that artworks 'articulate the state in which [humans] find themselves historically'.[32] But he does so in a way that seems almost accidental. It is as if, had he known what he was doing, he wouldn't have been able to do it, or perhaps wouldn't have wanted to. What Bacon does – and what we, as spectators, must therefore respond to – is to render visible not vague 'intensities' but the real abstract forces operating on and through human beings, disfiguring them, mutilating their very nature. *Look what the world has made of us*, Bacon's figures appear to silently exclaim. But this has nothing to do with providing a conventionally 'realistic' depiction of things. Indeed, we are here reminded of Bertolt Brecht's line that 'the situation is now…so complex that a simple "reproduction of reality" says less than ever about reality itself.'[33] Representing what is will therefore require not empirical accuracy, but instead excess and exaggeration. Only the hyperbolic caricature, a self-consciously constructed surplus, comes close to revealing what would otherwise remain hidden: the coldness at the core of the system itself.

Cold World

Samuel Beckett's late novella *The Lost Ones* (1970) begins with the line: 'ABODE WHERE LOST bodies roam each searching for its lost one.'[34] This abode is 'a flattened cylinder fifty metres round and sixteen high'; its walls and floor are made of 'solid rubber'. The lost ones, two hundred in total, 'one body per square metre', exist in a state of overcrowded 'gloom'. Most are engaged in the futile task of climbing ladders to reach the various niches and dead-end tunnels within the cylinder. While the temperature inside the space oscillates every four seconds between 5°C and 25°C, in social and subjective terms what we encounter here is a thoroughly *cold world*: shrivelled 'bodies brush together with a rustle of dry leaves'; those with the 'stomach still to copulate strive in vain'; missing rungs from the ladders are used to commit or repel violence.

The most troubling violence in the text, however, comes not from the lost bodies condemned to roam around the cylinder, but from the disembodied voice of the unnamed narrator. Like a nineteenth-century colonial anthropologist, it speaks in an unnervingly dispassionate tone – dissecting the 'customs' of the 'little people' who inhabit the abode, imagining 'a perfect mental picture' of their 'entire system'. What unfolds in Beckett's text then is an interrogation of the abstract violence enacted by this voice, showing how it opens on to a stalled dialectic of coldness. We might elaborate this as follows. While most of the cylinder's inhabitants still believe in the possibility of a 'way out', any exit initially appears blocked by the all-powerful narrator. As the text grows dense through increasingly elaborate 'explanations', however, the narrative voice hacks away at its own authority: its 'certitudes' become 'doubtful', its 'data' fails to add up, its power eventually reveals itself to be what it always was – *a sinister fiction*. The horrifying spectacle of the inside thus points towards the possibility of an outside. And yet, ultimately, the lost ones remain trapped in their cold abode. Constantly on the move but consigned to stasis, they are quite literally written into silence, and so unable to produce a collective sense of self – a 'we' – that might enable them to traverse their abstract dominion.

Bacon provides a different, though related, take on this dialectic of coldness. The artist sets out from a frozen vision of the social world – one in which human relations are, in Marx's phrase, characterised by 'reciprocal isolation and foreignness'.[35] But Bacon sees this situation as simply given, rather than socially mediated. He doesn't grasp how the subject is constituted by the cold forces of capital, specifically the real abstractions of 'value' and 'exchange'.[36] It is, however, this very *indifference* to the social dimension, the refusal of politics as such, that allows Bacon to depict the socially disfigured subject with a unique and unsettling accuracy.

We might put this point another way. What Bacon unwittingly makes visible is a specific *temporal dimension* of socially produced 'second nature'. This second nature, simply put, is the internalisation of the economic laws that govern society: their appearance as a kind of fated necessity or alien objectivity, holding sway over human beings but seemingly cut off from any human origin. Undergirding second nature is the exchange principle which, as Adorno points out, is in one respect a mere 'appearance' or 'illusion'; 'at the same time, however, this illusion is the most real thing of all, the magic formula that has bewitched the world.'[37] The domination of human beings by the exchange abstraction not only 'degrades subjectivity', turning individuals into mere 'agents of the law of value',[38] it also produces a particular temporal split: on the one hand, frenetic activity and constant disquiet; on the other hand, stuckness and stasis. This paradoxical state is described by Walter Benjamin, borrowing a phrase from the poet Gottfried Keller, as one of *petrified unrest*.[39]

It is this condition of petrified unrest that Bacon's work uncannily and hyperbolically captures. In *Three Studies for Portrait of Henrietta Moraes* (1963), [fig. 27] the artist uses a limited palette of crimson and white; the background is an unnerving inky black. The right-hand panel is perhaps the most arresting. Violent brushstrokes and smears capture Moraes's robust shoulders and upper chest from which her head emerges, as if emerging through a vaginal opening. The scene is one of controlled chaos – the figure appears to be giving birth to itself. And yet, the whip of black around the neck resembles a tight nuchal cord; the grey and blue pallor of the skin indicates a lack of oxygen (cyanosis); the left eye is open but blank, devoid of life. When Benjamin uses 'petrified unrest' as the 'formula' for Baudelaire's 'life history' it functions as an allegorical expression of the value system itself: a life of agitated movement which, at the same time, is frozen into place – one that 'knows no development.'[40] This simultaneity of movement and stasis is precisely what Bacon crystallises into an image. In the Moraes portrait, excess animation fuses with ice-cold stillness, producing someone or something that is disturbingly *undead*.

Petrified Unrest

Describing Bacon as an accidental painter of real abstractions finds a direct parallel in some of Louis Althusser's remarks about the Italian artist Leonardo Cremonini. For Althusser, Cremonini is 'not an abstract painter' but 'a *painter of abstraction*' – that is, a painter of 'the real abstract', the 'real relations' that obtain between persons and their things, or more accurately between things and their persons.[41] Cremonini does not directly paint 'living conditions', 'social relations', or 'class struggle'; rather, he renders visible 'the *determinate absence*' which governs them. In the *Grundrisse*, Marx famously says that 'individuals are now ruled by *abstractions*.'[42] These abstractions, however, as Althusser points out, can never be depicted by their presence, but only 'negatively' by their 'traces and effects'.[43]

An even more specific connection between Bacon and Cremonini concerns the treatment of the human face. Cremonini subjects his faces to what Althusser calls 'determinate deformation', whereby all coherent expression and individual subjectivity is removed. The faces thus become 'anonymous', 'inexpressive', the mere trace of the abstract forces which dominate their world.[44] We, as spectators, therefore cannot immediately 'recognise' ourselves in Cremonini's paintings. It is, however, precisely this space of non-recognition that opens up the possibility that we might come to *know ourselves* – know ourselves, that is, as constituted by the cold world of real abstractions. By staging this dialectic, Cremonini, as Althusser remarks in a final lyrical flourish, follows the path opened up:

> by the great revolutionary thinkers...the great materialist thinkers
> who understood that the freedom of [human beings] is not achieved

by the complacency of [their] ideological *recognition*, but by *knowledge* of the laws of their slavery, and that the 'realisation' of their concrete individuality is achieved by the analysis and mastery of the abstract relations which govern them.[45]

In light of Althusser's observations, the affinities between Bacon and Cremonini become striking and profound.[46] Both artists succeed in capturing what defies direct representation; and success, in both cases, is intimately tied to the fact that depicting the absent presence of capital – specifically its subjective and temporal effects – was never the intended aim.[47] As with the patient in psychoanalysis, it is as if truth could only ever emerge indirectly, by some kind of glorious accident. But far too little has been made of the politics of Bacon's modernism. Indeed, speaking about his work in this way still seems to violate some secret art-historical prohibition. This silence should, however, only spur us on.

Bacon's faces – like Cremonini's – aren't masks concealing a more 'authentic', more 'human' subject. There is, strictly speaking, nothing beyond the determinate deformations, no pure first nature hiding behind the mutilated second nature that has been socially produced. The deformations are, moreover, not indicative of a sickness in the depicted individuals, but rather of a society in which the individual is, in Adorno's apt phrase, 'neutralised', turned into nothing more than a frozen 'exhibition piece'.[48] The fact that the deformations remain a constant throughout Bacon's oeuvre, doesn't mean that his work makes no progress.[49] Rather, it indicates that there is no simple escape from the state of petrified unrest, from the exchange world of mythical ever-the-sameness. If an alternative future is to be constructed then a *determinate deformation* – that is, *a determinate negation* – of the present state of things will be necessary, a mass unleashing of human creative forces. If Bacon's work hints indirectly in this direction, then it does so only by serving as a potent reminder that *what would be different has not as yet begun*.[50]

But this, finally, presents us with a question regarding the politics of modernism today. According to Althusser, critical reflection on art produces self-knowledge; and this knowledge plays a crucial role in the formation of political consciousness. Yet such a position would seem to rehearse precisely the kind of theoretical 'humanism' that its author rejects, ascribing a straightforwardly educative function to the work of art. Without severing the connection between art and politics, what, then, would an alternative, less didactic position look like? To answer this question we might begin by staging a surprise return to the very figure with which we started – *the gambler*.

In a series of stunning reflections on the gambler, Walter Benjamin notes that by placing their bets at the last moment, at a critical 'moment of danger', the gambler arrives at a new level of alertness: one captured by the term 'presence of mind' (*Geistesgegenwart*).[51] This, for Benjamin, is a thoroughly dialectical concept: it involves a 'precise awareness of the present moment', out of which the future – whose energy resides in the still incomplete past – is itself made accessible. Presence of mind is not, therefore, the fantasy of pure immediacy; nor does it have anything to do with contemporary notions of 'mindfulness' or so-called 'presence culture'. It is, on the contrary, political through and through. It marks the difference between the present understood as mere empty duration (just one damn thing after another) and the present grasped as a 'point of explosion': a time filled with 'now-time' (*Jetztzeit*).[52] In an extraordinary theoretical twist, then, Benjamin thus manages to connect the temporality of the gambler to that of the revolutionary materialist historian.

In a similar spirit, might we not take the temporal experience of the gambler as an allegory for our own possible experience of the modernist art work? Riffing on Benjamin's remarks on *Geistesgegenwart*, could we not say that the modernist work 'elevates' the subject 'beyond itself', forcing it to 'let itself go', whilst simultaneously fostering a particular attentiveness that is capable of *foreseeing the present*?[53]

In the case of Bacon, the paintings provoke presence of mind precisely by bringing us to see the cold world of real abstractions made flesh. They call our attention to how social relations mutilate the subject, confining it to a state of petrified unrest. But to see this with the alertness of presence of mind is also to see behind and beyond it. The monstrous world of abstract economic forces, despite its appearance as something 'alien', remains at root a *human world* – one which individuals reproduce 'behind their own backs'.[54] '*They don't know it, but they do it*':[55] it is human beings themselves who unwittingly inflict the wounds from which they suffer. Of course, works of art cannot, by themselves, prefigure a new political order, nor can they negate the existing one. But they might nevertheless still have a role to play in interrupting capitalism's business as usual. By making visible the ideological world from which they emerge, they simultaneously remind us of the conditions from which we have failed to emancipate ourselves. If modernism lives on today, it is only because we are still living in what Marx famously called 'prehistory', a stage prior to the creation of an actual, flourishing human society.

1   Michael Peppiatt, *Francis Bacon: Anatomy of an Enigma* (London: Constable, 2008), p. 148; Mark Stevens and Annalyn Swan, *Francis Bacon: Revelations* (London: William Collins, 2022), p. 258. On the reference to Dostoevsky in this quotation, see Fyodor Dostoevsky, *Notes from the Underground & The Gambler* (Oxford: Oxford University Press, 1991). For a neat psychoanalytic reading of Dostoevsky's novel, see John Forrester, *'Transference and the Stenographer: On Dostoevsky's The Gambler', in The Seductions of Psychoanalysis: Freud, Lacan, Derrida* (Cambridge: Cambridge University Press, 1990), pp. 260-85. For a number of important early psychoanalytic texts on gambling, see Jon Halliday and Peter Fuller (eds.), *The Psychology of Gambling* (London: Pelican, 1977).

2   As Stevens and Swan comment, drawing on testimony from Lucian Freud: 'The cars would begin massing in Cromwell Place after hours, which threatened to attract the attention of the police. As a result, Bacon "had scaffolding put up and bogus window cleaners as lookout men, because it was illegal, quite an elaborate thing...He took a lot of trouble"', *Francis Bacon: Revelations,* op. cit., p. 219.

3   Peppiatt, *Anatomy of an Enigma,* op. cit., p. 145.

4   Anatole France, *Le Jardin d'Epicure,* cited in Walter Benjamin, *The Arcades Project*, trans. Howard Eiland and Kevin McLaughlin (Cambridge, MA: The Belknap Press of Harvard University Press, 1999), p. 498.

5   Michael Peppiatt, 'An Interview With Francis Bacon: Provoking Accidents, Prompting Chance', *Art International 8* (1989): 28-33 (30).

6   David Sylvester, *The Brutality of Fact: Interviews with Francis Bacon* (London: Thames & Hudson, 2016), p. 59.

7   Ibid., p. 123.

8   Ian Hacking, *The Taming of Chance* (Cambridge: Cambridge University Press, 1990), p. 1.

9   Ibid., p. 2.

10   Ibid.

11   Ibid., pp. 146-47. On the cultural, intellectual, and ideological development of chance, see also Gerda Reith, *The Age of Chance: On Gambling and Western Culture* (London: Routledge, 1999); Thomas M. Kavanagh, *Enlightenment and the Shadow of Chance* (Baltimore, MD: The Johns Hopkins University Press, 1993).

12   Friedrich Nietzsche, *Thus Spoke Zarathustra: A Book For Everyone and No One*, trans. R. J. Hollingdale (London: Penguin, 1969), p. 186. Nietzsche's thinking on chance gets developed in the American pragmatist tradition. See, for example, C. S. Peirce 'The Doctrine of Necessity Examined', in *The Essential Peirce: Selected Philosophical Writings 1867–1893*, vol. 1, ed. N. Houser and C. Kloesel (Bloomington, IN: Indiana University Press, 1992). Stéphane Mallarmé, *Collected Poems and Other Verse*, trans. E. H. & A. M. Blackmore (Oxford: Oxford University Press, 2006), pp. 139-181. On Mallarmé's modernist masterpiece, see also Paul de Man, 'Lyric and Modernity', in *Blindness and Insight: Essays in the Rhetoric of Contemporary Criticism* (Minneapolis, MN: University of Minnesota Press, 1983). Alain Badiou returns to Mallarmé's *Un Coup de dés* throughout his works. See especially Alain Badiou, *Being and Event*, trans. Oliver Feltham (London: Bloomsbury, 2013), pp. 191-98 (Meditation Nineteen). Badiou's conception of the relation between event and chance, is neatly captured in the following remark from an interview with Peter Hallward: 'singular truth has its origin in an event. Something must happen, in order for there to be something new. Even in our personal lives, there must be an encounter, there must be something which cannot be calculated, predicted or managed, there must be a break based only on chance.' See Peter Hallward, *Badiou: A Subject to Truth* (Minneapolis, MN: University of Minnesota Press, 2003), p. xxv. Ferdinand de Saussure, *Course in General Linguistics*, trans. Roy Harris (London: Duckworth, 1983), pp. 69ff. For an exploration of chance in Duchamp, which pivots around the *3 Standard Stoppages*, see Herbert Molderings, *Duchamp and the Aesthetics of Chance: Art as Experiment* (New York, NY: Columbia University Press, 2010). Duchamp regarded the *3 Standard Stoppages* as one of his most important works. It involved three threads, one metre in length, dropped horizontally, from a height of one metre, onto three canvases. The threads were then fixed to the canvas with varnish. This was, as Duchamp noted, his first use of 'chance' as a 'medium'. In his 1924 'Manifesto of Surrealism', André Breton defines surrealism as follows: 'SURREALISM, n. Psychic automatism in its pure state, by which one proposes to express-verbally, by means of the written word, or in any other manner-the actual functioning of thought. Dictated by thought, in the absence of any control exercised by reason, exempt from any aesthetic or moral concern.' See André Breton, 'Manifesto of Surrealism', in *The Manifestoes of Surrealism*, trans. Richard Seaver & Helen R. Lane (Ann Arbor, MI: University of Michigan Press, 1972), p. 26. Georges Bataille, *Guilty*, trans. Bruce Boone (Venice, CA: The Lapis Press, 1988), pp. 72, 71, 72.

13   Sigmund Freud, 'Psychopathology of Everyday Life', in *The Standard Edition of the Complete Psychological Works of Sigmund Freud, Vol VI*, trans. James Strachey (London: Vintage Books, 2001), p. 242.

14   Sigmund Freud, 'Leonardo da Vinci and a Memory of his Childhood', in *The Standard Edition of the Complete Psychological Works of Sigmund Freud, Vol XI*, trans. James Strachey (London: Vintage Books, 2001), p. 137.

15   Freud, 'Psychopathology of Everyday Life', *SE VI*, op. cit., p. 257. While this sounds impeccably neat, we should of course be immediately suspicious: for it is language itself – and by extension the unconscious *structured like a language* – that problematises any strict separation of inside and outside. Indeed, topologically speaking, what we take to be most intimate turns out to have the quality of exteriority, something radically foreign; and it is this disruption of the conventional split between 'internal' and 'external' that Lacan designates with his term 'extimacy'. See Jacques Lacan, *The Seminar of Jacques Lacan, Book VII. The Ethics of Psychoanalysis*, trans. Jacques-Alain Miller (London: W. W. Norton & Co., 1992), p. 139. See also Nadia Bou Ali and Surti Singh (eds.), *Extimacy* (Evanston, IL: Northwestern University Press, 2024).

16   Friedrich von Hayek, *The Road to Serfdom* (Chicago, IL: University of Chicago Press, 1944),

pp. 204-05. For a critique of Hayek's political-economic nonsense and bad philosophising, see István Mészáros, *Beyond Capital: Toward a Theory of Transition* (New York: Monthly Review Press, 1995), pp. 198ff.

17 Theodor Adorno, *History and Freedom: Lectures 1964-1965,* trans. Rodney Livingstone (London: Polity, 2008), p. 97. On this point, see also Marx writing in the Grundrisse: 'The social relation of individuals to one another as a power over the individuals which has become autonomous, whether conceived as a natural force, as chance or in whatever other form, is a necessary result of the fact that the point of departure is not the free social individual.' Karl Marx, *Grundrisse: Foundations of the Critique of Political Economy,* trans. Martin Nicolaus (London: Penguin, 1973), p. 197.

18 Edgar Allan Poe, 'The Facts in the Case of M. Valdemar', in *The Portable Edgar Allan Poe,* ed. J. Gerald Kennedy (London: Penguin, 2006), pp. 71-79.

19 See Elaine Scarry, *On Beauty and Being Just* (Princeton, NJ: Princeton University Press, 1999). For a well-aimed response to Scarry, which takes issue with the author's conservative neo-Kantianism, see Joan Copjec, *Imagine There's No Woman: Ethics and Sublimation* (Cambridge, MA: The MIT Press, 2004), pp. 169-74.

20 Theodor Adorno, *Philosophy of Modern Music,* trans. Anne G. Mitchell & Wesley V. Blomster (London: Bloomsbury, 2007), p. 169.

21 Clement Greenberg, '1968: Interview Conducted by Edward Lucie-Smith', in *The Collected Essays and Criticism, Modernism with a Vengeance, 1957-1969, Volume 4,* ed. John O'Brian (Chicago: Chicago University Press, 1995), p. 278.

22 Kenneth Burke, *Permanence and Change: An Anatomy of Purpose* (Oakland, CA: University of California Press, 1984), p. 112.

23 Ibid., p. 113.

24 See Theodor Adorno, *Hegel: Three Studies, trans. Shierry Weber Nicholson* (Cambridge, MA: The MIT Press, 1993), p. 59; and Theodor Adorno, *Aesthetic Theory,* trans. Robert Hullot-Kentor (Minneapolis, MN: University of Minnesota Press, 1997), p. 69. For a critique of the 'immediatist'

emphasis of contemporary culture, see Anna Kornbluh, *Immediacy, or The Style of Too Late Capitalism* (London: Verso, 2024). This book is a brilliant defence of the tradition of Marxist critical theory against the 'new nihilism' of vibrant materialism, auto-theory, Afro-pessimism, and all the rest. However, the overall argument turns out to be too simplistic: it essentially pits 'good' mediation against 'bad' immediacy, thus passing over precisely the kind of dialectical relation that both Hegel and Adorno insist upon. As the latter notes: 'One can no more speak of mediation without something immediate than, conversely, one can find something immediate that is not mediated. But in Hegel the two moments are no longer rigidly contrasted. They produce and reproduce one another reciprocally...' (Adorno, *Hegel: Three Studies,* op. cit., p. 59).

25 Adorno, *Aesthetic Theory,* op. cit., pp. 118-128.

26 Aristotle, *Physics,* trans. Robin Waterfield (Oxford: Oxford University Press, 1999), pp. 42-48. See also Jonathan Lear, *Aristotle: The Desire to Understand* (Cambridge: Cambridge University Press, 1988). In alternative versions of the *Physics,* and in some of the secondary literature, *tuchē* gets translated as 'luck', 'fortune', 'fate' or 'contingency'; and *automaton* as 'accident', 'necessity', or 'chance result'.

27 Aristotle, *Physics,* op. cit., p. 45.

28 Ibid.

29 Jacques Lacan, *The Seminar of Jacques Lacan, Book XI, The Four Fundamental Concepts of Psychoanalysis,* trans. Jacques-Alain Miller (London: W. W. Norton & Co., 1981), pp. 53ff.

30 Ibid., p. 55.

31 See Mladen Dolar, 'Tyche, Clinamen, Den', *Continental Philosophy Review* 46 (2013): pp. 223-39.

32 Theodor Adorno, *Aesthetics: 1958/59,* trans. Wieland Hoban (London: Polity, 2018), p. 77.

33 Cited in Anthony Squiers, *Bertolt Brecht's Adaptations and Anti-capitalist Aesthetics Today* (Leiden: Brill, 2025), p. 150.

34 Samuel Beckett, 'The Lost Ones', in *The Complete Short Prose, 1929-1989* (New York: The Grove Press, 1995), p. 202.

35 Karl Marx, *Capital: A Critique of Political Economy, Volume I,* trans. Ben Fowkes (London: Penguin, 1990), p. 182.

36 On the notion of 'real abstraction', see Alfred Sohn-Rethel, *Intellectual and Manual Labour: A Critique of Epistemology* (London: Macmillan, 1978). For a still highly insightful discussion linking Sohn-Rethel (and the critique of political economy) to psychoanalysis (and the question of the unconscious), see Slavoj Žižek, *The Sublime Object of Ideology* (London: Verso: 1989), pp. 3-55.

37 Theodor Adorno, 'Sociology and Empirical Research', in *The Positivist Dispute In German Sociology,* trans. Glyn Adey and David Frisby (London: Heinemann, 1976), p. 80.

38 Theodor Adorno, *Negative Dialectics,* trans. E. B. Ashton (London: Routledge, 1990), p. 178; Theodor Adorno, *Minima Moralia: Reflections from Damaged Life,* trans. E. F. N. Jephcott (London: Verso, 2002), p. 229.

39 Benjamin, *Arcades Project,* op. cit., p. 319. As Benjamin notes in his dossier on Baudelaire: 'The close of "La Destruction" (published in 1855 under the title "La Volupte"!) presents the image of petrified unrest. ("Was like a Medusa-shield, / image of petrified unrest" – Gottfried Keller, "Verlorenes Recht, verlorenes Glück.") The idea of petrified unrest in Benjamin has been little discussed, but see Eric L. Santner, *On Creaturely Life: Rilke, Benjamin, Sebald* (Chicago, IL: University of Chicago Press, 2006), pp. 80-81.

40 Benjamin, *Arcades Project,* op. cit., p. 329.

41 Louis Althusser, 'Cremonini, Painter of the Abstract', in *Lenin and Philosophy and Other Essays* (Delhi: Aakar Books, 2006), p. 158. Althusser's essay has received surprisingly little attention. Notable exceptions include Michael Sprinker, *Imaginary Relations: Aesthetics and Ideology in the Theory of Historical Materialism* (London: Verso, 1987), ch. 10; Benjamin Noys, *The Persistence of the Negative: A Critique of Contemporary Continental Theory* (Edinburgh: Edinburgh University Press, 2010), pp. 167-69; Alberto Toscano, 'Materialism Without Matter: Abstraction, Absence, and Social Form', in Rebecca Colesworthy & Peter Nicholls (ed.), *How Abstract Is It? Thinking Capital Now* (London: Routledge, 2016), pp. 63-69.

42 Karl Marx, *Grundrisse,* op. cit., p. 164.

43 Althusser, 'Cremonini', op. cit., p. 162.

44 Ibid., p. 163.

45 Ibid., p. 165.

46 Bacon was acquainted with Cremonini's work. In December 1953, Bacon wrote to his friend, the gallerist and dealer Erica Brausen, suggesting that she invite W. H. Auden to write an article on Cremonini, ahead of the artist's show at Brausen's Hanover Gallery in London. In the event the essay for the exhibition was written by Stephen Spender, not Auden. The letter is reprinted in the catalogue for the 2024 exhibition, held at Galerie T&L in Paris, *Leonardo Cremonini dans l'oeil de Francis Bacon: histoire d'une amitié.* (Thanks to Martin Harrison for sharing this item with me.)

47 Althusser says that there is a productive split between Cremonini's 'ideological project' and what materialises on the canvases. This 'ideology' concerns 'the immediate relation between man and nature'; but what Cremonini actually paints (and certainly in his later work) is 'the *difference*' from this ideology – not the 'similarities' between 'man' and 'nature', but, rather, human beings as 'marked' by real abstractions. See Althusser, 'Cremonini', pp. 160 and 161. A similar split might also be seen to be at work in Bacon. While Bacon describes himself as simply 'recording' 'facts' about his subjects and communicating the 'feeling of life', with all its 'violence' and 'intensity', the paintings themselves can be seen to break free from this high humanist pathos. To put the point very simply: Bacon's extreme individualism becomes an extreme materialism.

48 Adorno, *Minima Moralia,* op. cit., p. 135.

49 According to John Berger, 'Bacon questions nothing, unravels nothing. He accepts that the worst has happened. His lack of alternatives, within his view of the human condition, is reflected in the lack of any thematic development in his life's work.' See John Berger, 'Francis Bacon and Walt Disney', in *About Looking* (London: Bloomsbury, 2009), p. 123.

50 Adorno, *Negative Dialectics,* op. cit., p. 145. Citation slightly modified.

51 Benjamin, *Arcades Project,* op. cit., p. 512. See also Walter Benjamin, 'Notes on a Theory of Gambling', in *Selected Writings, Volume 2, Part 1, 1927-1930,* trans. Rodney Livingstone et al. (Cambridge, MA: The Belknap Press of Harvard University Press, 2005), pp. 297-98. I agree with Fredric Jameson that Benjamin's reflections on the temporality of the gambler constitute 'some of his most extraordinary pages'. See Fredric Jameson, *The Benjamin Files* (London: Verso, 2020), p. 93. To briefly outline parts of Benjamin's broader theory of the gambler: he notes the similarity between the gambler and the factory worker on the assembly line: the reflexive mechanism that the machine triggers in the worker appears again in gambling, 'for there can be no game without the quick movement of the hand by which the stake is put down or a card is picked up. The jolt in the movement of a machine is like the so-called *coup* in a game of chance.' While gambling and wage labour would appear to be starkly opposed activities, they are in fact, as Benjamin argues, intimately aligned: 'the drudgery of the labourer is, in its own way, a counterpart to the drudgery of the gambler. Both types of work are equally devoid of substance… The process of continually starting all over again is the regulative idea of gambling, as it is of wages for work.' (See Walter Benjamin, 'On Some Motifs in Baudelaire', in *Selected Writings, Volume 4, 1938-1940,* trans. Edmund Jephcott et al. (Cambridge, MA: The Belknap Press of Harvard University Press, 2006), pp. 330-31.) As with capitalist work, then, gambling is here tied to the empty temporality of repetition and the general disintegration of human experience. But this, as Benjamin reveals, is only one side of the story. The intoxication of the gambler, as he goes on, in a powerful shifting of the gears, 'depends on the peculiar capacity of the game to provoke *presence of mind* through the fact that, in rapid succession, it brings to the fore constellations which work…to summon up a thoroughly new, original reaction from the gambler.' (See Benjamin, *Arcades Project,* op. cit., pp. 512-13.) What Benjamin is thus aiming at with his theory of gambling is to imagine an overcoming of the capitalist labour process from within, and with it a transformation of time and experience. As the very embodiment of the world of exchange, the gambler, for Benjamin, dialectically prefigures its overcoming.

52 See Benjamin, 'On The Theory of Knowledge, Theory of Progress' (Convolute N), *Arcades Project,* op. cit., pp. 460-88; Walter Benjamin, 'On the Concept of History', in *Selected Writings, Volume 4,* op. cit., pp. 389-97.

53 As Benjamin puts it: 'Presence of mind as a political category comes magnificently to life in these words of Turgot: "Before we have learned to deal with things in a given position, they have already changed several times. Thus, we always perceive events too late, and politics always needs to foresee, so to speak, the present"'. Benjamin, *Arcades,* op. cit., pp. 477-78.

54 See Sohn-Rethel, *Intellectual and Manual Labour,* op. cit., p. 33. Herbert Marcuse gives another formulation of this point when he says: 'The constitution of the world occurs behind the backs of individuals; yet it is their work'. See Herbert Marcuse, 'Philosophy and Critical Theory', in *Negations: Essays in Critical Theory* (London: May Fly Books, 2009), p. 111.

55 Karl Korsch, *Karl Marx* (Leiden: Brill, 2015), p. 15. This is a modified translation of a phrase that appears in Marx, *Capital: Volume I,* op. cit., pp. 166-67. To further develop the idea of a subject's 'not knowing' about its role as an economic actor, we might introduce the fruitful psychoanalytic notion of disavowal. For an excellent analysis, see Alenka Zupančič, *Disavowal* (London: Polity, 2024).

*Thanks to Peter Buse, Dany Nobus, and Jamieson Webster for insightful comments on an earlier version of this essay.

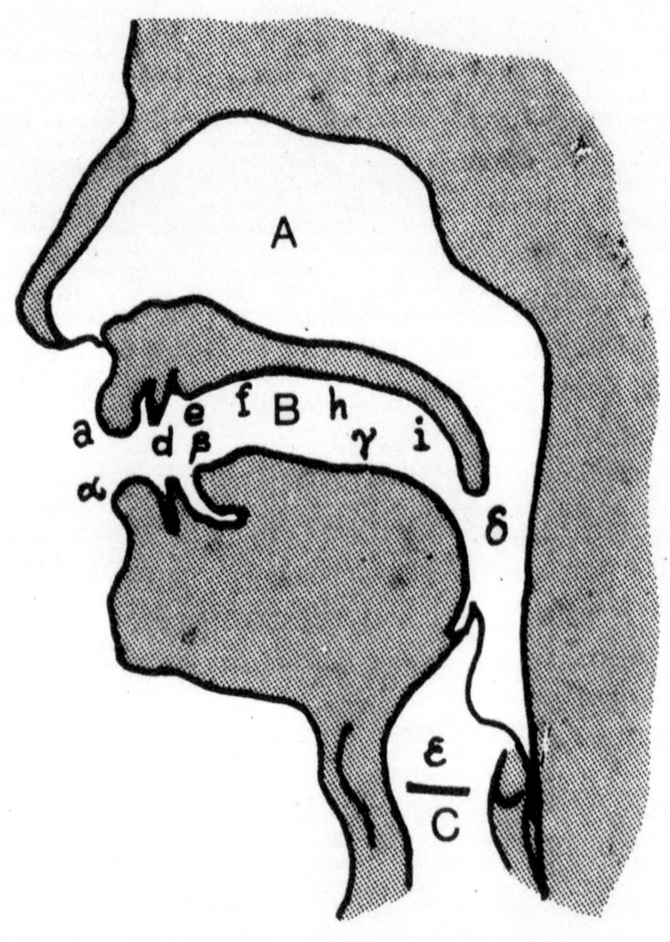

fig. 10 Ferdinand Saussure, *Course in General Linguistics; Appendix: Principles of Physiological Phonetics*

SAVING FACE: BACON BETWEEN EAR, NOSE AND THROAT

Jamieson Webster

If the doctor looks down a child's throat or carries out some small operation on him, we may be quite sure that these frightening experiences will be the subject of the next game…
Sigmund Freud, 1920

Before turning to Francis Bacon, let's set the stage for the opening act of psychoanalysis. When the iodoform gauze was at last unfurled from Emma Eckstein's nasal cavity, it totalled at least half a metre – the length of an average umbilical cord. Its removal left behind a swollen, infected void. A foul odour filled the room, followed by a gush – and then a gush again – of blood. Freud fled. He was overwhelmed not by this gushing of blood (nor by the patient's bulging eyes, pale face, or slowing pulse) but by a surge of 'strong emotions' that he recounted to his good friend and fellow medical colleague, Wilhelm Fliess – the surgeon responsible for leaving 'the foreign body' lodged inside Eckstein upon removing one of her turbinate bones:

> So we had done her an injustice; she was not at all abnormal, rather, a piece of gauze had gotten torn off as you were removing it and stayed in for fourteen days, preventing healing; at the end it tore off and provoked the bleeding. That this mishap should have happened to you; how you will react to it when you hear about it; what others could make of it; how wrong I was to urge you to operate in a foreign city where you could not follow through on the case; how my intention to do my best for this poor girl was insidiously thwarted and result-ed in endangering her life – all this came over me simultaneously.[1]

Well, accidents happen. Modern medicine was still in its infancy. But just before they removed the gauze, Freud had a thought: 'There is something inside; I shall not pull it out lest there be a hemorrhage; rather, I'll stuff it some more…'[2] But, they had to remove it – 'pulled at something like a thread, kept on pulling.'[3] And with that, psychoanalysis was born – from the very stuff that it will come to be made of, or unmade by.

Freud attempts to absolve Fliess of guilt for nearly killing the girl: 'you did it as well as one can do it.' 'I really should not have tormented you here.' After recounting this tale he says he felt ashamed. Of what? Perhaps because he did write to torment him with the scene of his own torment. Freud calls Eckstein 'my child of sorrows', and confesses, 'I felt miserable'. 'Strong emotions were welling up. She was not abnormal.' I can think of a no more important revelation for the founder of psychoanalysis, than this – 'she was not abnormal'.

Wilhelm Fliess – Freud's intimate confidant and, in many ways, his own quasi-analyst – was an ear, nose, and throat doctor. And so it is fitting that when Freud fled the room to compose himself with a glass of cognac, it was Emma Eckstein who greeted him on his return with the cutting remark: 'So this is the strong sex.'[4] Even after all that, she found her voice. She skewered Freud. Her voice was the only one in a room full of men stuffing bodies with gauze, with blame, with names – and she named the problem: sex.

The birthing scene of psychoanalysis was Emma Eckstein's mangled face – and she remained disfigured for the rest of her life. Freud would then have to come face to face with what he didn't want to know: the 'weaker' sex, her complaints, her sexuality, her voice. From this primal medical failure, psychoanalysis would have to learn to listen rather than look, to follow voice rather than seek visible pathology.

By the time Freud wrote *The Interpretation of Dreams*, he had steeled himself. In his infamous specimen dream that opens the book Freud finally looked unflinchingly into the throat of Irma (who stands in for Emma) to ask himself about all this 'stuff': medical malpractice, drug use, suffering, conscience, death. Freud thought to himself, 'It seemed as if I had been collecting all the occasions which I could bring up against myself as evidence of a lack of medical conscientiousness.'[5] Freud wanted to blame Irma/Emma: *it really is all your fault, these pains of yours; if you would just listen to me you would get better*. But instead, he found his own pangs of conscience.

Lacan famously said of this moment that Freud found something horrendous. Everything was there in her throat. It was the inside-out of the head. The gulf of the mouth that swallows everything. It was death.

Everything blends in and becomes associated in this image, from the mouth to the female sexual organ, by way of the nose… there's a horrendous discovery here of the flesh one never sees, the foundation of things, the other side of the head, of the face, the secretory glands par excellence, the flesh from which everything exudes, at the very heart of the mystery, the flesh in as much as it is suffering, in as much as its form in itself is something which provokes anxiety.[6]

Here, words ceased. But this space allowed Freud to finally hear himself. To turn towards language. From one angle, this is a heroic tale – at least as told by Lacan – with Freud following a trail of words from the sight of this impossible THING toward the Valhalla of the symbolic and the possibility of psychoanalytic interpretation. He discovered the meaning of dreams. Dreams were not just images, they were a ciphered, symbolised wish.

The equivalence in the 'solution' he was searching for in Irma/Emma's cure moved him from solution as substance (cocaine, tissue) towards solution as word. Freud found his resolve to be a psychoanalyst; to listen. And yet how could these words he proffered or heard, themselves not carry in them something deadly? Wasn't this the deadliest transmission – blame, guilt, judgement – beyond the reality of death? 'How will you react when you hear about it?' Freud said to Fliess. Hearing might be worse than seeing something maimed.

Lacan eventually adds an extra step in the cure, not only to hear and be heard, but also 'the desire for a speech with nothing beyond.'[7] We might like this idea of a solution to our problems found in speaking, but speaking was also our problem. Freud proffered to us the solution of the word at the place of suffering flesh, but it came like a final judgment and unleashed an even more primal fury that still had to find a limit. Lacan pushes Freud towards this – what he called headlessness. We are at the end of saving face when a voice has nothing beyond it.

A similar reckoning can be seen in Francis Bacon. Much psychoanalytic and philosophical interpretation of Francis Bacon's work focuses on the question of the image and what falls outside of its fascinating grasp – trauma, violence, or life. The focus is on what, broadly speaking, Lacan termed the real. In one sense, the terrain of images has magnified exponentially in the contemporary landscape since Bacon's time. Even Bacon wondered how painting could disrupt and bring something new to viewers after Picasso, the avant-gardes, two world wars, movies and photography. All while remaining wedded to figuration within the history of painting. I want to take another approach to Bacon's work, thinking not about the beyond of images or the imaginary or identity, but of our relationship to the symbolic and to language and meaning more broadly, as evinced by this primal scene of psychoanalysis. What if we imagined Bacon's question as one about the voice?

Beginning in this scene of disfiguration, faces, and language at the dawn of psychoanalysis, we could move beyond so many questions regarding the mask and its horrific underside, the painting of affect as despair or shock in Bacon. The trajectory from Emma Eckstein's voice cutting through medical authority to Bacon's reinvention of portraiture maps a fundamental shift in how we understand the relationship between bodies, language, and visual representation. Where traditional portraiture is thought of as capturing psychological interiority or social position, Bacon's portraits reveal the body and face as the site where language performs its most fundamental intensities and transformation.

Emma Eckstein's observation – 'So this is the strong sex' – continues to resonate through Bacon's work as a challenge to all forms of authority that claim to know the truth of subjects without listening to them, without understanding that everything said is spoken. The spaces between ear, nose, and throat mark the sites where the question of how to listen remains always urgent, always unresolved. I see Bacon's paintings staging an uncanny dimension within language and, with Lacan, ask whether he sought a beyond of language, touching 'on the real by losing all meaning'.[8]

According to Freud in his *Project for a Scientific Psychology*, speaking begins with *Schreien*—or crying out, howling, shouting. Importantly, this is also the beginning of babbling, singing, and all those pleasures in making sounds that lead to song, wit, writing. Perhaps the uncharacteristic triptych of Mick Jagger portraits by Bacon becomes exemplary. [fig. 46] Who else could be recognised both as a mouth and by the sounds of *that* mouth? Bacon took very few commissions, and for those he did, he had met the subject in question. But he never met Mick Jagger. And Mick Jagger is the only broadly public icon that he painted.

I would be hard pressed not to say that Bacon was interested in the mouth that defined an entire era of Rock and Roll; that put generations in a trance. In the triptych, Bacon charts the progression of the mouth – from closed, to parting lips revealing teeth, to a full-throated burst. Mick Jagger was a singer with an incredible range and ability to shift registers from melodic to shouts and growls, from smooth and sensual to gritty and aggressive. It's not a question of screaming, but tone, rhythm, sensuality. In the pictures where the mouth opens, more and more we lose the eyes. While Warhol painted an icon, Bacon painted a mouth and a voice.

Where does a voice take place? Where does language take place? These questions trouble spatiality itself – the strange boundary between inside and outside – and push us to think of aesthetic composition beyond the figurative realism of the image. The disruption of the face in Bacon's work is not simply the sign of a psychological disturbance, but of a material one. What happens to a face when the mouth moves, when it opens? As Bacon remarked to David Sylvester in their interviews when asked about Giacometti trying to trap the gaze:

I don't think it's just the gaze[...]You're conscious of the whole structure of a person. I mean, one knows Giacometti is quite right that a skull is more abstract because it hasn't got eyes, but then you've got your nose, your mouth, your teeth, your tongue, your everything, your lips. You've got all those things, too. So he's limiting it very much when he said it's just the gaze.[9]

Bacon also said that he disliked surrealism because it seemed to him like illustration, lacking the qualities of painting that go beyond depiction of reality. One had to trap reality as it appeared, not narrativise or copy.

Many asked again and again – seemingly offended or continuously bewildered – how he could say that he was simply painting life and appearance given the nature of his use of distortion. As Bacon himself said,

> The violence itself is only a story, the violence would have to be *remade* through technical, new technical means in the paint itself to bring over its violence, otherwise it would be an illustration of violence... It's a violence that has been exacerbated within the nervous system and comes out in the paint.[10]

While much focus has been given to the question of violence in relation to his work, I'm interested in the idea of the problem being that violence is 'only a story'. Bacon insisted that nothing in his paintings was meant to tell a story or offer commentary on the world. In this, he moves us towards and away from discourse at once – towards the material of language as it hits the body, and away from the endless circulation of narratives. He wants something of the real speaking body, here and now.

Speaking is an act that is as continuous as it is discontinuous. Again, in speaking with Sylvester, Bacon turns to the task of painting in a way that brings the creation of an image close to the construction of a spoken sentence:

> I think a painter, if he's going to attempt to record life, he's got to do it in a much, much more intense and curtailed way. It has to have the intensity of, you can call it sophisticated simplicity[...] You have to abbreviate, abbreviate it, into intensity.[11]

From the standpoint of the symbolic, even as it organises a system of differentiation, it creates a virtual space where meaning is imagined as existing, granting places, erecting systems, that feels proximate to a world. None of this can be seen; none of this exists as such. Yet, one is included in it as a name, and its continual use by bodies is how memory lives on. 'If it's necessary for man to use speech to make discoveries or get his bearings, it's as a function of this natural propensity to decompose in the presence of the other', wrote Lacan.[12]

God, Lacan reminded us, is a voice that under no circumstances reveals its face. Lacan referred us to what in language is inextricable from the instances of embodied voices. But then there were the disembodied voices of thought that torture us. We learned from psychoanalysis that what sustains speech is an Other whom we address when speaking, who we desire to hear and know something about what we are saying, a virtual repository of meaning. While this may sustain *our* speech, the Other itself could not readily be sustained or grasped. And yet it appears from time to time. Importantly, there are material signifiers that wander about, fasten, surprise, congregate, raise the hairs on one's arms, and seemingly overdetermine us. Master strokes. As Darian Leader wrote: this primal mark interested Bacon – language reduced to its most singular and essential element.

At one point the linguist Ferdinand Saussure tried to map language according to where the sounds of letters were created in the mouth, nasal cavity, and throat.[13] [fig. 10]

I love this illustration. I feel as if it's a map for Bacon's work. When we think of language, we might want to begin with the hallowed halls of knowledge, swayed by the sight of libraries and the ease of associating language with a written text. But Saussure understood that we must begin elsewhere: with the body. With the mouth, tongue, palate, throat, nasal cavity. This is where language comes alive. Where it enters the world. Passed from generation to generation through vibration and air.

Each person's language is a strange subtraction from all possible sounds made in infancy, honed into the mother tongue that stamps us irreversibly. Is it such a leap, then, to imagine Bacon's portraits – as they capture the movement of a face in a single image – as also capturing the rhythm and assimilation of speech? The work of subtraction, and then all the additions of a lifetime? Can we see this rhythm – this cadence – defining his brushstrokes, those fugal marks across a face?

Of course, in name alone, Francis Bacon leads us naturally to think of animal carcasses in butcher shop windows. But these places are more symbolic than imagistic. We should remember that 'spilling your guts' means, precisely, talking too much. It is language – not image – that reduces something to a piece of meat, that transforms a pig into pork, a calf into veal, or, with a flick of the tongue, into a sow or a golden cow. Isn't this exactly what Bacon meant when he said a painter should remember his love of the colour of meat? While the hysteric – the vocal suffering of her sexual body – was the starting point for Freud, for Lacan it was the psychotic: the one for whom language returns from the outside and haunts.

It's not the idea of suffering flesh undoing the self-image that should occupy us, but rather the restaging of the subject's relation to language. The butcher shop reappears at the beginning of Lacan's reflections on psychosis. A woman tells him that her neighbour insulted her. It seems trivial, easy to dismiss. But Lacan presses her. The man had passed her in the hallway and muttered: *I've just come from the butcher.* Lacan immediately understood. The woman had received the message in an inverted form: she heard herself being called a pig. She smiled in agreement. We can smile, too – and hear Bacon.

In Lacan's reading of Daniel Paul Schreber's *Memoirs of My Nervous Illness*, we find a further frame for Bacon. Schreber was obsessed with nerves – the painful, pleasurable excesses of his body – and with the divine rays that emanated to bind him to others. But for Lacan, this wasn't about physiology. It was about the body's painful encounter with language. Schreber's 'nervous illness' was a crisis of the linguistic order – what he called *nerve-contact*. Bacon might well have said the same. He once described his paintings as the patterns of one's nervous system – a repeated phrase too often misread in neuroscientific terms.

Lacan isolates several key moments in Schreber's passage through language. The first is what he called the *bellowing miracle.* Schreber felt compelled to shout. His mouth became intensely present to him – so much so that anything in it had to be spat out:

> ...we see in this shouting the mouth's motor participation in speech reduced to its most extreme aspect. If there is anything by means of which speech comes to be combined with an absolutely a-signifying vocal function, and which nevertheless contains all possible signifiers, it must surely be what it is that makes us shiver in a dog's baying at the moon.[14]

This is the beginning of all language – Freud's *Schreien*. The scream is, at first, a-signifying. It is almost entirely motoric: mouth opening, body tensing, air forced through lungs and larynx. We don't know why a baby cries, so we interpret. We impose significance on a scream. Could this be where Bacon begins, but begins to move further afield? All those screaming popes renounced.

Lacan next turns to what he calls 'the call for help.' But this isn't Schreber's own cry – it comes from the Other. Sometimes these cries would leap into his mouth; more often, they appeared as divine nerves trailing behind them a kind of comet's tail. The call was animated and anxiety-inducing. Schreber recognised meaning, but it came from elsewhere. The cries returned, but their meaning was more like an emission – something discharged, trailing off, then vanishing. Lacan linked this to abandonment. It wasn't clear whether it was their appearance or disappearance that was more disturbing.

But this is the beginning of a system: the linguistic order where every meaning contains its opposite. A mother's coming will, under this structure, always also include her going. Freud called this 'the antithetical meaning of primal words.'[15] In this comet's tail I can't help but hear Bacon's infamous and oft-repeated line:

> I would like my pictures to look as if a human being had passed between them, like a snail, leaving a trail of the human presence and memory of past events as the snail leaves its slime.[16]

This trail of slime is also the lived residue of the loved Other's presence – and absence – marked in speech. To signify, at first, means only that someone was *here*. That something passed through. This is how a shadow is cast. Freud reminded us that children aren't afraid of the dark if they can hear a voice. And then, someone disappears for good. 'I've done a lot of self-portraits, really because people have been dying around me like flies and I've nobody else left to paint but myself,'[17] says Bacon.

Following these disappearing traces, Schreber began to describe the incessant sounds of birds and insects surrounding him. It's difficult not to hear the question of 'the birds and the bees' – that is, of sex. We're close now to language as an *eroticised field* – an attempt to make meaning about what we cannot articulate: enjoyment, desire, love, reproduction. And with it comes absurdity, stupidity, vulgarity, humiliation. Of course it does. Schreber tried to minimise these sounds – or at least to find respite from their convergence, their prickling, their tickling.

In Bacon's works closest to sexuality – *Two Figures* (1953*)*, [fig. 20] *Two Figures in the Grass* (1954*)*, [fig. 21] *Two Figures on a Couch* (1967), [fig. 31] *Two figures with a Monkey* (1973) [fig. 40] – it's often said that the bodies wrestle and fuse. But the action also happens between their faces. One's mouth is often there, open – as if speaking. The other taking in. Mouths are close to ears. The hint of aggressivity, if there is one, is undeniably tied to what can't be heard; though the two figures in the grass seem almost to whisper to one another. The monkey's excited noises can certainly be heard, accentuating the silent whispers of the figures above.

We are always in the conundrum of the voices of others, and yet painfully alone with our own, and what we say, want to say, or hear. Confronting the *real* of voice must be close to the way voices land on the nervous system. Bacon spoke of nothing else, really; as if he were a conductor grounding voice into flesh and nerve. He was, unlike so many painters, loquacious. Witty. A real talker. And as for those tales of sado-masochistic love, one might remember that *beat* also refers to rhythm – something musical. Freud certainly played on this polyphony when he titled his paper 'A Child is Being Beaten'. As Darian Leader notes, the passage through the symbolic involves the body undergoing the *blows and beats* of language, assimilating an Other cadence. This is how we give voice a place.

Lacan notes that Schreber finally found relief by translating this erotic field of speech into space. A more spatial apprehension of the world emerged for him. The calls came towards him from the horizon, circled his head, and stabbed in from behind. He called this a 'trans-space', linked to the apprehension of the signifier in this field of meaning. Language, Lacan says, is spatial in that it places us in a sequence. It grants temporality. Any sense of support or coherence must come from this temporal quality of language – not from any grasping of an image, whether of the world or of oneself.

We cannot see the entirety of ourselves. And yet, with the signifier, we have an apprehension of totality – a virtual space from which meaning arises and in which it is organised. This is one of Lacan's most counterintuitive and ingenious insights: that spatial support for the body arises not from the visual field but from language. This, he argued, was always the hysteric's mistake – turning the field of speech into images which caused her bodily disintegration. Her cure begins when talking turns those images back into speech. Bacon notes in 1971:

> I think as I want the paint to speak as strongly as it were, as it can, on its own account, not necessarily saying anything, but, as my, all my art is based on figuration. As I want the paint in itself to have a very strong quality, that may give it a feeling of. That I am also trying to say, saying something about people in extremities.[18]

'Speak as strongly as it were[...]on its own account' and 'not necessarily saying anything'. This is a vision of the psychoanalytic cure at its *strongest*. The space of its work.

I keep returning to the spaces of Bacon's paintings. So many interpreters want to assign psychological meanings to these spaces – glass boxes, wrestling rings, operating theatres, prisons, stages, prosthetic cages. But what captivates me is their *spatial quality*: space in the act of spatialising. This is another way of saying that meaning is always framed – held within a context it must use to signify. But with Bacon, the framing is literal. *Language takes place in a framed space.*

As we know, Bacon always framed his paintings and put them under reflective glass. He himself says that whatever people made of his backgrounds, they existed only to help something appear. One could say these spaces were designed to isolate – to create intensity and compactness, to abbreviate in the sense he meant. This is very different from isolation as imprisonment. Even if meaning is a kind of prison. Importantly, meaning never arrives. There is no final meaning to be reached.

Schreber's final phase, like so many psychotic structures, culminated in a fantasy of the end of the world – not because the world was ending, but because the *erotic field* of speech had to stop. It had gone on long enough. Lacan insisted: meaning always continues. It is infinite. The end of the world is a fantasy that attempts to stop meaning because only a limit can produce peace. Lacan called this 'the peace of the evening', set against the anxiety we typically associate with nightfall.

Language elides an end. Meaning, belief, must by themselves find a limit. Only then can there be peace. Only then can we escape the fantasy of final judgment – guilt. This *real* of language appears again in one of Lacan's final texts, *L'Étourdit*. We must listen for the speaking that is forgotten behind what is said. If we give up on meaning, on judgment, on totality or finality – what remains? Mouths moving, breathing, speaking, calling, reaching out, trailing off, shutting up.

Judgment, as we know, is always a scene of speaking: an accounting for oneself, of one's existence, to an Other. It's the final freeze frame – just before all sound comes to a stop. How can we not, eventually, long for speech to stop? It's as if we are suspended – torn between a tender longing for language and the quiet that follows. Violence plays a role here, yes – but it's the middle of the story, and maybe the least interesting part. This trajectory was in Freud's dream of Irma/Emma. He found his fear of vengeance, or the *law of talion* – an eye for an eye. But beyond this monstrous scene of speech was Lacan's 'peace of the evening' – when the sun sets like a mouth closing.

What if flesh in Bacon's paintings isn't primarily the fantasy of violently suffering flesh but rather the *impossible horizon* of flesh at peace? Bacon pushing there – what Lacan imagined as the silence that follows the scream. Yes, this moment is close to apocalyptic visions, the end of the world. But we must shift the violence of the image towards this voice with nothing beyond it. In Bacon's later portraits, the figures seem less like faces on the verge of screaming, and more like faces that have gone silent. Despite the brushstrokes that continue to ripple across them, these are not mouths about to open – they are mouths that have stopped.

There's a rhythm in Bacon between the gesture of the brush and the gesture of the face. Their improbable collision produces something increasingly not quite expressive, not quite still. But a stillness nevertheless there, as if promised. *Self-Portrait* (1971), [fig. 36] *Portrait of Michel Leiris* (1976), [fig. 41] *Triptych* (1991) [fig. 51] come to mind. In the two portraits the face is serene, eyes and mouth still, as if to hold presence behind the curved brushstrokes breaking up space in the foreground. These strokes don't take the face with them as they do in *Three Studies of Henrietta Moraes* (1969), for example. [fig. 33] Distance is taken from what ripples a surface. *Triptych* (1991) was one of the last works that Bacon completed and has been described as having an elegiac, meditative calm. [fig. 51] Notably the faces are not distorted and yet carry the same uncanny quality of much of his work.

Milan Kundera once wrote that Bacon, like Beckett, closed an era rather than opening one. Bacon himself remarked that among his contemporaries, he had no one to talk to. He wasn't painting during Picasso's ascendancy, or wartime collectives. Bacon was isolated. What, for Bacon, was at the limit of twentieth-century horror? Kundera said it was the face:

> The face that harboured 'that treasure, that nugget of gold, that hidden diamond' which is the infinitely fragile self-shivering in a body; the face I gaze upon to seek in it a reason for living the 'completely futile accident' that is life.[19]

This shivering treasure is the signifier at its most real and most embodied. When Lacan read Socrates's *Symposium*, he named this treasure the *agalma* – the jewel-like object from which desire springs. A place always lost to us, returned to by chance – we can only circle it. Try to tighten the rings around its absence. I see Bacon *there*. With no face left to save. 'The thing is one can't really talk about painting, only around it. After all if you could explain it why would you bother to do it?'[20] Bacon notes.

Some characterise the imagistic and figurative disintegration in Bacon's work in terms of the primal scene – witnessing something violent and passionate that shouldn't be seen, well before it can be understood. We might remember however, that one often didn't see anything. One *heard*. Sounds, breathing, screaming, moaning, gagging, laughing, humming. The sphinx, if she was anything, was a voice. She spoke fate – death within life. Bacon often said he was trying to access something essential from the ancient Greek texts. He felt 'close to the ancient world'. And what were these texts, if not rare records of oral tradition?

Bacon loved Aeschylus's *Oresteia*, often quoting the line: 'The reek of human blood smiled out at me.' It's a sentence of pure speech, of poetry. It is synaesthetic: a smell that smiles. A line passed between nose, eyes, ears, and mouth. Bacon's furies are straight from Aeschylus – and he often painted them headless. A fury, in Bacon's hands, becomes an *acephalic* creature. Early versions sometimes retained ears and mouths, a neck or throat – exaggerating their quality as voices. Later, in works like *Oedipus and the Sphinx After Ingres* (1983),[fig. 47] there's only a wound where the head once was. The sphinx, on the other hand, is still, enigmatic, and feminine, like *Sphinx, Portrait of Muriel Belcher* (1979). [fig. 43] Language, Lacan writes, riddles us like a Sphinx. As analyst, he says, 'I sphinx my not-all in you.'[21]

For Bacon, the furies were spoken judgment – vengeance, sacrifice, fate. Their splayed, cylindrical forms remind me of something between the nasal turbinate bones and the cochlea – between smell and sound. At the site of the head's undoing – at the limit of figure and face – there's a sense of necessity that moves us beyond mere visage. Bacon, of course, anticipates this, and makes this attack on the head a question of beauty:

> I think in this case, it certainly is; mind you, like all chance things it's luck in the quality of the damaging. Luck comes into the quality of the damaging; it could completely ruin this head. But you see, it so often happens in these heads to the nose, for instance, as it protrudes. Well, as you know, many people are improved in their looks when they've had their nose broken and pushed in. That's again a curious thing if you've ever looked at boxers' heads. Sometimes their good looks have been enormously improved by having their noses broken. I mean it's very strange that all these beauty parlours[...] don't have someone just bash their heads about a bit[...] After all, the Africans did remarkable things by cutting their face and very often made marvellous elongations of the face by the way they cut it.[22]

How is it that damage brings out an unknown beauty – so contradictory to conventional ideals? It must be because we can't *feel* form until we reach its limits. An element of chance, of necessity, gets superimposed, and suddenly everything changes.

Psychoanalysis stakes its wager on the surprise of speech – on the chance interruption – that always demonstrates the limit of meaning. Bacon, too, more and more, played with moments of chance. He courted chance in his work and allowed it to determine whether a painting would survive. He often said he worked until he was just short of wanting to destroy a painting. If he failed to reach this moment, he'd ask someone to remove the canvas from his studio before he destroyed it himself – as he did with hundreds of paintings.

Bacon was, of course, an avid gambler. Gambling debts kept him painting. Or perhaps painting kept him gambling. Lacan tied the passion for gambling directly to language, elaborating on Freud's idea that gambling was a confrontation with fate or destiny. Lacan positioned gambling at the juncture between the symbolic and the real. He described the 'automatic stupidity' of discourse – its droning, binary logic, its endless chains of meaning. One can talk shit to the very end. What interrupts us happens by *chance* – a cut, a break in speech that forces a reckoning. Suddenly, we must look back and take stock. All bets are in. Our losses and gains are revealed. Lacan writes: 'The gambler's passion is nothing but that question asked of a signifier, figured by the automaton of chance.'[23]

This is judgment – but not as moral reckoning. Rather, it's the *retroactive effect of meaning*, produced by virtue of stopping. We ask for meaning to stop. We ask that the ledger be drawn:

> In the game of chance no doubt he will test his luck, but also he is going to read his destiny in it. He has the idea that something is revealed there, which belongs to him – and all the more so given that there is no one confronting him.[24]

Meeting with chance during a gamble, one is, according to Lacan, finally alone. We are not caught in the endless anticipation of meaning from some other. No one is there, and yet *something* is revealed. This is how the gambler touches the signifier in its purest form.

Gambling for Bacon is a way to start again – like getting rid of a painting. A moment to read his destiny one more time. Find the aloneness he sought in both painting and play. Bacon himself linked gambling and painting through the idea of chance:

> I think that every artist or every plastic artist certainly, and I, no I would say every artist, hopes that the inevitability of the form that is given to him by chance will go on recurring for him. Because of course I always expect chance to work for me, even when I go into a casino expect to win and this doesn't by any means happen very often, as in painting, but I always expect, or each time I start painting I think a marvellously unresolved, unthought-out image will come out of, out of what you could call my hope in my despair. You could say that working with chance is working, in a way, with the despair of not being of not being able to logically make this image, because if I made it logically it would be an illustration of my idea.[25]

There is a draining of enjoyment at this point – a stillness – because something is given. It is given, it works, without anyone's intervention. Without logic as it were. Bacon calls this working with chance, *my hope in my despair*.

I see him stumbling out of the casino in the early morning. The telegrams asking for money will resume. The need to paint, to gamble again, will return. But not yet. In this moment – he is leaving, losing, letting go. I imagine him loving this sleep most.

'In trying to do a portrait, my ideal would really be just to pick up a handful of paint and throw it at the canvas and hope that the portrait was there,'[26] says Bacon to Sylvester. This hopeful handful of paint becomes the portrait in *Jet of Water* (1988), [fig. 50] a late painting that is often celebrated for its force and dynamism. This jet is also Bacon playing with the moment of chance, the spray of paint, that he had long worked. If *Jet of Water* has force, his two *Sand Dune* paintings (from 1981 and 1983) [fig. 45], [fig. 48] show this force's dissipation and stilling. A kind of dissolution of form, but still a difference, like one sand grain and another, close to what remains of a person in their portraits. 'At the end of the day, it's all we want. Voluptuousness,' Francis Bacon told Melvyn Bragg in 1985. He continues, 'Yes, a state of voluptuousness. Whatever it is. Everything else is a falling away.'[27]

What can we say of a voice with nothing beyond it? What falls and allows for a sense of peace and stillness? Perhaps it's confronting the most intimate rhythm of all: breathing. The suspended breath between speech and its response. Voice itself arises from this from air held, shaped, released. A column of air manipulated in the void between the ear, nose and throat. We live through this rhythm. And silence is always coupled with breath—at least while we are alive. Our dependence on breath, and our aloneness in breathing, is something Bacon knew intimately as a lifelong asthmatic. His asthma marked his childhood and his violent conflicts with his father, who saw him as weak. As fate would have it, asthma was the culprit in Bacon's death, exacerbating the pneumonia he developed on a trip that led to his heart-attack. He was travelling against doctor's orders. He gambled with going anyway.

Thoré said of Bacon's hero Velázquez: 'It is a matter of 'creating a void' around figures and material things so that they may appear in the air. Velázquez never risks a positive color in his backgrounds, always neutralized by mixed and elusive colorings...'.[28] Air *is* the speech where we do not appear and yet it is ours. In Bacon living elements certainly took place at a mouth that almost seemed to be speaking, or faces that were moving, gesturing, close to confused material. I sense precipitant meaning and its shadows, close to what Bacon said of his screaming popes:

> I did the whole thing series of the Popes for a curious reason – I bought a book on diseases of the mouth when I was quite young – it had always fascinated me, and also I'd been hypnotized by Velázquez's

portrait of Innocent X and at that time I thought that with the color of the portrait and the mouth, the saliva and the glitter of the mouth, I would be able to make a marvelous image –but I never succeeded in doing it. When the Pope was screaming, it wasn't screaming; I wanted to make the scream into something which would have the intensity and beauty of a Monet Sunset.[29]

But then again, he claims to have regretted painting them. Velázquez didn't need more perfecting. What, then, was the beauty and intensity of a scream – not as horror, but as something else? Is it not voice?

In one sense, this could be the central question of all of Bacon's work. He wasn't painting subjective emotion or mere negative sensation. The scream belonged to the mouth, its glitter and the shine of saliva. To disease rendered in vivid colour. To sunsets. To pleasure. Quotidian, singular, and registered on a face. What we see in a face is a *voice*, not a scream which is simply its origin.

The intensity of Bacon's brush strokes seems more and more to wrap the face around a void, certainly the void that is there between ear, nose and throat. This wrapping of the face around a void becomes equivalent with what Bacon called 'essence' in his late portraits. For this reason, these are for me the better reference when it comes to Bacon, with Mick Jagger as a hallmark. As Robert Melville wrote in the *London Review of Books*, in his piece 'Bacon's Furies':

> It was Bacon's turn to portraiture in the early 1960s, making studies of the faces of actual people, that brought about the most radical transformation of his brushwork, its most drastic turns and twists. It was by this means that he hoped to bring out hidden likenesses, and although the outcome often looked extremely brutal, as if he were destroying the last shred of dignity in some of his closest friends, the effects could be awe-inspiring.[30]

His evolving twists and turns of the brush are linked for me to the cadence of language and voice at the place of the face. As for brutality, Bacon himself said in 1964 when asked about teeth and fear: 'I simply wanted for a moment to record people when they laughed and talked. That's all it is.'[31] And later, quoting Paul Valéry, man wants 'the grin without the cat'.[32]

*I am indebted to the research and editorial assistance of
Kasen Scharmann for this work on Bacon and voice.*

1   Sigmund Freud's Letter to Wilhelm Fliess on March 8, 1895 in *The Complete Letters of Sigmund Freud to Wilhelm Fliess, 1887–1904*, ed. Jeffrey Moussaieff Masson (Cambridge, MA: Harvard University Press, 1985), pp. 118–20.

2   Ibid., pp. 118.

3   Ibid., pp. 119.

4   Ibid., pp. 119.

5   Sigmund Freud, *The Standard Edition of the Complete Psychological Works of Sigmund Freud, Volume IV.* 'The Interpretation of Dreams: Part I.' (1900), ed. and trans. James Strachey (London, UK: Hogarth Press and the Institute of Psychoanalysis, 1953), p. 111.

6   Jacques Lacan, *The Seminar of Jacques Lacan, Book II: The Ego in Freud's Theory and in the Technique of Psychoanalysis 1954-1955*, ed. Jacques-Alain Miller, trans. Sylvana Tomaselli (New York, NY: WW Norton & Co., 1991), p. 154.

7   Jacques Lacan, *L'étourdit* 'Second Turn: The Discourse of the Analyst and Interpretation', trans. Cormac Gallagher (Lacan in Ireland, 2010), p. 12.

8   Ibid.

9   In *Francis Bacon Retrieved: Lost Words/New Writing*, ed. Martin Harrison (New York: Estate of Francis Bacon Publishing; Thames & Hudson, 2025), p. 123.

10 Ibid., p. 87.

11 In David Sylvester, *The Brutality of Fact: Interviews with Francis Bacon* (New York: Thames & Hudson, 1988), p. 176.

12 Jacques Lacan, *The Seminar of Jacques Lacan, Book III: The Psychoses (1955-1956)*, ed. Jacques-Alain Miller, trans. Russell Grigg. (New York, NY: WW Norton & Co., 1993), p. 229.

13 Saussure, F. *Course in General Linguistics* ed. Charles Bally and Albert Sechehaye, trans. Roy Harris (Chicago, IL: Open Court, 1986), p. 42.

14 Lacan, The Seminar of Jacques Lacan, *Book III*, op. cit., p. 140.

15 Sigmund Freud, *The Standard Edition of the Complete Psychological Works of Sigmund Freud, Volume XI.* 'The Antithetical Meaning of Primal Words', (1910) ed. and trans. James Strachey (London, UK: Hogarth Press and the Institute of Psychoanalysis, 1953), p. 155.

16 Cited in *Theories of Modern Art: A Source Book by Artists and Critics*, ed. Herschel B. Chipp (University of California Press, 1982), p. 621. (From an interview with David Sylvester, *Sunday Times Magazine* 14 July 1963, pp. 13-18.)

17 In Sylvester, op. cit., p. 129.

18 In *Francis Bacon Retrieved*, op. cit., p. 97.

19 Milan Kundera, 'The Painter's Brutal Gesture' in *Bacon: Portraits and Self-Portraits* (New York: Thames & Hudson, 1988).

20 Michael Peppiatt, *Francis Bacon – In Your Blood – A Memoir*, (London and New York: Bloomsbury Publishing, 2015).

21 Jacques Lacan, *L'étourdit* 'First Turn', trans. Cormac Gallagher (Lacan in Ireland, 2009), p. 21.

22 In *Francis Bacon Retrieved*, op. cit., p. 100.

23 Jacques Lacan, 'Seminar on "The Purloined Letter"', (1956) in *Écrits: The First Complete Edition in English*, trans. Bruce Fink (New York, NY: WW Norton & Co., 2006), p. 28.

24 Lacan, J. *The Seminar of Jacques Lacan, Book III*, op. cit., p. 229.

25 In *Francis Bacon Retrieved*, op. cit., p. 101.

26 In Sylvester, op. cit., p. 107.

27 In Francis Bacon interview with Melvyn Bragg for ITV, South Bank Show (1985).

28 Théophile Thoré-Bürger on Velázquez, quoted by Roberto Calasso in *La Folie Baudelaire* (New York: Penguin, 1998), p. 109.

29 Statement in *Francis Bacon: A Self Portrait in Words* (ed. Michael Peppiatt) New York: Thames & Hudson, 2024), p. 37.

30 Robert Melville, 'Bacon's Furies' in *London Review of Books* Vol 3, No 6, April 1981.

31 Francis Bacon speaking with Pierre Koralnik (1964) in Peppiatt, *Francis Bacon: A Self Portrait in Words*, op. cit..

32 Francis Bacon speaking with Julian Jebb (1965) in ibid..

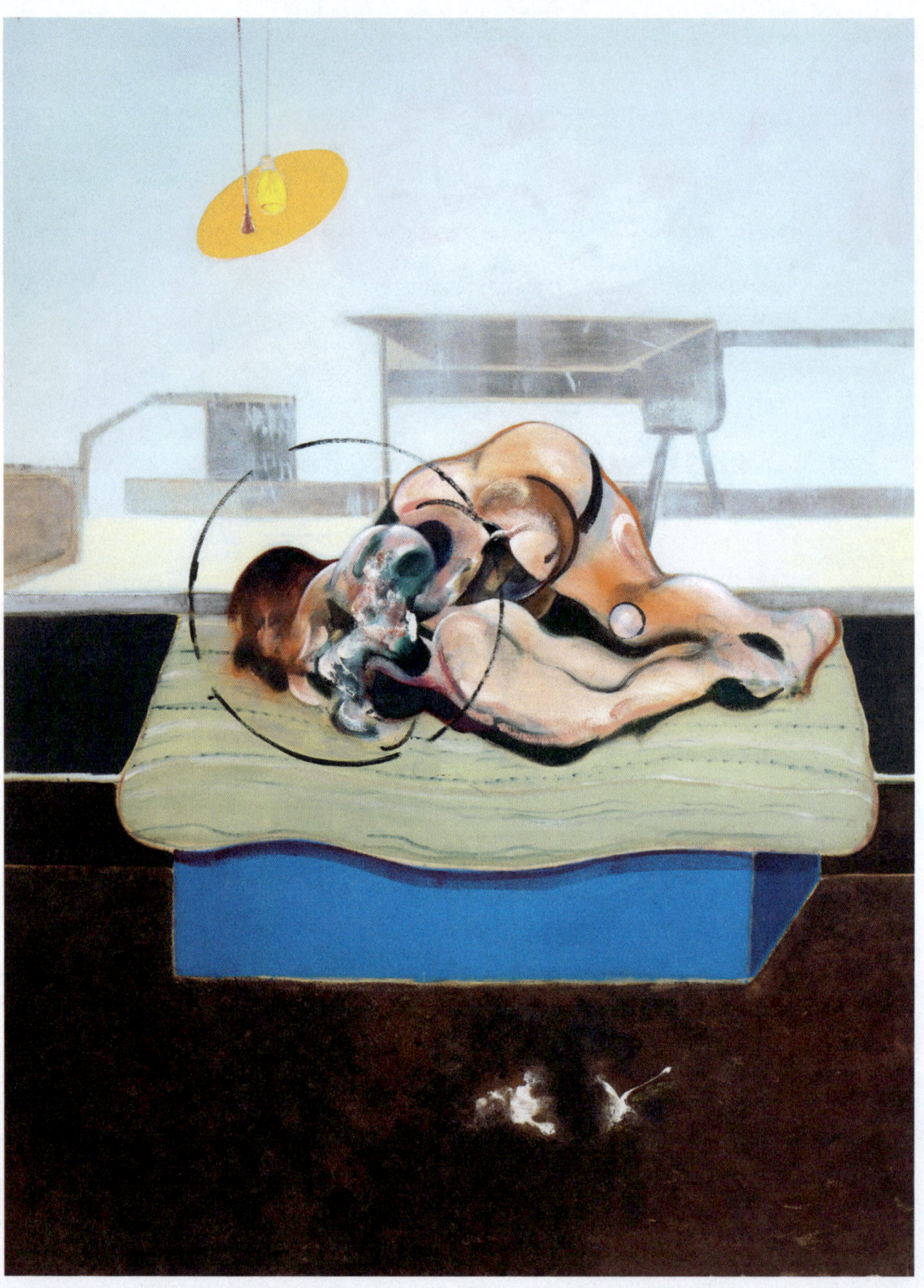

fig. 11 *Three Studies of Figures on Beds*, 1972 (centre panel)

BACON'S ONTOLOGY OF APPEARANCE

Alenka Zupančič

If, according to textbook presentations of Kant, we only have access to 'appearances' (*Erscheinungen*), that is to things as they appear to us and not as they are in themselves, it seems that Francis Bacon extends this impossibility, or at least difficulty, to appearances themselves. Appearances cannot be taken for granted. Clearly, Bacon's interrogation does not spring from the same epistemological issues as Kant's, so the comparison is limited. But it is interesting to think about how, from the point of view of Bacon's art, the problem (of what is 'true') becomes intrinsic to appearances, and splits them from within. Moreover, the question spills over and touches the very existence, or being, of appearance(s).

We are used to the divide between true and false appearances, which suggests that the former are faithful to the thing of which they are appearances, whereas the latter are its distortions. In other words: appearances can be deceiving, or not. But this is not Bacon's question. For him, the real question is the difference between two kinds of 'true' appearances, the ones that are technically true (based on some sort of correspondence or correlation, what he calls 'illustration'), and ones that are at the same time true and made (up), which he calls a 'made appearance':

> The mystery of painting today is how can appearance be made. It can be illustrated, it can be photographed, but how can this thing be made so that you catch the mystery of appearance within the mystery of the making? (Sylvester 1999, 105)

> And the way I try to bring appearance about makes one question all the time what appearance is at all. The longer you work, the more the mystery deepens of what appearance is, or how can what is called appearance be made in another medium. (Sylvester 1999, 118)

When discussing his nude figures – specifically those of the figures of couples on beds [fig. 11] – Bacon describes his process as 'grafting' the contours of bodies that affected him and says that he wanted to paint onto the bodies in Muybridge's photographs of human figures in motion. [fig. 15] Through this artifice he, in his words, 'manipulated Muybridge bodies into the form of the bodies I have known'. Yet we are not only dealing with a superposition or 'grafting' of two kinds of bodies (Muybridge's and the one whose appearance Bacon strives to 'make'). A significant further element in this 'making of the appearance' is what Bacon calls a 'disruption all the time of the image', its distortion – he describes the whole procedure as 'an elliptical way of coming to the appearance of that particular body'. (Sylvester 1999, 118)

This persistent questioning of the mystery of appearance – of what appearance is and of how appearance can be made – presupposes, or at least implies, a peculiar ontology in which appearance exists as something independent of the 'thing'. The relationship between the thing and its appearance unfolds across a radical gap that severs all immediate connections between them. They are related (for we are speaking of a 'true' or 'right' appearance), yet not in any direct way.

If we were to look for a philosophical predecessor of this peculiar ontology, we would find it in a perhaps surprising place. Or perhaps not so surprising, since we are speaking of Baltasar Gracián, the seventeenth-century Spanish Jesuit priest, philosopher, and baroque prose writer – a contemporary of Velázquez and Rembrandt, two major sources of Bacon's inspiration. Indeed, one could add a fourth point of reference to this curious constellation of Francis Bacon, the baroque painters, and Baltasar Gracián: namely Jacques Lacan. Lacan not only wrote some remarkably powerful pages on baroque art; he also referred to Gracián in one of the most famous and intriguing passages of *Television*, where he compares the position of the analyst to that of a saint.[1] Serge André comments on this passage in his compelling essay 'Être un saint', (André 1999) in which he draws on Gracián and his notion of appearance to elucidate Lacan's enigmatic claim – linking the analyst's position to the question of crafted appearance. In this reading, the 'made appearance' (of the analyst) is a form of the *objet a*: the appearance that enables the subject to ultimately relinquish the pursuit of the enjoyment she believes she lacks and imagines would complete her, and instead to discover and establish her desire precisely at the site of that lack – instead of giving in to need or the compulsion to fill it.

As we can see, these references form a rather dense and complex knot. What I propose to do in this essay is to loosen it just enough to reveal the logic of its entanglement – and to show how Bacon's art can be seen as emblematic of this curious knot.

1. La montre

Let us begin with Baltasar Gracián. Of particular interest is his *Oráculo manual y arte de prudencia* from 1647 (literally *Manual Oracle and Art of Discretion*, commonly translated as *The Art of Worldly Wisdom*). This 'manual' consists of 300 aphorisms, or maxims, each accompanied by a brief commentary. The final aphorism reads: 'In a word, be a saint' – the very lines later evoked by Lacan in *Television*. Another work of relevance here is *El Discreto* (translated into English as *The Compleat Gentleman*).

The English translation of *Oráculo manual* by Joseph Jacobs, first published in 1892, was a huge commercial success, with many reprintings over the years. A new English translation by Christopher Maurer (New York: Doubleday) became a national bestseller in the U.S. in 1992, and sold almost 200,000 copies. The first French translation, by Amelot de La Houssaye (*L'homme de cour*), was already published in 1684. In 1924 a revision and reprint of this translation, with a preface by André Rouveyre, attracted a wide readership, and was very much admired by André Gide. This also seems to be the version that Lacan had read.

I'm bringing this up because Amelot de La Houssaye's translation introduces a very interesting and intriguing term (and emphasis) that Serge André insists on in his reading of and commentary on Lacan's usage of the 'saint' reference: *la montre*. Gracián's 'art of prudence' rests on three artifices: silence, absence, and appearing. An essential ingredient of the latter is what he calls (in the French translation) *la montre* – and here we encounter an important resonance with the etymology of the word monster, to which we will return later. The term is rooted in the Spanish *ostentación*, which is justifiably rendered in English as 'appearance' rather than 'ostentation'. It refers to the strategic display of one's qualities. As Serge André observes, 'the art of appearance [*l'art de la montre*] proves that appearing [*le paraître* – also 'seeming'] is truly the criterion of being'. (André 1999, 174) In *El Discreto*, Gracián states that 'in many cases appearance is more important than reality. Appearance is a kind of supplement proper to fill up a vacuity or emptiness'; appearance, he continues, is 'absolutely necessary, and gives things in some measure a second existence'. (Gracián 1730, 114–15)

The reference to a 'void' and a 'second existence' (or 'second being') is absolutely crucial. As André also points out, *la montre* – or appearance – is not about dissimulating some being, but about revealing it as inessential and pointing to a gap within it. (André, 174) The point, then, is not that appearance 'fills in' a void (in the sense of covering or concealing it), but rather that appearance emerges at the site of this vacuity, as a form of this vacuity – making the vacuity itself *appear as something*.

It is in this sense that we could say that appearance is essentially a 'second being' – or what Lacan, playing on the French word for appearing (*paraître*), calls 'para-being' (*par-être*), being beside (being). (Lacan 1999, 45) And is the Lacanian *objet a* not precisely such a 'second being': a 'nothing' that nevertheless is, and which we also refer to as a *je ne sais quoi* that makes a thing what it is?

André's reading of Gracián rightly begins from the latter's concern with how to prevent and ward off envy, and it insists on a crucial difference between envy and desire. Like Gracián's hero, the analyst must at all costs avoid appearing as the possessor of some enjoyment, of some surplus substance that would stir up enjoyment and arouse envy. Instead, the task is to bring the subject to desire 'a nothing'.

But what interests us in this discussion specifically in relation to Bacon is another aspect of it, namely the peculiar ontology at stake in this interrogation of appearance and its artifice. And it is also and precisely here that the gap constitutive of desire takes place.

In the maxim 130 of *Oráculo manual y arte de prudencia* Garcián proposes a very intriguing notion of this 'showing', appearing or seeming. The maxim is titled '*Hacer y hacer parecer*' – 'Do and seem to do', (or, in Mauer's translation, 'Do, but also seem').

What occurs here is a most interesting separation and redoubling: 'to do' and 'to seem to do' are two distinct things, and the French term *la montre* refers to the latter. Gracián emphasises that it is not sufficient merely to possess qualities; one must also make them visible, 'show them off in the right way' (which is itself an *art*, a matter of *manner*). Moreover, this requires that one make use of, and rely upon, contingencies – things that belong to the concrete configuration in which one finds oneself, and which Gracián calls 'circumstance'. Deploying a wordplay between *sustancia* and *circunstancia*, he writes: 'No basta que la sustancia, también se requiere la circunstancia.' This is maxim 14 of the *Oráculo*, rendered in English (by Maurer) quite ingeniously as: 'Both reality and manner. Substance is not 'stance' enough: you must also heed circumstance.'

The idea is to underscore the importance of not only being virtuous or doing virtuous things but also of *appearing so*, because this appearance itself has its own agency, its own capacity to act on things, its own '(second) being'. This appearing is not simply 'showing off', boasting with one's qualities, flaunting or parading (them), as in 'promoting oneself (as virtuous)' – this would rather steer things in the wrong direction of envy. Instead, it is about making the quality appear as (almost) independent object, something that exists and acts (exercises influence) on its own. It is also not simply something like a false appearance (to appear virtuous while one is not): 'Do, but also seem' does not imply an opposition between doing or being something and appearing so, nor simply their indifference to each other, but rather a connection and a gap; or a *repetition across a gap*. So that the appearance is not appearance of some (positive) substance, an evocation of enjoyment that stirs envy, but the appearance of a nothing that can sustain a desire.

To 'seem' or to appear is a creative repetition of being (and hence a 'being' in its own right), not something that emanates directly from being/substance or constitutes its direct expression. There is a *gap* between substance and expression or appearance, but they are nevertheless related across this gap, they don't just break apart. (The appearance is not just a 'spontaneous', immediate image of the former, which is why 'false appearances' exist; at the same time the difference between a 'true' and a 'false' appearance is not in the artificiality, 'fabrication' of the latter, because the former also involves an artifice.)

To make this 'substance' visible is an art and an artifice, an *elliptical art*, one could say with Bacon. Substance is not 'stance' enough – without a proper appearance it is devoid of an essential dimension of its being: this essential part may well be 'a nothing', yet it is still essential, and recognisable as such. This is the art of '*making* appearances', and of a singular 'sameness' that exists across a gap. It is almost as if the appearance externalised something essential to substance, something not directly visible – even not directly present – in it, which is precisely the accident of its 'circumstance'. Something in being that is itself not (being), something in being 'more' – but also 'less' – than being.

This is why 'making things seen', making them appear, as a rule involves showing *less than all*; more precisely, the *art* of showing less than 'all' is not simply a matter of concealing or leaving some things out, but of bringing in the gap, the void, *as something*. Gracián is quite explicit about this: 'The truths that matter most to us are always half-spoken...' (maxim 25), or 'The half is much more than the whole' (maxim 170). But we could also see this clearly in Bacon, in his 'interruptions' and distortions of images, their appearing chipped, hollowed out, lacking a part, or *leaking a part* (where the leak then appears as a 'surplus'), like in *Triptych – August 1972*. [fig. 38]

This is precisely what Bacon alludes to when talking about 'disruption all the time of the image', its 'distortion', as 'an elliptical way of coming to the appearance of that particular body'. (Sylvester 1999, 118) 'Elliptical way' could be understood as the way of following, pursuing 'something' that eludes us at every stage, and then it suddenly gets caught in an image, or a figure. (Bacon often talks about 'setting a trap' for this thing.) Another way of putting this would be to borrow one of Lacan's characterisations of the *objet a* as the 'something in you more than you' and to say that Bacon was precisely after painting the 'something in his subjects more than his subjects'; his painting is about the pursuit of the *objet a*, and about the artifice of catching it on canvas. We will return to that after a short excursion into the phenomenon of monsters.

2. Monsters

Lingering in the background of the questions of appearing and of *la montre*, is also the occurrence of 'monsters', particularly if we take into account the rich and interesting etymology of the term, which is related to 'appearance', but with an important additional twist. This etymology should prevent us from understanding 'monsters' simply in the sense of (deformed, horrific) evil creatures.

In classical Latin, *monstrum* could be *anything extraordinary* – often a sign or portent, such as a malformed animal or child, which showed ('(de)monstrated') or signalled that something was out of balance in the world. Etymology also points to *monere*, 'to warn'.

This moreover relates 'monsters' to what psychoanalysis – following Marx on this notion – calls symptoms: something signalling, pointing to some deeper disorder, by way of giving body to that disorder, bringing it to light, making it appear. Hysterical symptoms are a very good example of this: in spite of their subjective character and of being, strictly speaking false, they also constitute objective pointers, they point to some truth. They function as *la montre*. They point not simply to some personal, individual pathology, but to a 'disorder in (social or family) heaven'.

There is a possible way of establishing a link between art and monsters understood in that sense, a way in which the art itself, the works of art, become 'monsters' of a certain kind, 'things that show', or display. Yet one needs to be precise here: it is not so much that art shows things, as it makes (its) things show something; *it creates things that show*. In other words, we are not suggesting that art 'functions as a symptom', one could rather say that art 'creates symptoms', that it 'makes symptoms', in the same sense that it makes appearances. We could thus paraphrase Bacon and say: 'The mystery of painting today is how can symptom *be made*' – how can something that is not visible in any immediate way, but is nevertheless part of the what is there, appear? Art of 'making symptoms' is part of the art of making appearances. Some possibly terrible things or 'illnesses' lack symptoms, precisely in the sense that they lack appearances.

Of course, not all art is about making some *wrong*, or some 'illness', appear, much of it is concerned with making appear something 'positive', a *je ne sais quoi* that engages our desire. So perhaps we should simply say – returning to the etymology of the term monster – that art is about making appear something surprising and *extraordinary*, in the midst of the ordinary.

In this vein, we could thus propose another notion, or another emphasis of the term *monstrum*, which is *the art of* – quite literally – *making appearances*. And this brings us back to Francis Bacon. If we speak of 'monsters' in relation to Bacon it is therefore not to refer to the 'horrific' or the 'bestial' that his paintings are often associated with, but rather to this obsessive interrogation of 'what is an appearance' and 'how can appearance be made' – how can genuine monsters/appearances be made?

In Bacon we often find a vacillation, in one and the same painting, between a saturation with some substance (like 'raw flesh', the 'Thing') and emptying out of the same substance (its leakage, which then gives body to his figures). [fig. 38] In a different way, in the *Three Studies for Figures at the Base of a Crucifixion* [fig. 1], crucifixion itself (and hence the body of Christ) is conspicuously absent (we only see the three 'Furies'), yet there is a thread that connects Christ and the centre panel, namely the blindfold, allegedly derived from Matthias Grünewald's *Mocking of Christ,* 1503. We could thus say that the suffering of the flesh, obfuscated in the (usually) sublime image of the crucifixion, is brought to the surface, it appears in this elliptical way. It is also this that would connect Bacon to Baroque, at least in the Lacanian reading of Baroque as 'exposition of the filthy truth of Christianity' – the suffering bodies evoking jouissance. (Lacan 1999, 107)[2]

The blindfold may be seen as a prime example, or marker, of what Bacon calls 'accident' or 'chance' and what Gracián terms 'circumstance'. Bacon was insistent that the ultimate 'resemblance' – the recognition of the *je ne sais quoi* that makes you you – must be brought in by some happy accident, an accidental detail. Gracián likewise insists, as we have seen, that 'substance is not 'stance' enough – you must also heed circumstance'. In other words, one must attend to that which 'stands around'. In the case of Bacon's painting, circumstance becomes the starting point: the crucifixion is approached by way of painting 'the three figures at the base of the crucifixion', and then, through an evocative, 'elliptical', and accidental detail (the blindfold), the entire scene appears as the substance itself – as crucifixion. The Fury in the middle is Christ's suffering body; or, perhaps more radically, the Furies are Christ's suffering body. Bearing in mind that the Furies are ancient Greek goddesses, it would not be far-fetched to discern here an echo of a suggestion Lacan makes in *Seminar VII*: namely, that the sublime image of the crucified Christ came to occupy the void left behind, in the hearts of Christians, by the death of the pagan gods. Lacan further suggests that 'those gods who are dead in Christian hearts are pursued throughout the world by Christian missionaries.' (Lacan 1992, 262)

What we find in both Gracián and Bacon and their thinking about the problem of appearance thus also offers a very interesting way of thinking about the relationship between the *structural* (or substantial) and the circumstantial or *accidental* ('substance is not 'stance' enough'

– you also need the 'circum', the around, that which 'stands around').
Taken just 'in-itself', the substance lacks the gap that necessitates and
instigates its relating to its concrete surrounding, bringing out 'that in
being more than being' – to paraphase Lacan's dictum 'something in
you more than you'. (Lacan 1998, 263)

3. Appearance and Change

Let us now return to a point made previously: art is the art of making
(unexpectedly) appear something *extraordinary*, in the midst of the ordinary. And by making this extraordinary thing appear, art changes our
perception, and the very substance of our 'instincts'. In the *Interviews*,
Bacon raises the following simple yet crucial question:

> Why, after the great artists, do people ever try to do anything again?
> Only because, from generation to generation, *through what the great
> artists have done, the instincts change*. And, as the instincts change,
> so there comes a renewal of the feeling of how can I remake this
> thing once again more clearly, more exactly, more violently. You see,
> I believe that art is recording; I think it's reporting. And I think that
> in abstract art, as there's no report, there's nothing other than the
> aesthetic of the painter and his few sensations. There's never any
> tension in it. (Sylvester 1999, 67, my emphasis)

This last point about abstract art, which Bacon keeps repeating throughout the *Interviews*, associating abstract art and its 'patterns' with an
(undisciplined) catching and displaying of all sorts of emotions that
artists usually have in abundance *(Interviews*, 67)*, can be judged as
largely irrelevant for understanding and appreciating abstract art (particularly of the very different forms that it can take), but it is a very useful
indication of the difference that Bacon aims at establishing here, and of
how he wants to situate his art and the *tension* that sustains it. We could
say that in Bacon's eyes, abstract art is bound to the logic of a direct
'expression' of a substance – in this case of 'emotions' or feelings. This
is why 'it always remains on one level' and lacks tension: the patterns
are an expressive prolongation of emotions or feelings. There is no gap
here. His art, on the other hand, comes closer to the Gracián ontology
of appearance as something that exists across a gap from the substance
(a gap between doing, or feeling, and seeming or appearing), so that the
essence of a substance needs to be 're-created', repeated across this
gap with the help of some artifice and circumstance/accident. There
must be a creation of a 'second being', to use Gracián's wording, which
brings out 'that in substance more than substance'. In other words, this

're-creation' reveals a tension or split within substance itself. Substance is not necessarily, or simply, 'what it is' or 'what is'. And this brings us to the first, crucial part of the above quotation.

Bacon speaks of instincts undergoing a change through the great works of art. We must be careful in how we understand the term 'instinct' here: it is not simply something one carries deep within oneself, as the proper or authentic 'you' that seeks expression, or that one may follow or not. For Bacon, 'instincts' are deeply relational: they refer to our mode and capacity of perceiving things and relating to them. Instincts are the drive behind the obsession to record something; they are not independent of that thing. They are like something through which we 'see' and perceive – an opening, an orifice. Great works of art transform our instincts: 'And, as the instincts change, so there comes a renewal of the feeling of how can I remake this thing once again more clearly, more exactly, more violently.' The Thing and the instincts (our capacity or 'way' of relating to the Thing) together form a dialectical 'substance', cracked by a feedback loop that alters not only the way we perceive some substance but the substance itself.

There is a difference between two kinds of images. There is image as resemblance ('illustration'), and there is an image that haunts me, say, in the appearance of a person, as something that I absolutely want to convey, record 'more clearly, more exactly, more violently', the image of 'something in this thing more than this thing'. It is something that I will be able to recognise (with surprise) as essential for that thing, without there being a direct resemblance between them.

We could also put it like this: Great art decides, creates what people see when they see things. It is not simply about expression, about 'expressing oneself' (as an artist) or 'illustrating' some reality; it changes instincts. But not only does art make our instincts change, it produces appearances ('second beings') that constitute the armature of this change. 'Instincts change', yes – but, paradoxically, what this change finally *amounts* to is decided not by the instinct itself, but by the new appearance that gives it form. Instinctual shifts remain vague and indeterminate unless and until they are crystallised in an image, in a figure that embodies them. It is only when changing instincts find (or are given) the 'right' image or figure that they become real, that they truly transform our way of seeing and living. This does not happen automatically. And it is great artists who create or decide what the new way of looking, of seeing things, will be – how things appear. And this (new) appearing does not merely accompany change, but *decides its very substance*: it constitutes the change, the difference that makes a difference. This is what we could call the 'political edge of art', which exists regardless of its direct political connotations, intentions, or ambitions.

I believe that realism has to be re-invented. (Interviews)

We have already noted that Bacon describes his way of working as an 'elliptical' approach to making the (right) appearance – a pursuit of 'something' that continually eludes us until it is suddenly caught in an image or a figure. We have further suggested that his art may be understood as the pursuit of the *objet a* within the things he paints, and as the invention of an artifice capable of 'catching it' on canvas.

'Catching it' has to be understood here quite literally and materially: it is about some fragment getting – accidentally, yet with the help of an artifice, a 'trap' – stuck in the canvas, and finding a way to organise and structure the appearance around it. This setting involves a particular ontology, a singular realism that Bacon himself names and describes eloquently. Here is a somewhat longer passage from the *Interviews,* which is philosophically quite remarkable:

DS It seems to me from all that you've been saying that in the end what matters most to you is not an immediacy in the work's reference to reality, but a tension between juxtaposed references to different realities and the tension between a reference to reality and the artificial structure by which it's made.

FB Well, it's in the artificial structure that the reality of the subject will be caught, and the trap will close over the subject-matter and leave only the reality. One always starts work with the subject, no matter how tenuous it is, and one constructs an artificial structure by which one can trap the reality of the subject-matter that one has started from.

DS The subject's a sort of bait?

FB The subject is the bait.

DS And what is that reality that remains, that residue? How does it relate to what you began with?

FB It doesn't necessarily relate to it, but you will have created a *realism equivalent to the subject-matter which will be what is left in its place.* You have to start from somewhere, and you start from the subject which gradually, if the thing works at all, withers away and leaves this residue which we call reality and which perhaps has something tenuously to do with what one started with but very often has very little to do with it. (182, my emphasis)

The metaphors here are quite suggestive: the subject matter is a bait placed within an artificial structure designed to capture some real.

This new 'realism' emerges as a residue – something that could, in fact, be interestingly related to the Lacanian notion of *déchet*. Baconian artwork as bound to a singular 'realism' of *trashitas*, of *déchariter*? The analogy with psychoanalysis is compelling: The 'subject matter' corresponds to the problems that a patient brings into the analytic situation. The artificial structure is the analytic dispositive itself: the analyst installed in the position of the subject-supposed-to-know, and functioning as a *manifestation* ('*la montre*') of the *objet a*. What remains at the end – the residue that 'passes', meaning that it can be transmitted to others independently of the analysand – is the singularity of that particular analysis. You begin with the bait, and you work – constructing an artifice designed to trap, to catch in the subject matter 'something more than the subject matter'. What remains in the trap is thus not simply the bait (the subject), but what this bait has, in the course of the work and with the aid of the artifice, both caught and transformed: some singular reality.

Here we rejoin Bacon, who insists that this reality is never a mere 'raw real' seized in the trap. Rather, it is a curious amalgam – a fusion of the 'brutality of fact' and of a 'lie' (something artificial). For this 'lie' can, paradoxically, be 'truer than truth':

> I believe that realism has to be re-invented. It has to be continuously re-invented. In one of his letters Van Gogh speaks of the need to make changes in reality, which become lies that are truer than the literal truth. This is the only possible way the painter can bring back the intensity of the reality which he is trying to capture. I believe that reality in art is something profoundly artificial and that it has to be recreated. Otherwise it will be just an illustration of something – which will be very second-hand. (Sylvester 1999, 172)

The whole setting of the artifice described by Bacon – beginning with a bait, setting a trap, and ending with a residue as articulation of some real – could almost be read, in psychoanalytic terms, as a correlate of the claim that *auto-analysis* is ultimately impossible. One needs an artifice and an exteriority through which, and only through which, one's 'interiority' becomes what it is – becomes, in fact, truer than one's 'personal truth'.

Bacon claims that his art is an art of 'guided chance' – which is not a bad description of psychoanalysis either. Analysis, too, begins from the insight that, when it comes to the unconscious, all chance is 'guided', that is, oriented by some impossible-real. This is precisely the 'real' that Bacon is after, as David Sylvester observes: 'an essential part of the force of a thing is that, while being unexpected, it also looks inevitable.' (Sylvester 1999, 179) This is to say that in the end, the question is not simply how one guides chance – for example, which chance occurrences one seizes upon and which one discards – but what necessity guides you in this guiding. You do not guide chance simply 'from yourself' (from your subjective inclination), but from the thing itself, from the way *it* inclines you. New realism is precisely this 'artificial' short circuit between the subject and the real.

This procedure differs from what is usually called 'correlation' or 'correspondence', because it depends on the ways in which you are already implicated in the real you seek to render. It is not a matter of standing outside reality and comparing your work to it, but of being caught up in the very process that produces the residue of the real – the 'That's it!' moment we have already encountered in Bacon's language of bait, trap, and guided chance.

This is also what is at stake in Bacon's repeated emphasis on the distinction between 'illustrative' and 'non-illustrative' art. Non-illustrative art is not a mere depiction, it delivers an unexpected recognition of the real – a shock of inevitability in something unforeseen.

Sylvester uses the term 'comparison' rather than 'correlation', but I believe he is pointing in the same direction. When something in great art moves us, it is not because we measure it against reality and admire the degree of likeness. It is because, in encountering it, we recognise something that could only have emerged through the interplay of chance and necessity – something whose force comes precisely from our implication in it:

> **DS** Is our response to [a great work of art] not a response to its inherent qualities, which obviously connect with our experience – very much so – but not in a way that amounts to our making a comparison of it with something else? If you say that a thing is like something in reality, you have to compare it with reality to confirm that. But isn't it the case, when we look at a great work of art and are moved by that we don't make such comparisons, that the work has a kind of power of its own which speaks to us? (172)

In this precise sense, we can say that the power of a great work of art lies in its capacity to create the reality of which it is the appearance. And yet, even if this reality comes into being right there and then, for the first time, we 'recognise' it – as if we had encountered it before, as if it were not the first time it struck us. This is the peculiar temporality at work in art (and in creation more broadly): a great work of art is an original that nonetheless recalls something we have already been looking at, though without ever having been able to see it. Now we see it. As Bacon puts it:

> The living quality is what you have to get. In painting a portrait the problem is to find a technique by which you can give over all the pulsations of a person. It's why portrait painting is so fascinating and so difficult. Most people go to the most academic painters when they want to have their portraits made because for some reason they prefer a sort of colour photograph of themselves instead of thinking of having themselves really trapped and caught. The sitter is someone of flesh and blood and what has to be caught is their emanation. I'm not talking in a spiritual way or anything like that that is the last thing I believe in. But there are always emanations from people whoever they are, though some people's are stronger than others. (173)

'Emanation' is the *je ne sais quoi* – the difference between mere representation (illustration, literal copy) and the thing itself. It is the *objet a*, though here not as bait or lure (one face of the *objet a*), but as residue, as the refuse of the subject(-matter). Trash or even shit? Yes, but with the additional twist that sublimation-as-creation brings into play, and which makes us exclaim something like: 'This shit is good!'

Could not an essential dimension of Bacon's painting – especially in the case of his portraits, one of his preferred genres – be captured by paraphrasing Lacan's prosopopoeia of love as desire: 'I love you, but, because inexplicably I love in you something more than you – the *objet petit a* – I mutilate you'? (Lacan 1998, 263) Namely, by rephrasing it as follows:

> *I love you, but, because inexplicably I love in you something more than you – the* objet petit a – *I paint you.*

This essay is a result of the research programme P6-0014 'Conditions and Problems of Contemporary Philosophy' and the research project N6-0286 'Reality, Illusion, Fiction, Truth: A Preliminary Study', which are funded by the Slovenian Research and Innovation Agency.

References:

Sorge André, 'Être un saint', in: *Connaissez-vous Lacan?*
(Paris: Seuil, 1999).

Lorenzo Chiesa, 'Exalted Obscenity and the Lawyer of God: Lacan,
Deleuze and the Baroque', in Lacan and Deleuze: a disjunctive synthesis,
pp.141–162 (Edinburgh: Edinburgh University Press, 2017).

Baltasar Gracián, *The Art of Worldly Wisdom*, trans. Christopher Maurer
(New York: Doubleday, 1992).

Baltasar Gracián, *The Compleat Gentleman*, trans. T. Saldkeld, 1730,
available in Internet Archive (https://dn790007.ca.archive.org/0/items/
compleatgentlema00gracuoft/compleatgentlema00gracuoft.pdf)

Baltasar Gracián, *L'Homme de cour,* trans. Amelot de la Houssaie
(Paris: éd. Champ Libre, 1972).

Jacques Lacan, *Television*, ed. Joan Copjec
(New York & London: W. W. Norton & Company, 1990).

Jacques Lacan, *The Ethics of Psychoanalysis*, trans. Dennis Porter
(London: Routledge, 1992).

Jacques Lacan, *The Four Fundamental Concepts of Psychoanalysis,*
trans. Alan Sheridan (New York & London: Norton & Company, 1998).

Jacques Lacan, *Encore*, trans. Bruce Fink
(New York & London: W. W. Norton & Company, 1999).

David Sylvester, *Interviews with Francis Bacon*
(New York: Thames and Hudson Inc., 1999).

Endnotes

1 "A saint's business, to put it clearly, is not caritas. Rather, he acts like trash (déchet- refuse, waste, garbage); his business being trashitas (il décharite). So as to embody what the structure entails, namely allowing the subject, the subject of the unconscious, to take him as the cause of the subject's own desire. In fact it is through the abjection of this cause that the subject in question has a chance to be aware of his position, at least within the structure. For the saint, this is not amusing, but I imagine that for a few ears glued to this TV it converges with many of the oddities of the acts of saints.
The saint is the refuse (rebut) of jouissance. (...)
The saint doesn't really see himself as righteous, which doesn't mean that he has no ethics. The only problem for others is that you can't see where it leads him.
(...)
The more saints, the more laughter; that's my principle, to wit, the way out of capitalist discourse – which will not constitute progress, if it happens only for some." (Lacan 1990, pp. 15-16)

2 For an extensive discussion of Lacan's reading of the Baroque see Chiesa 2017

PLATES

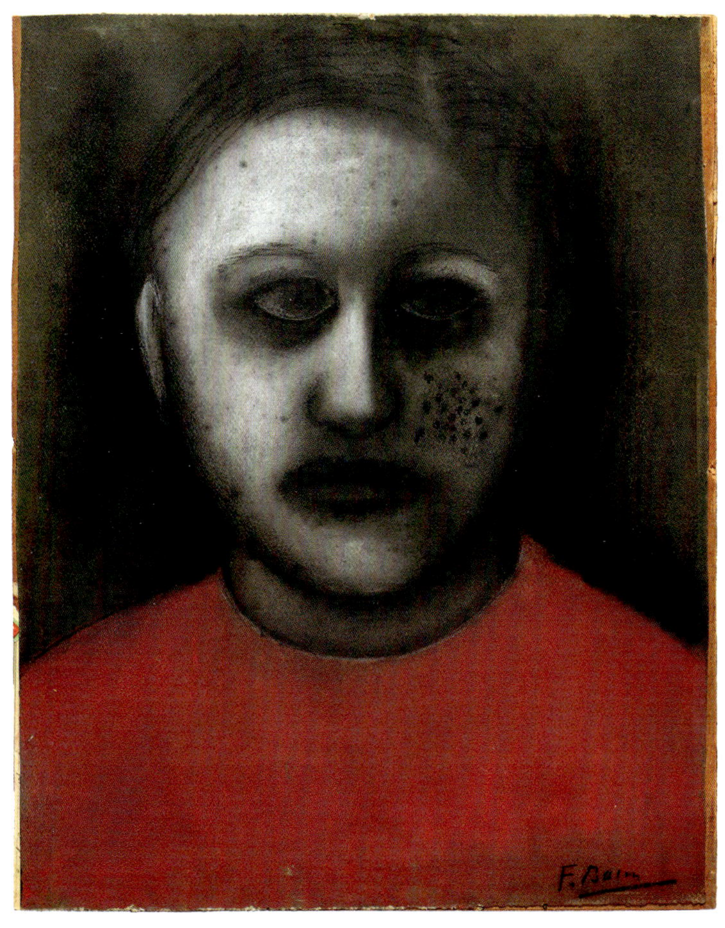

fig. 12 'Portrait', c. 1930

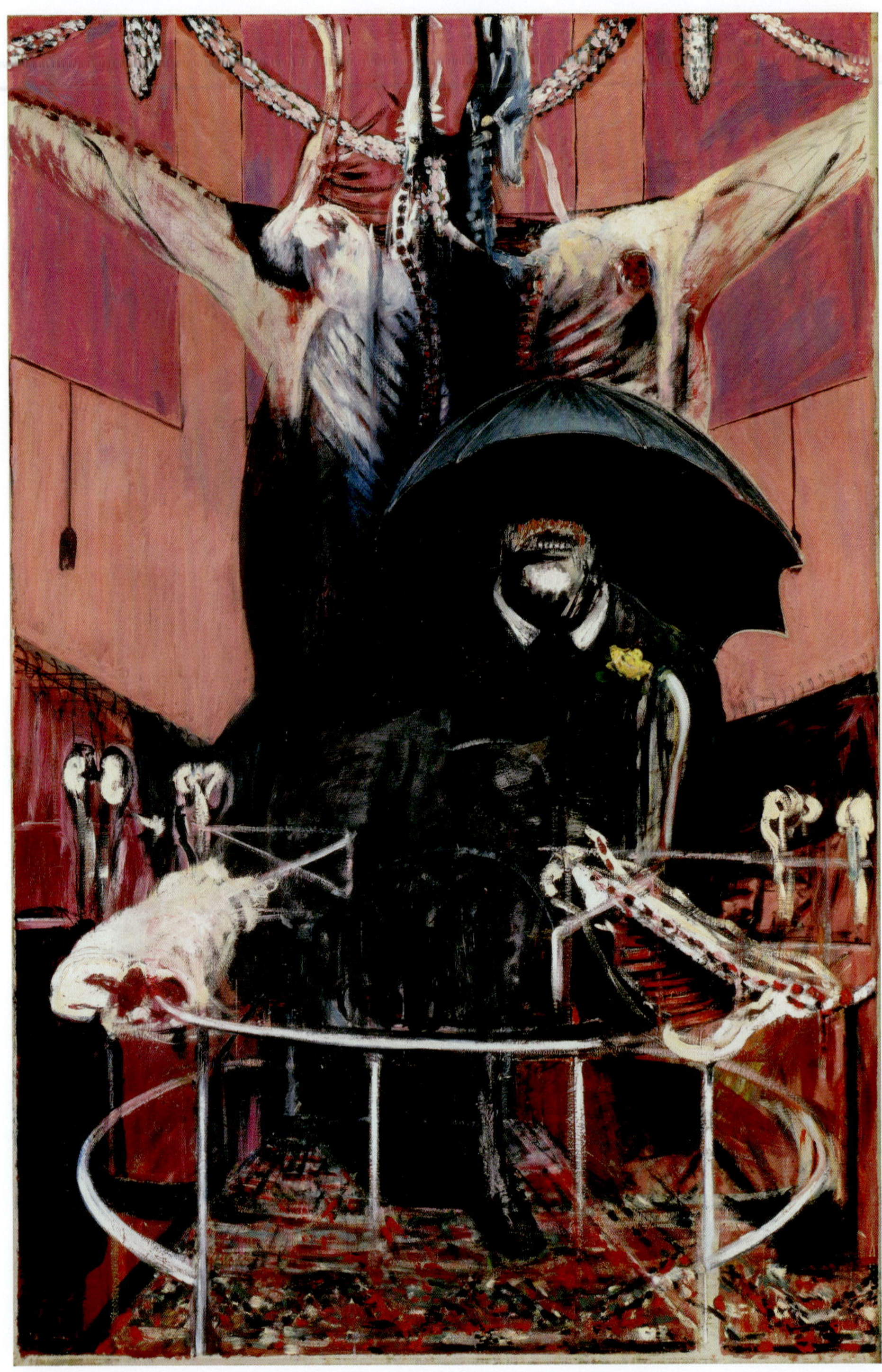

fig. 13 *Painting 1946*, 1946

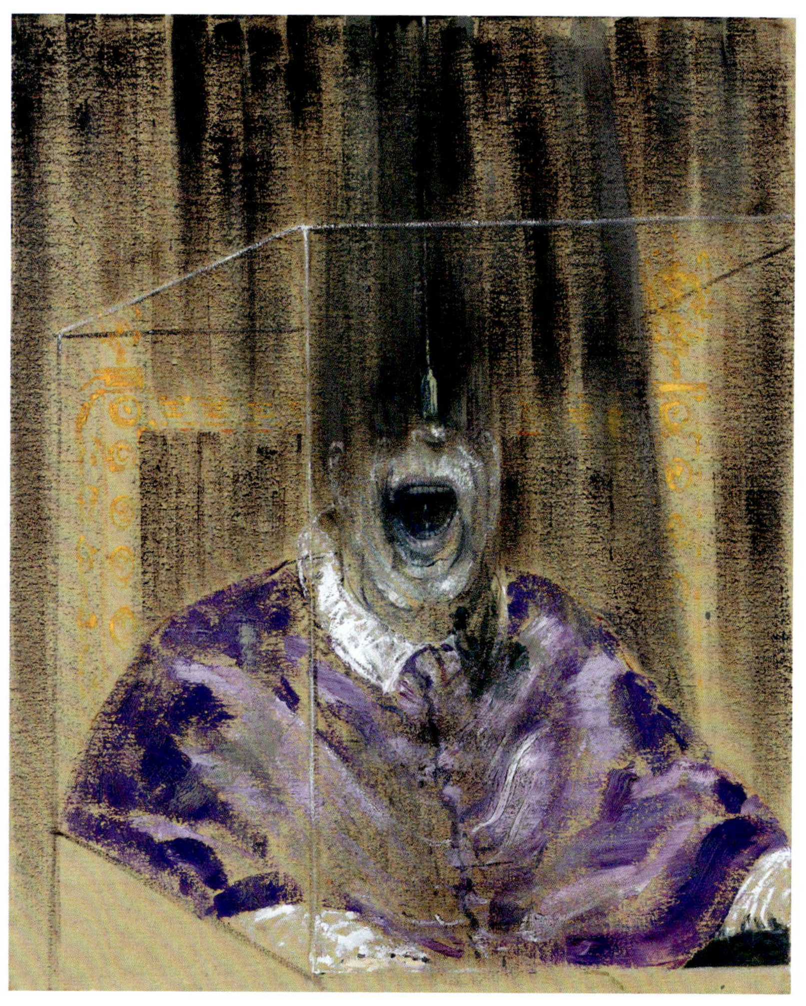

fig. 14 *Head VI*, 1949   **153**

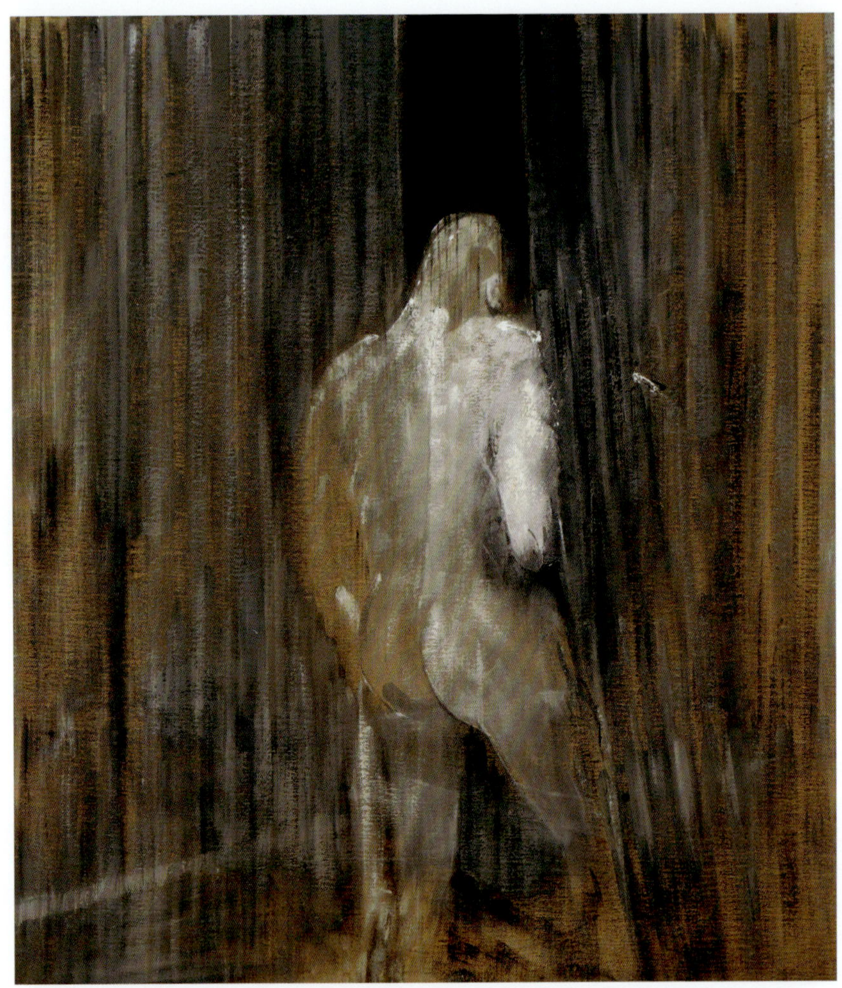

fig. 15 *Study from the Human Body*, 1949

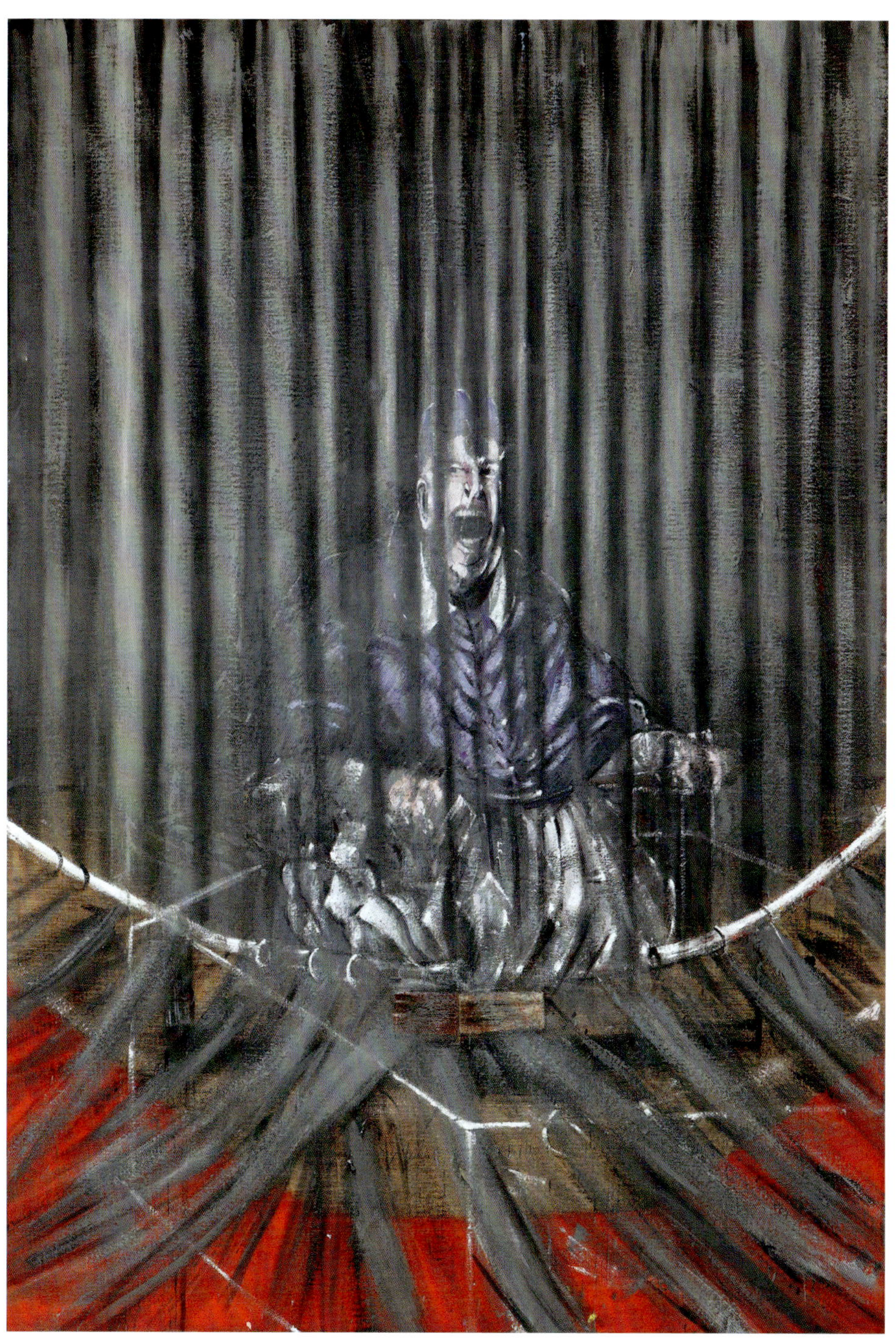

fig. 16 *Study after Velázquez*, 1950   **155**

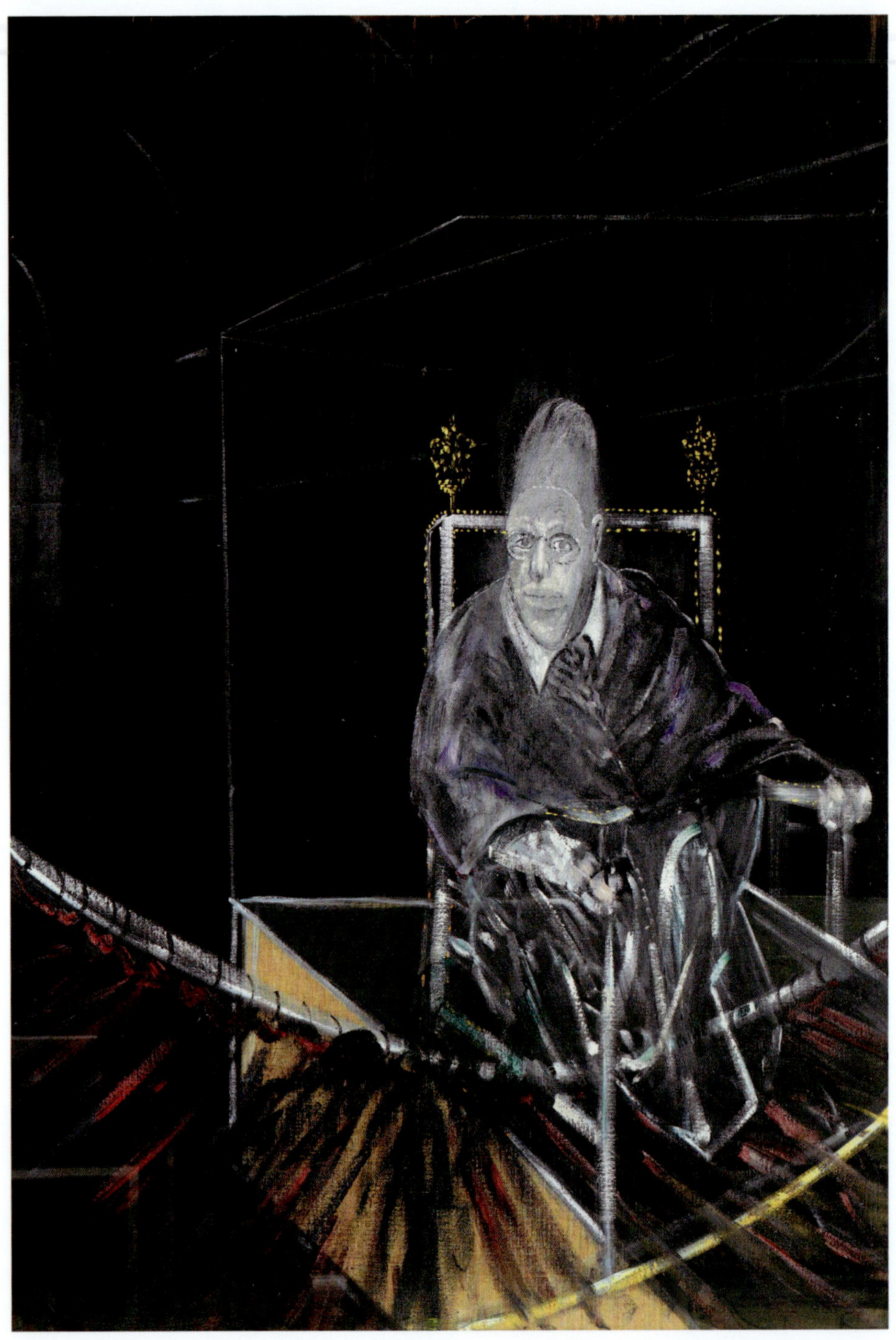

fig. 17 *Pope I*, 1951 **156**

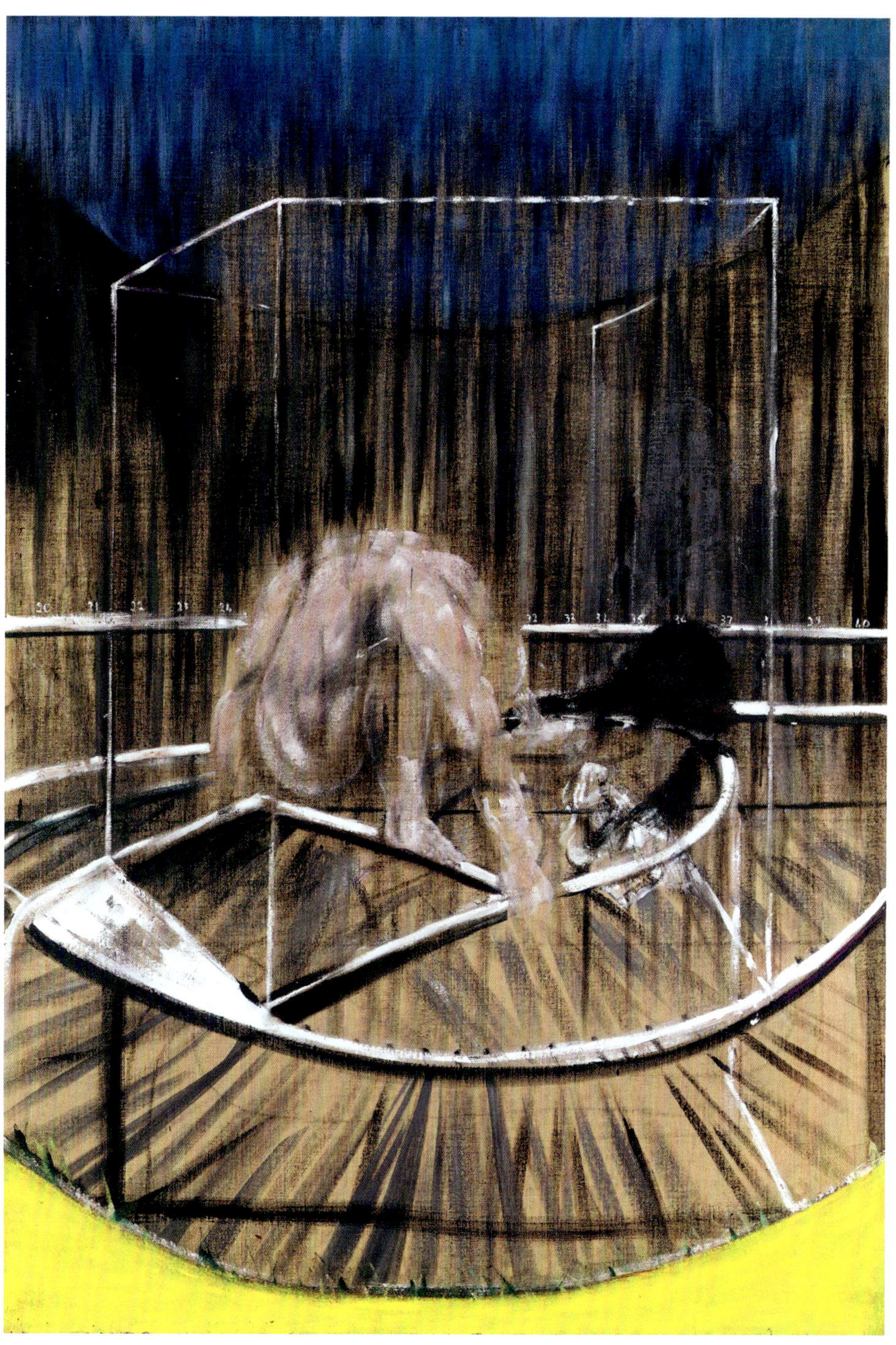

fig. 18 *Study for Crouching Nude*, 1952

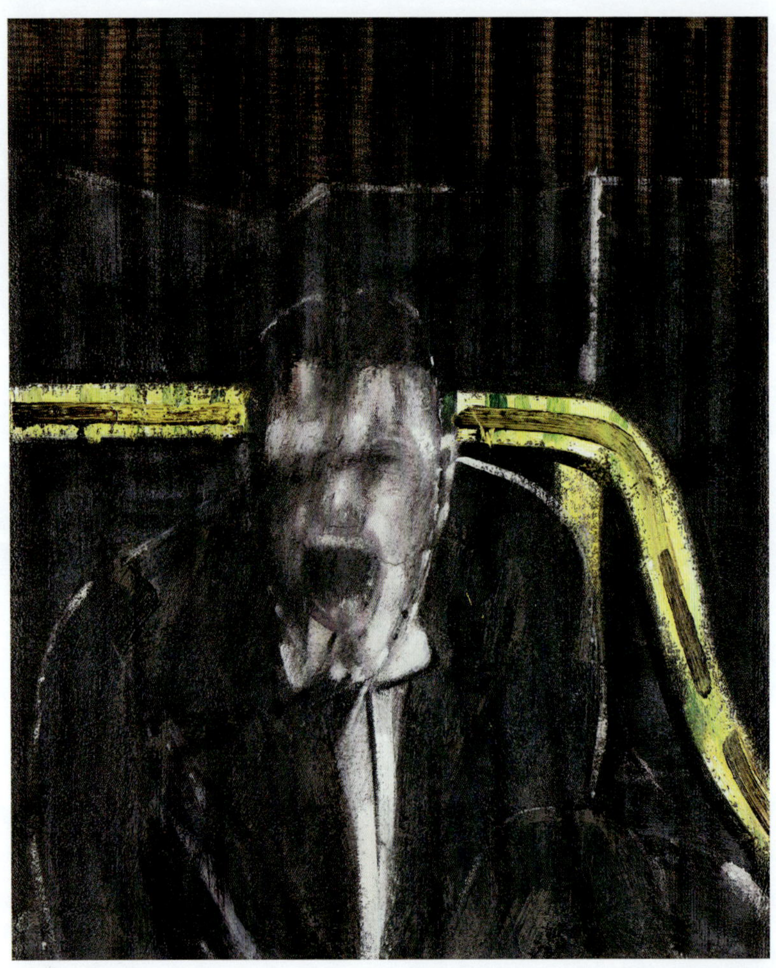

fig. 19 *Study for Head*, 1952   **158**

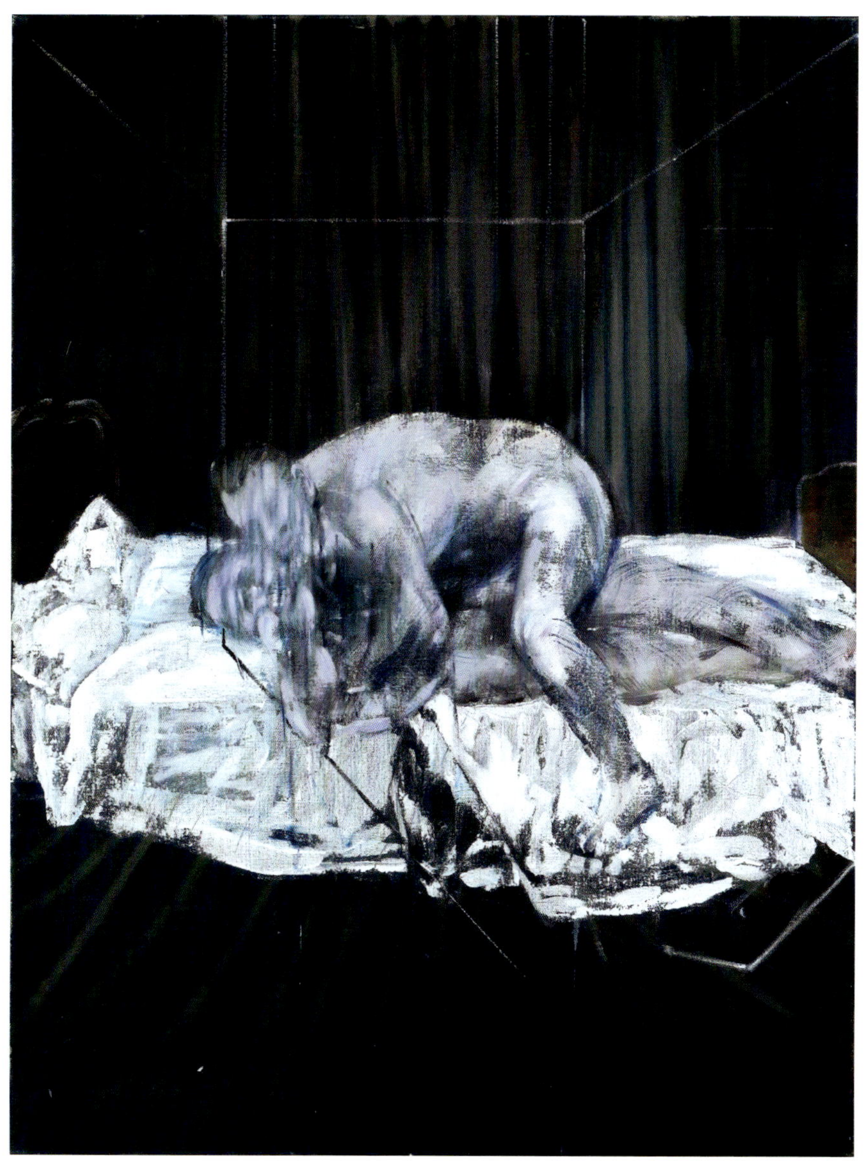

fig. 20 *Two Figures*, 1953   **159**

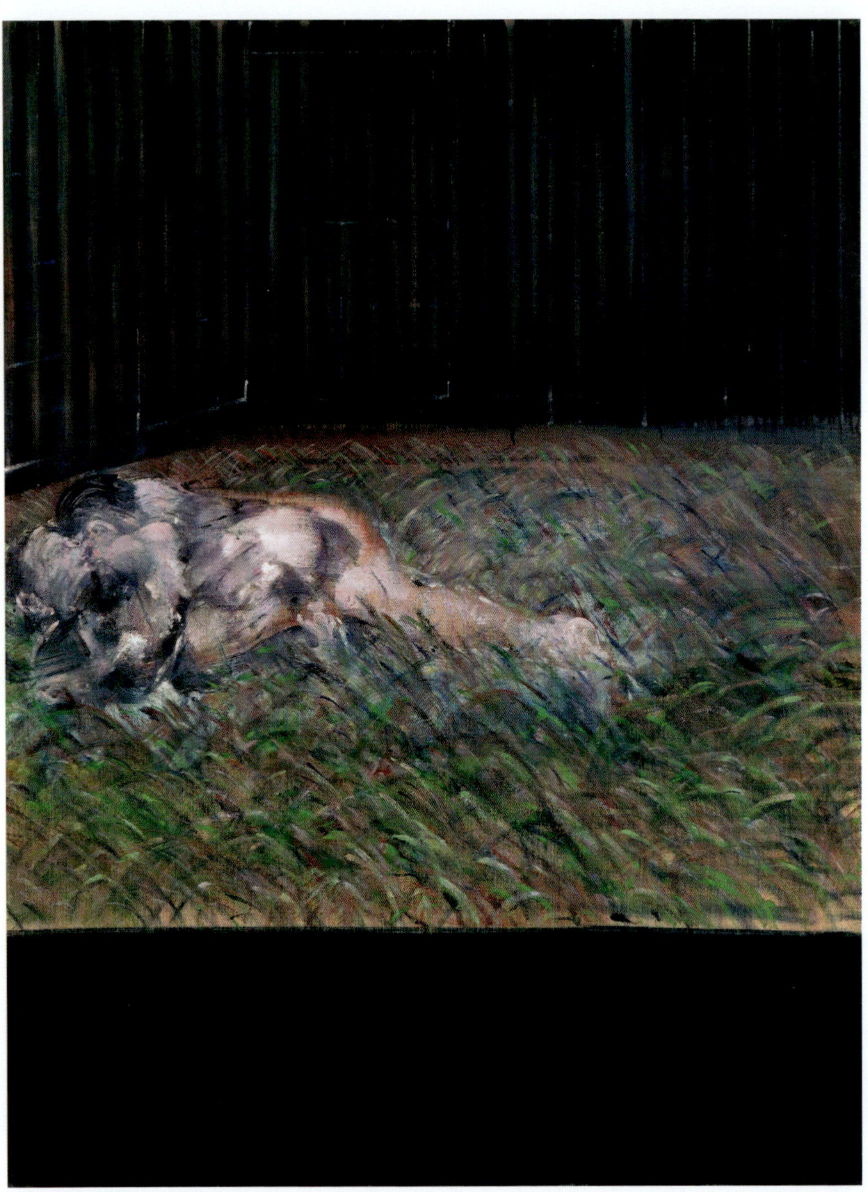
fig. 21 *Two Figures in the Grass*, 1954

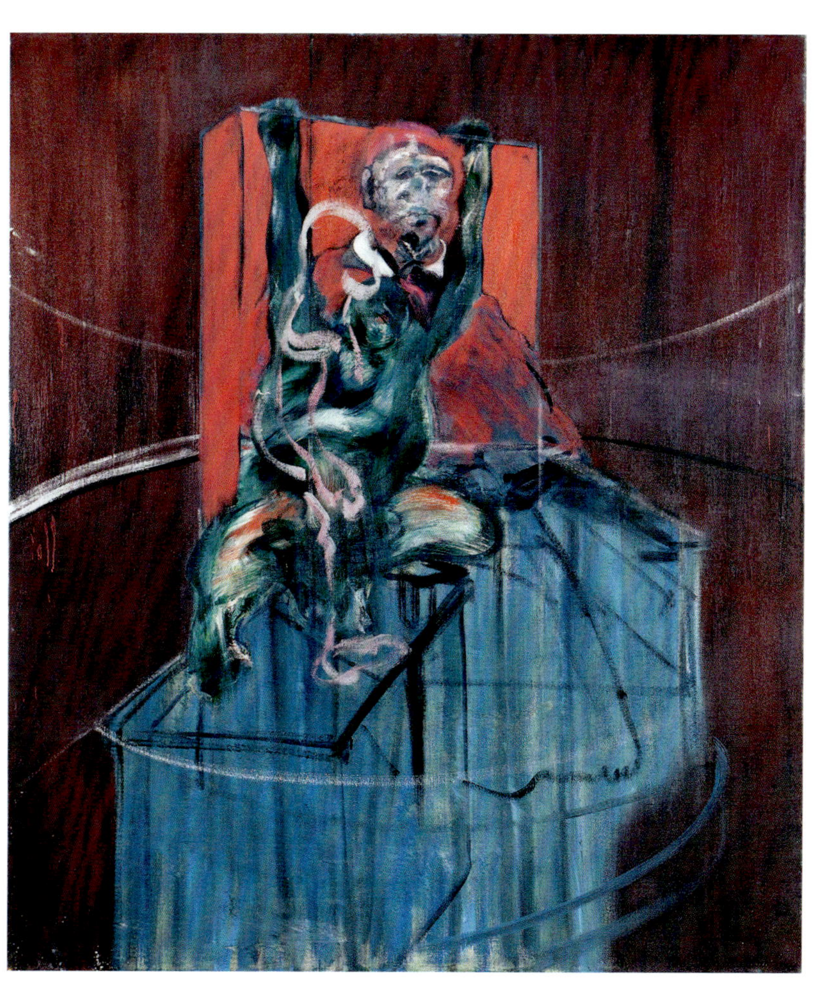

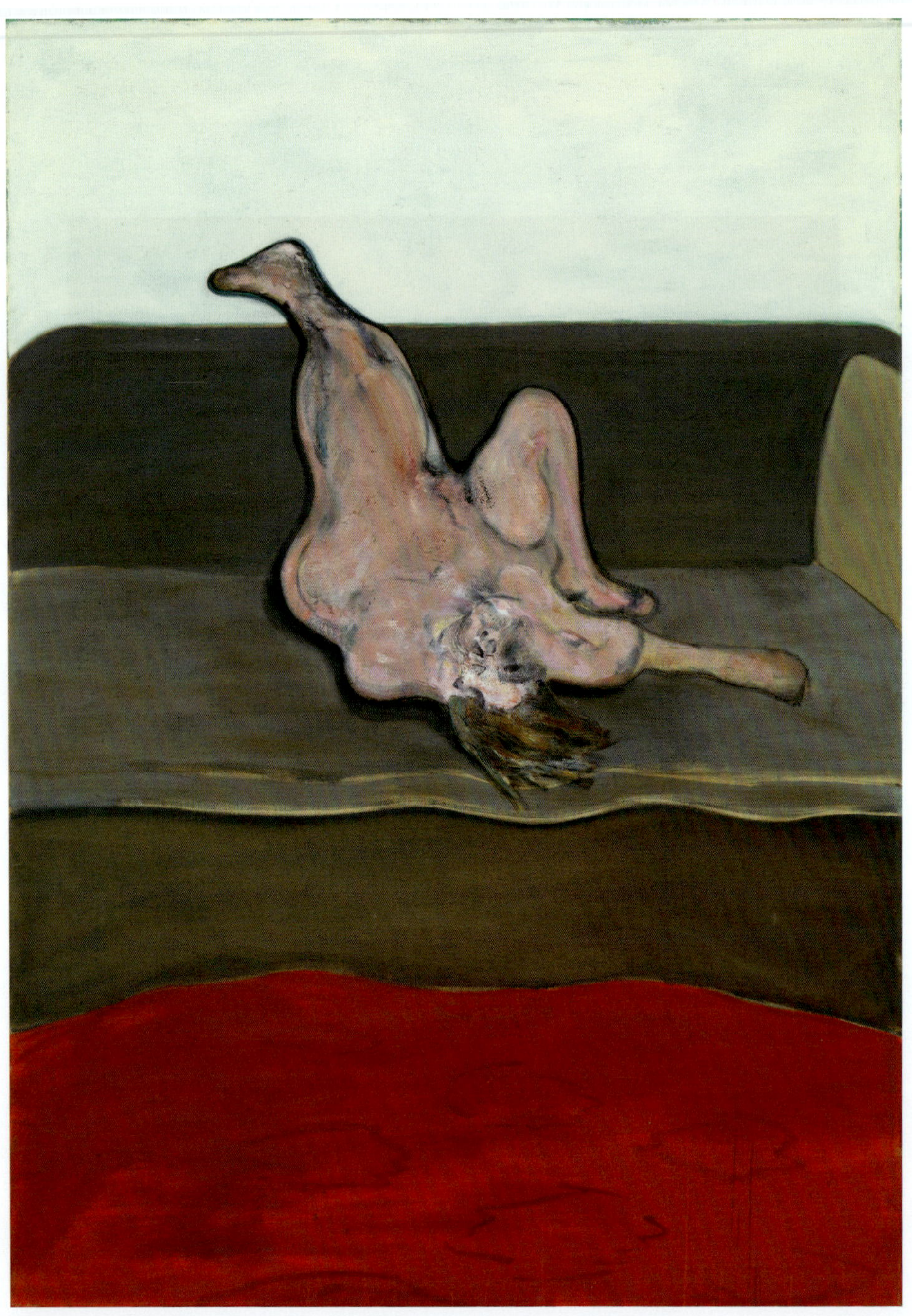

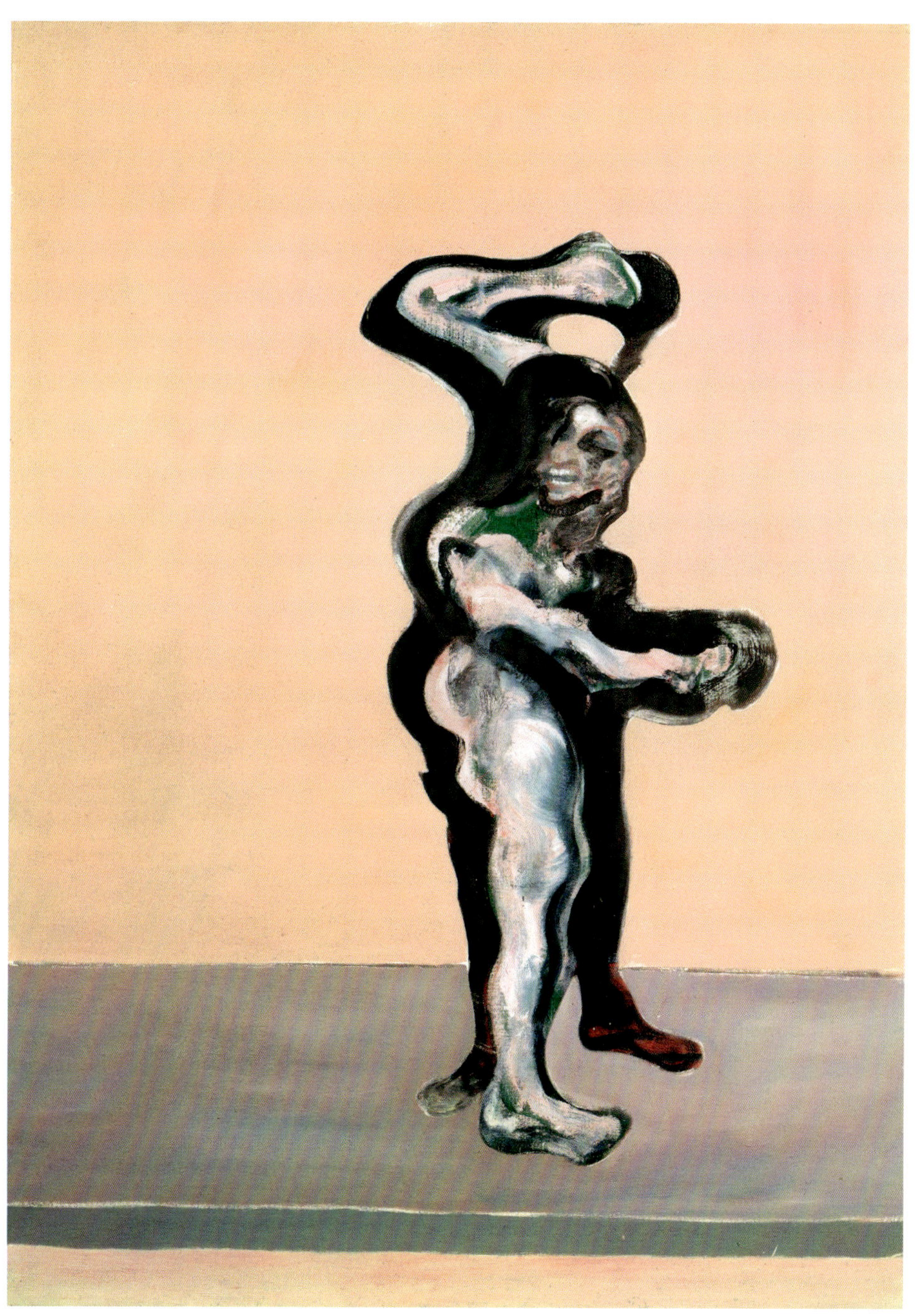

fig. 24 *Two Figures*, 1961

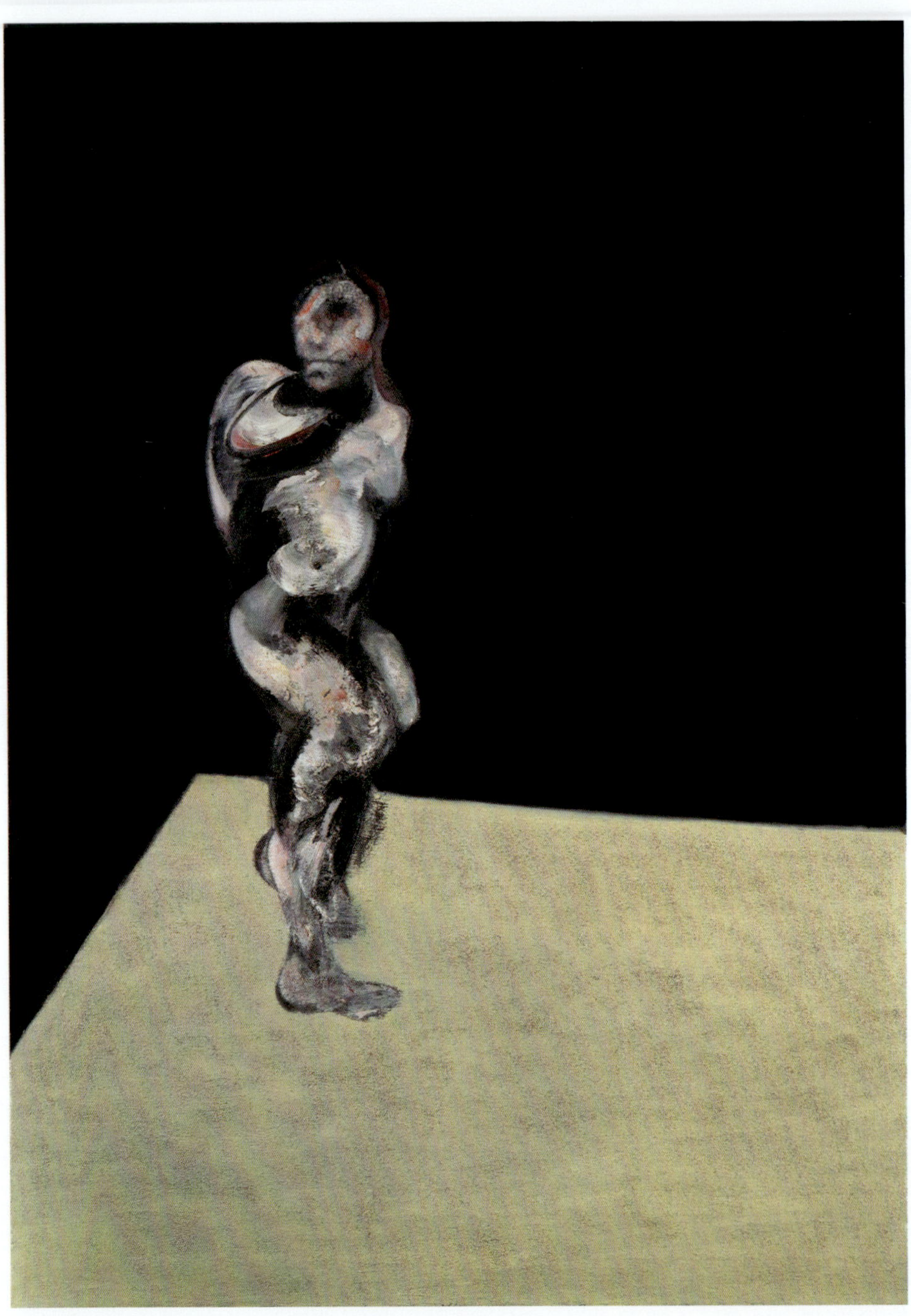

fig. 25 *Figure Turning*, 1962   **164**

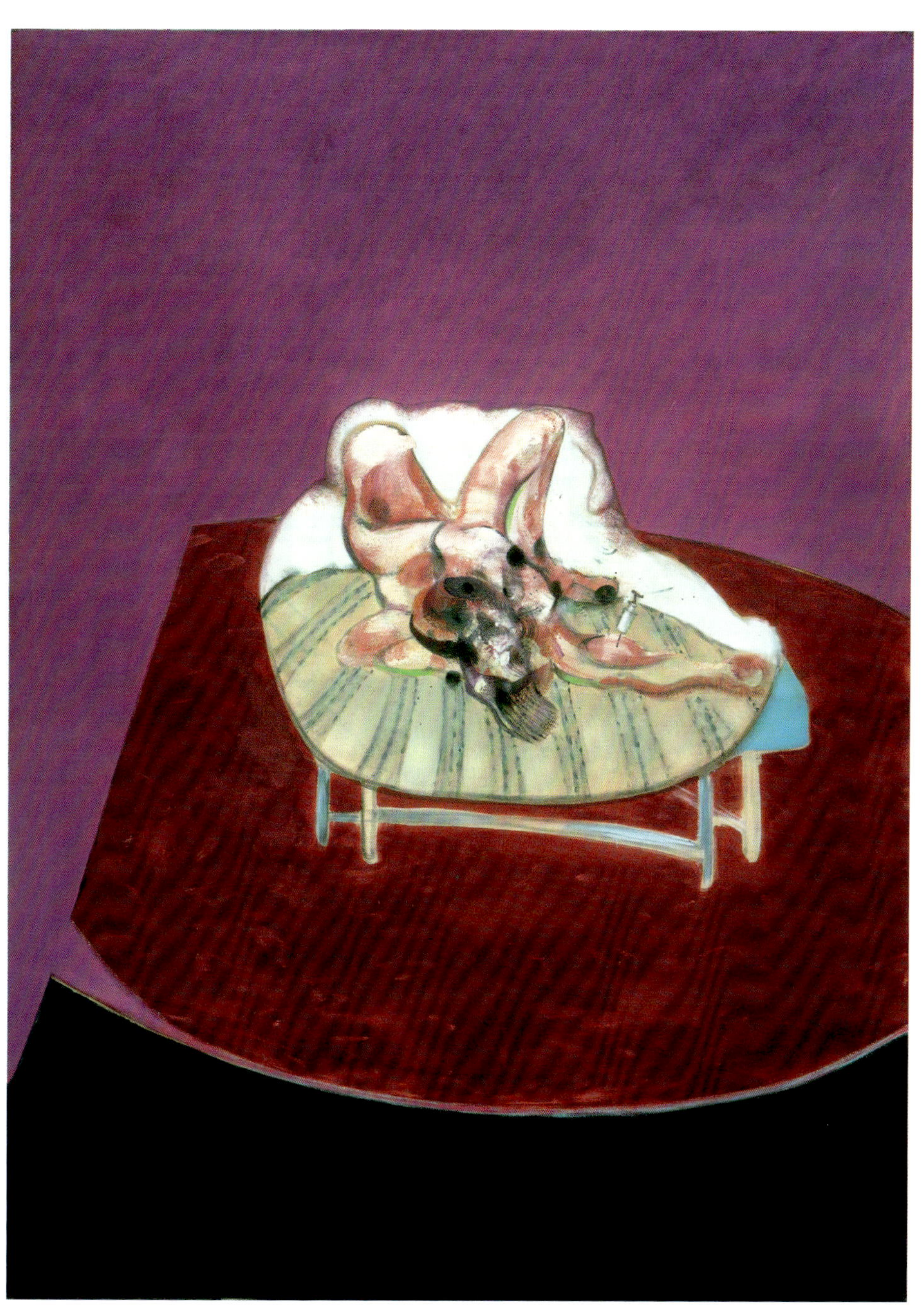

fig. 26 *Lying Figure with Hypodermic Syringe*, 1963

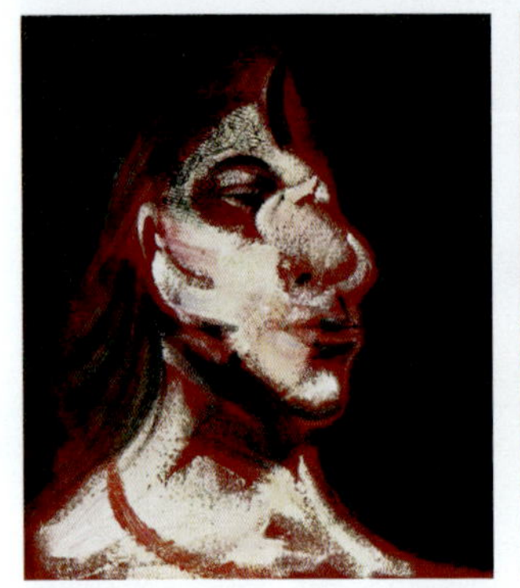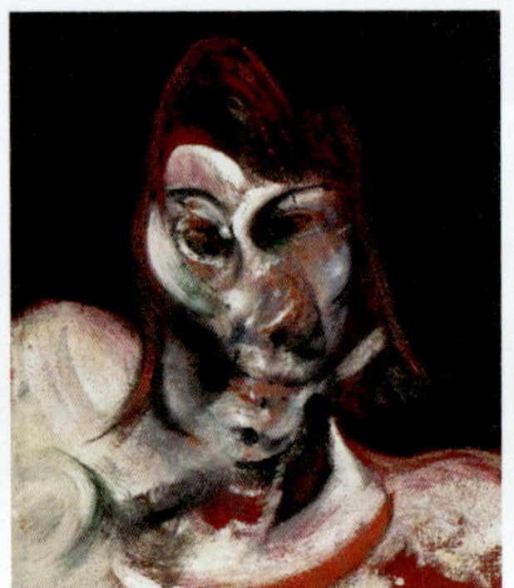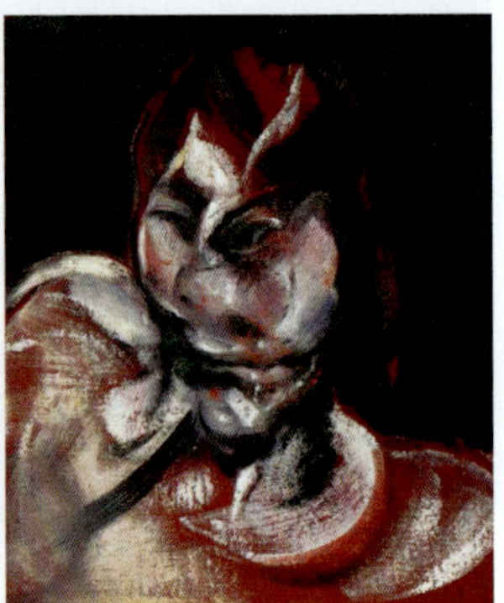

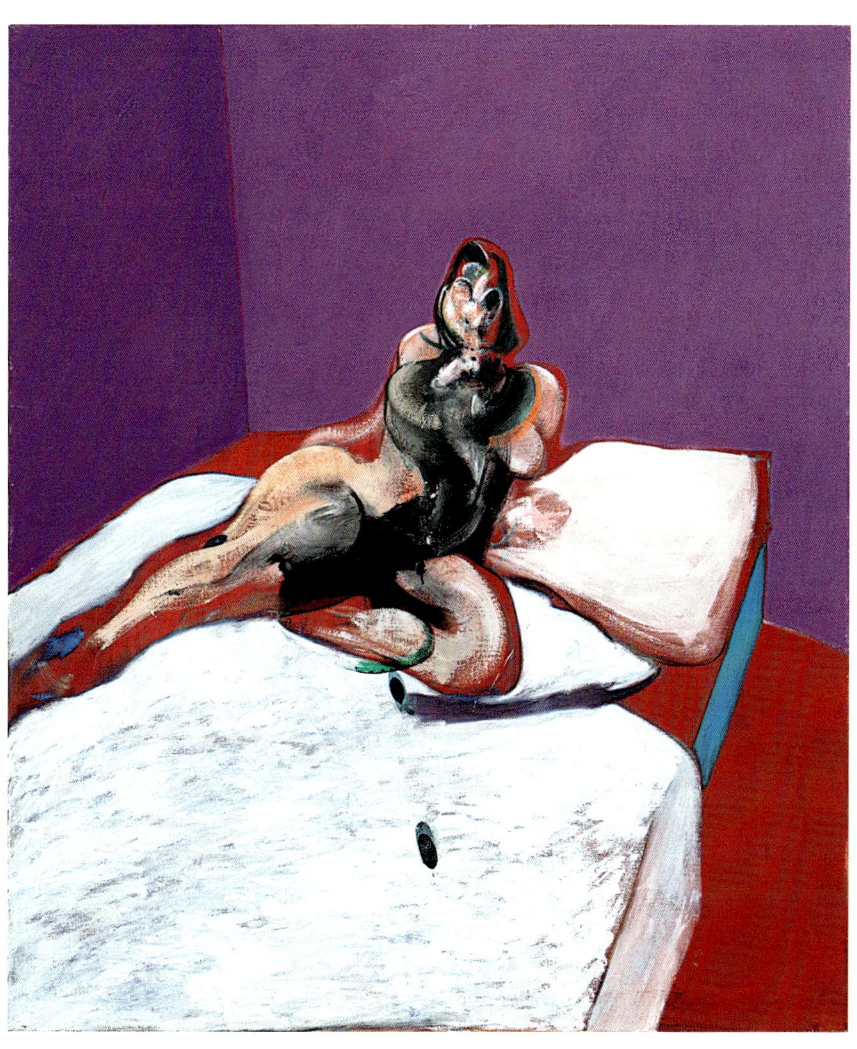

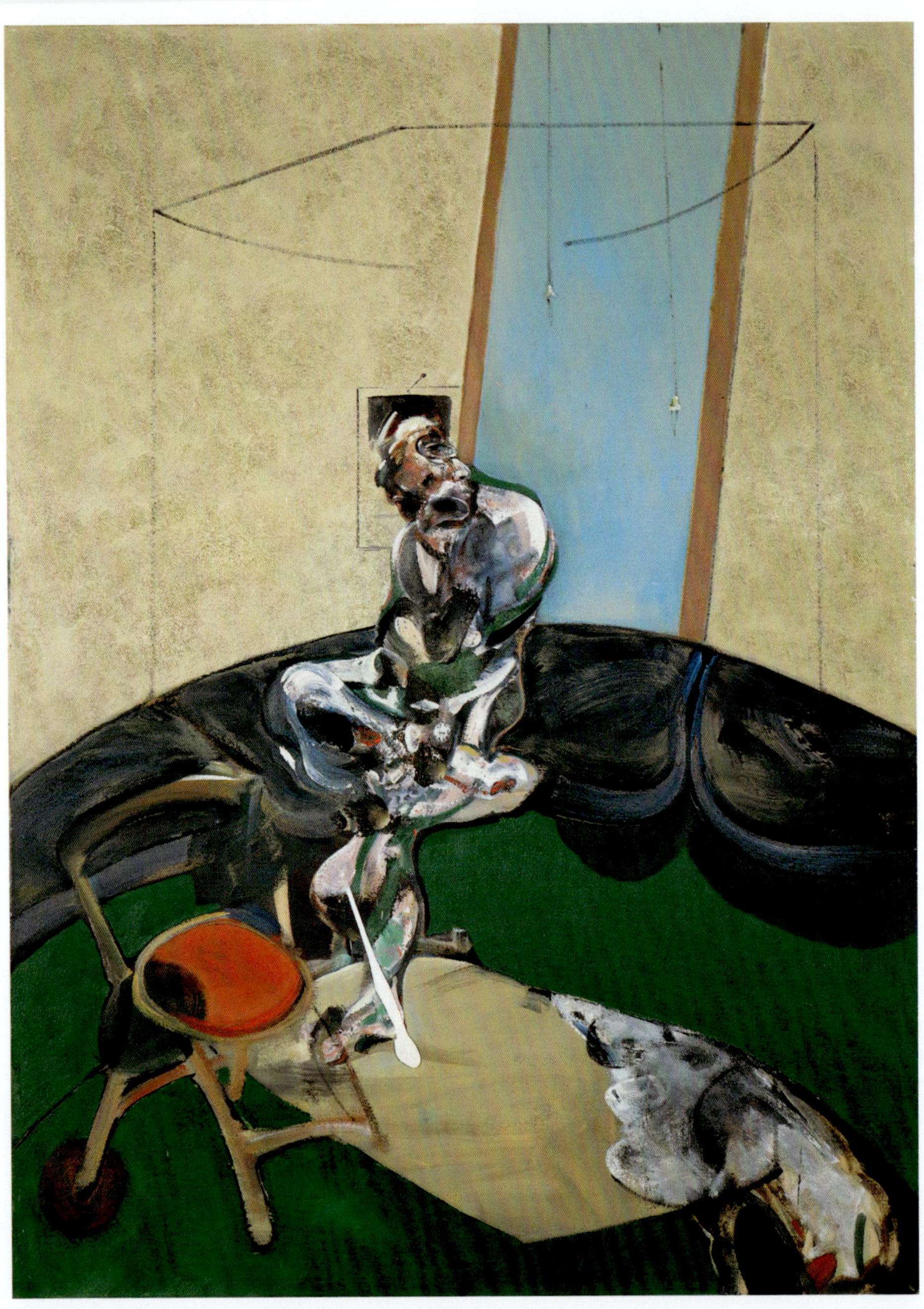

fig. 29 *Portrait of George Dyer Staring at Blind-Cord,* 1966

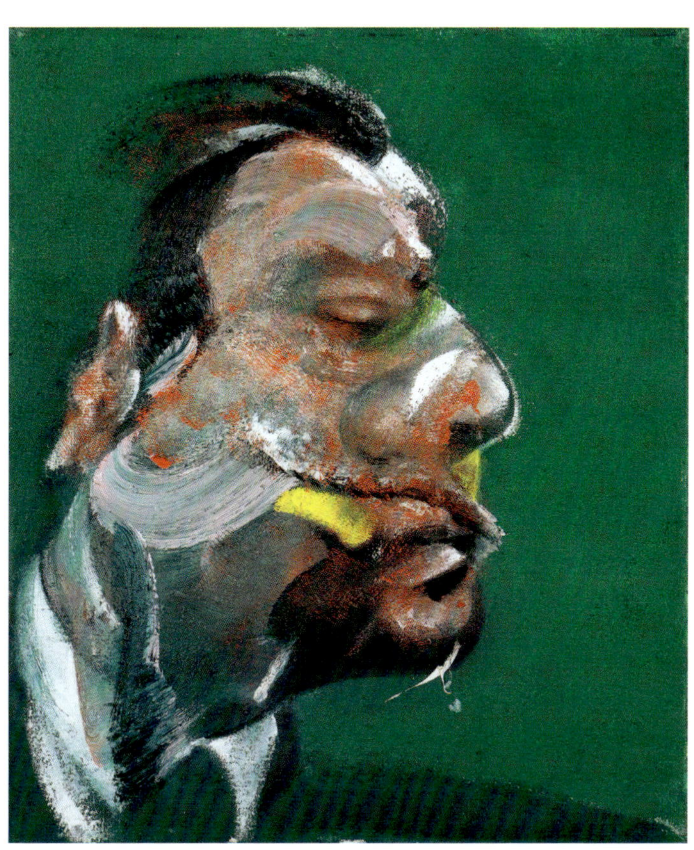

fig. 30 *Study for Head of George Dyer*, 1967

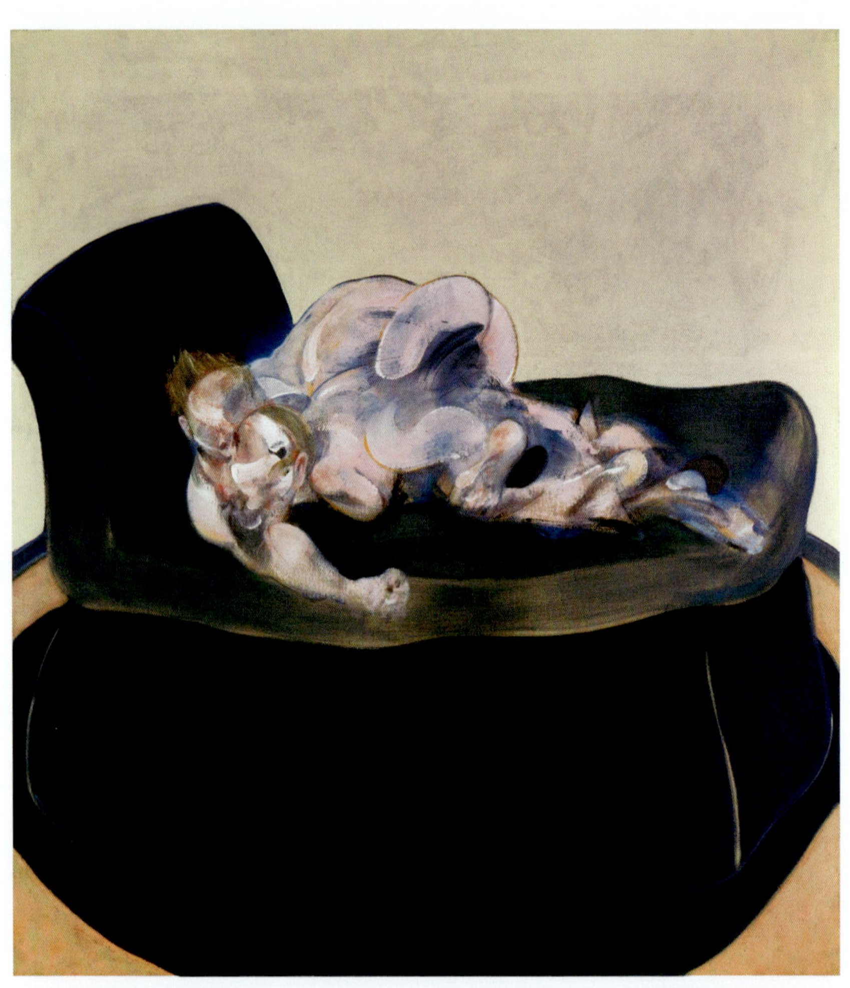

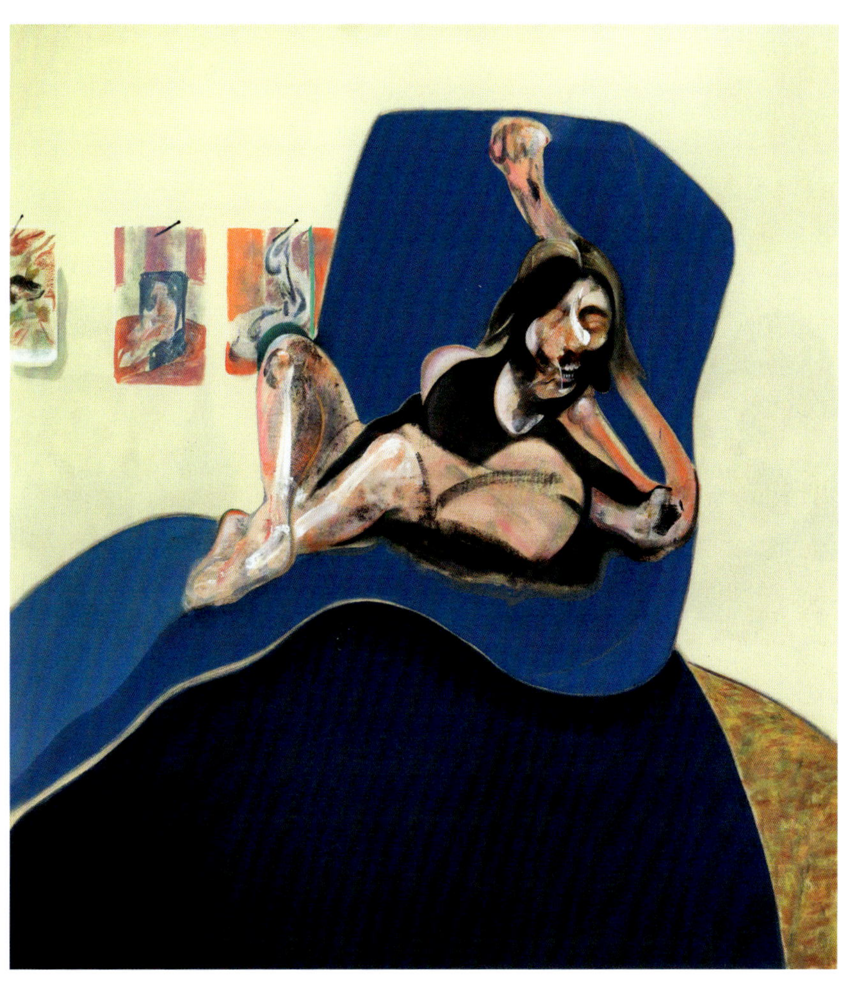

fig. 32 *Study for a Portrait*, 1967

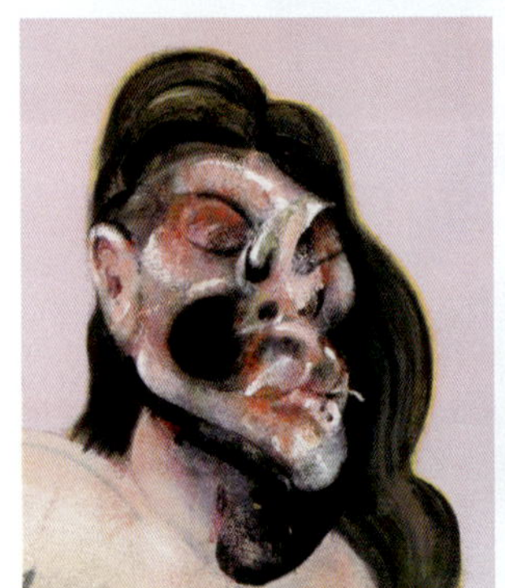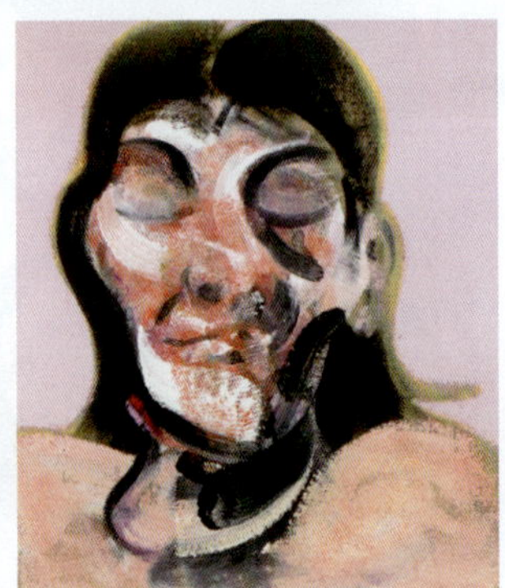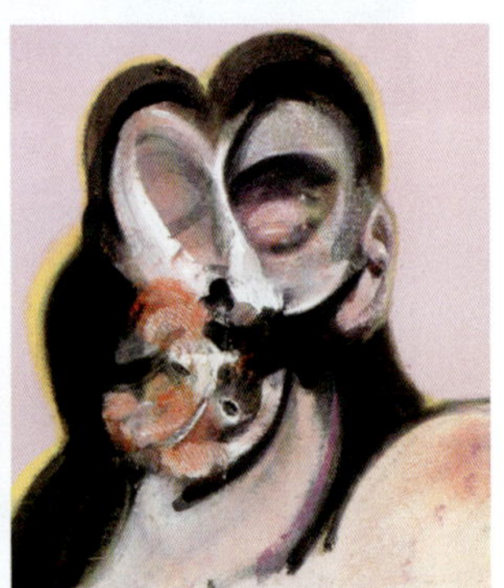

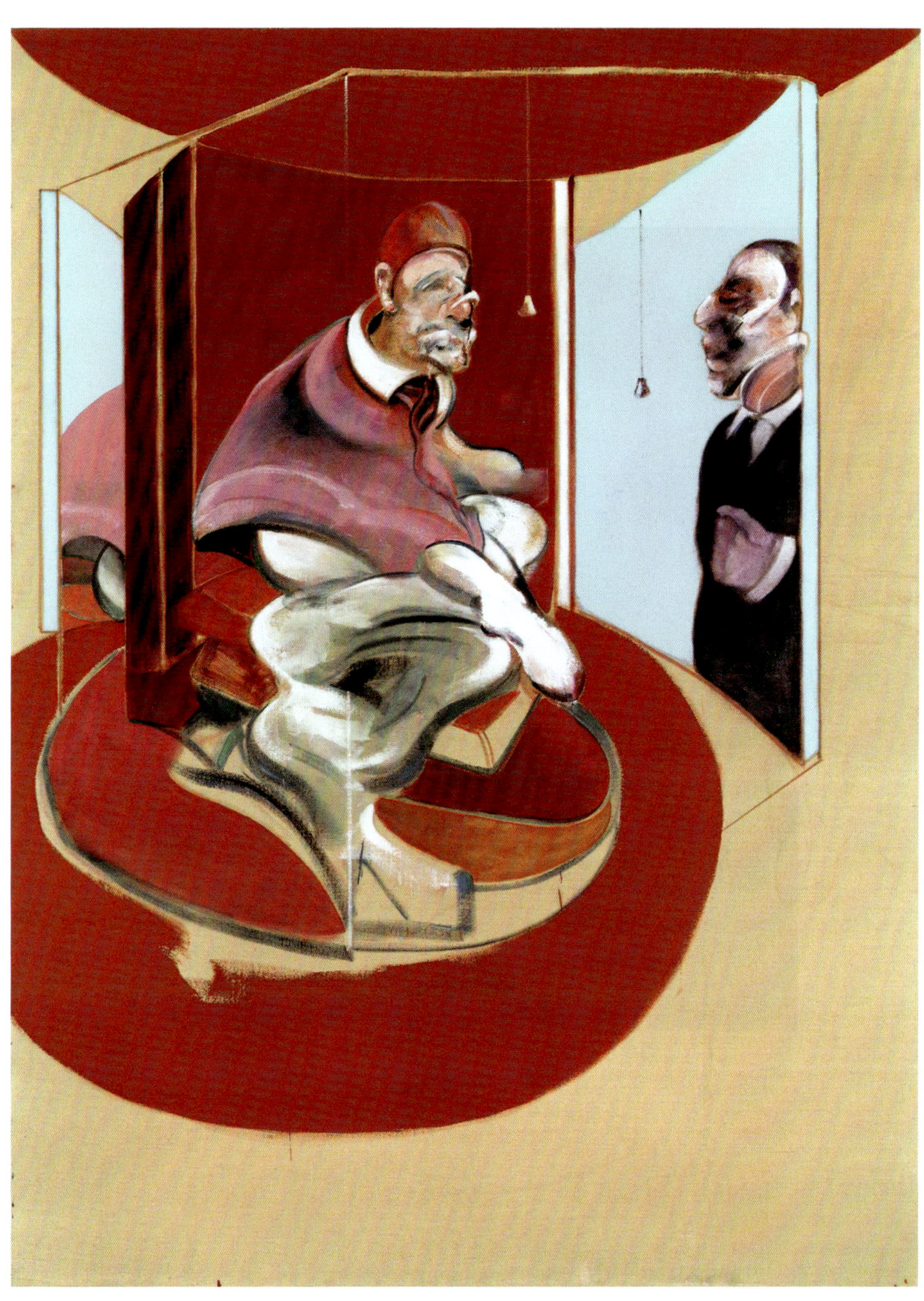

fig. 34 *Study of Red Pope, 1962, Second Version*, 1971

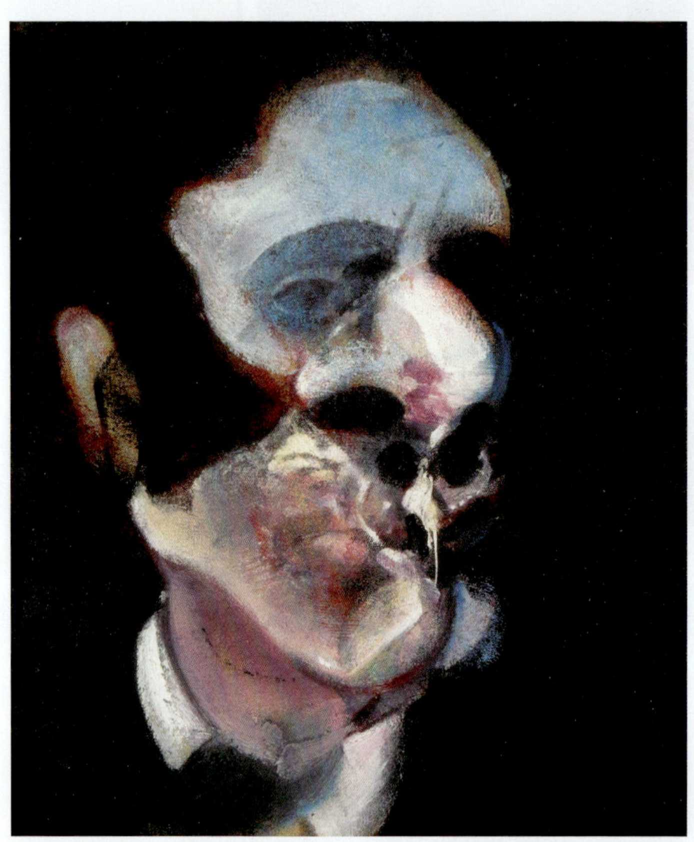

fig. 35 *Study of George Dyer*, 1970

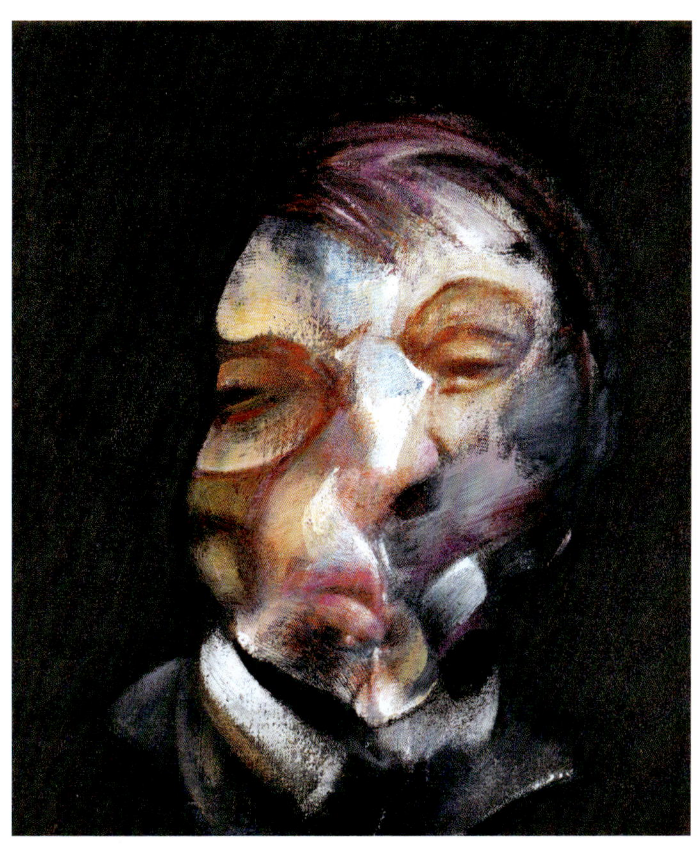

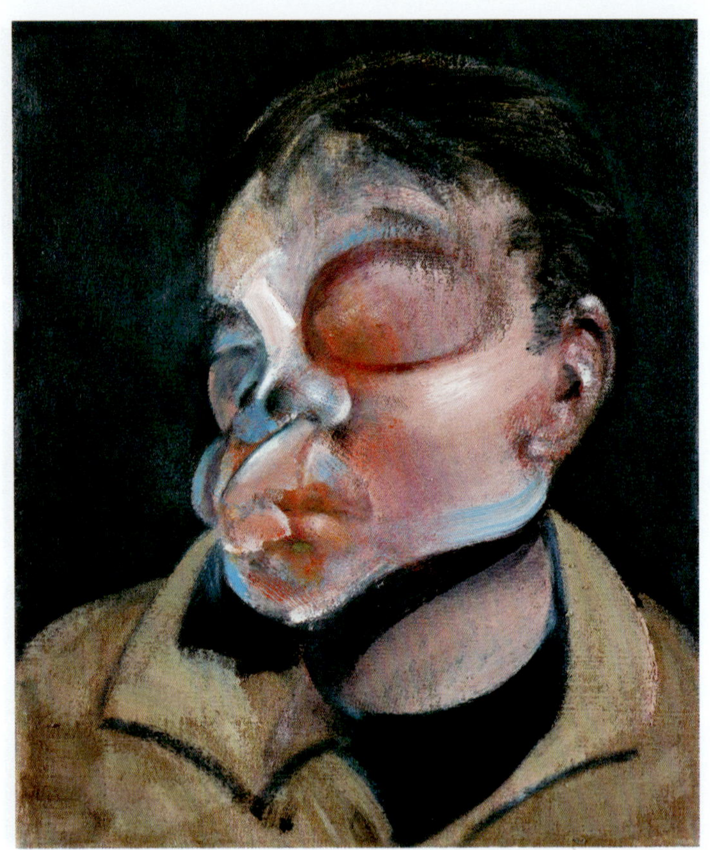

fig. 37   *Self-Portrait with Injured Eye*, 1972

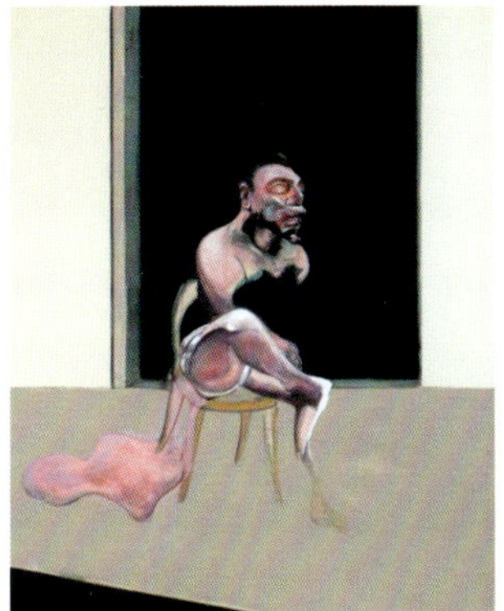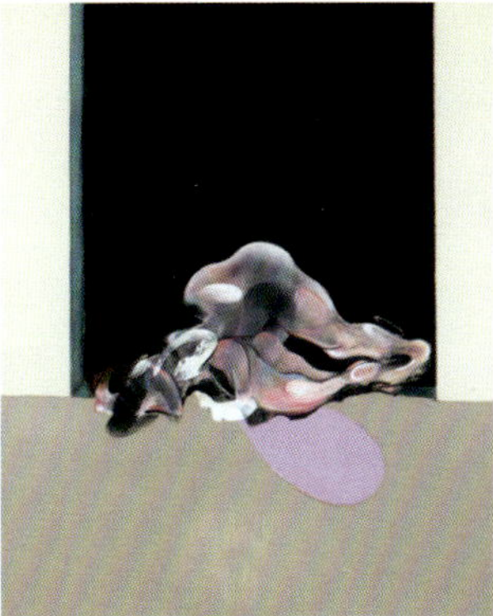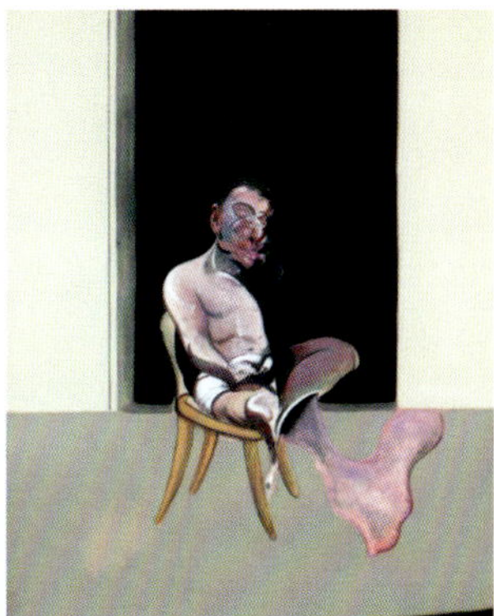

fig. 38   *Triptych August 1972*, 1972

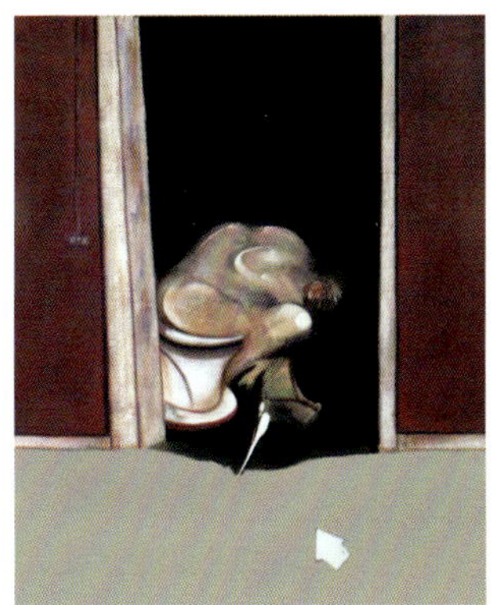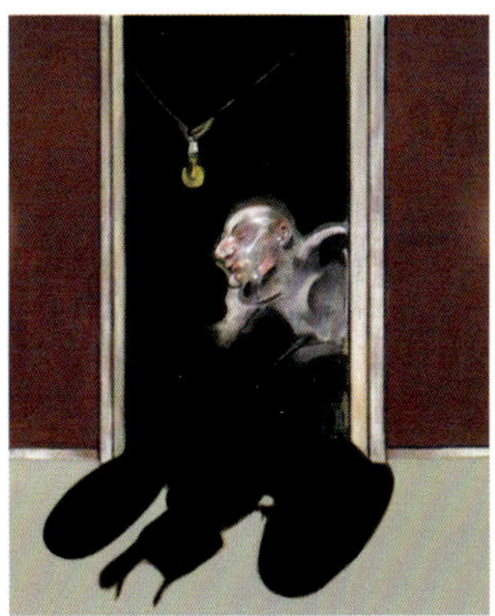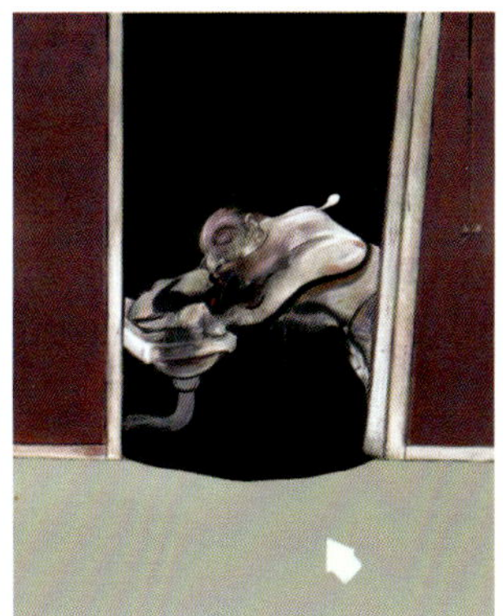

fig. 39   *Triptych May-June*, 1973

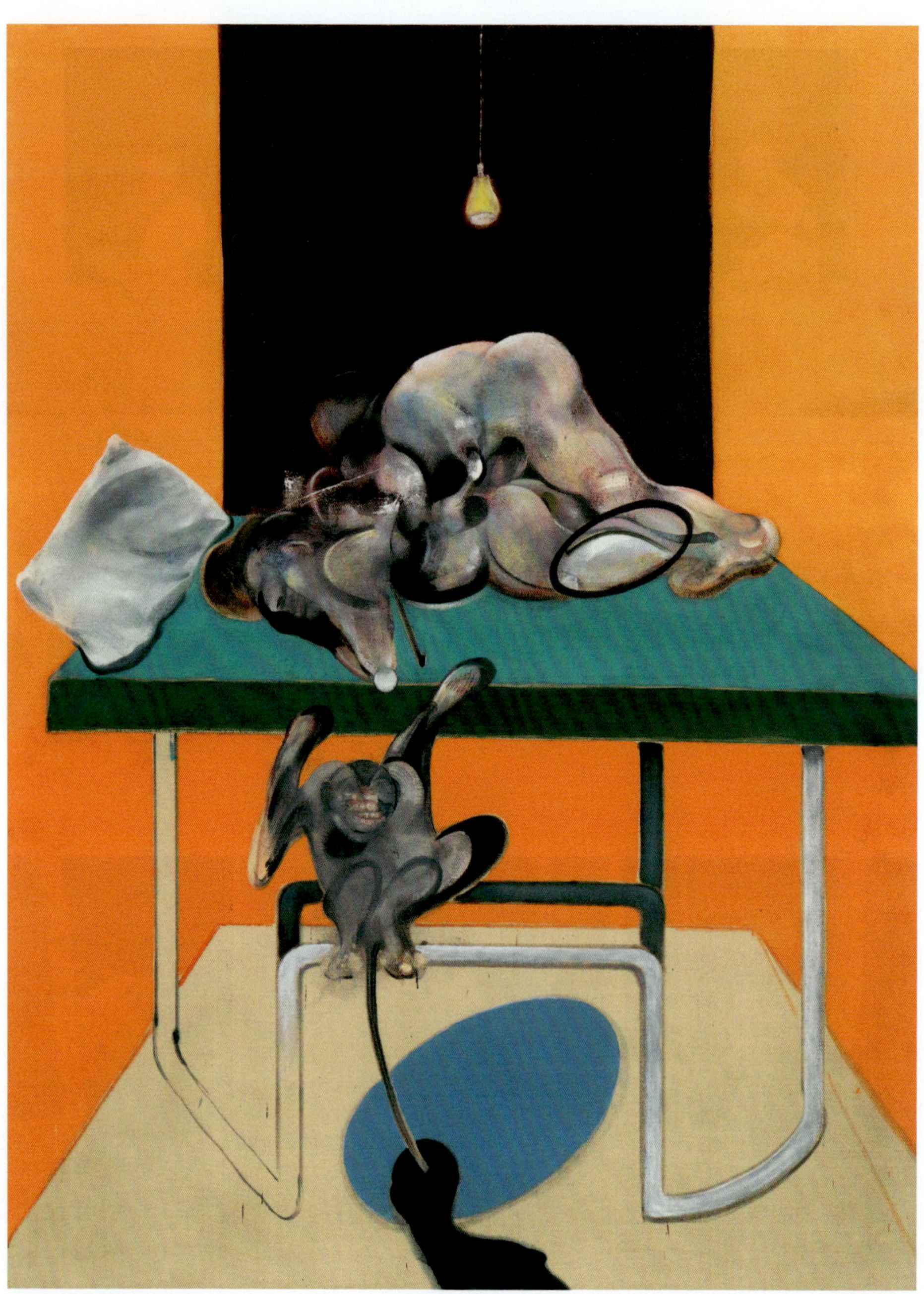

fig. 40 *Two Figures with a Monkey*, 1973

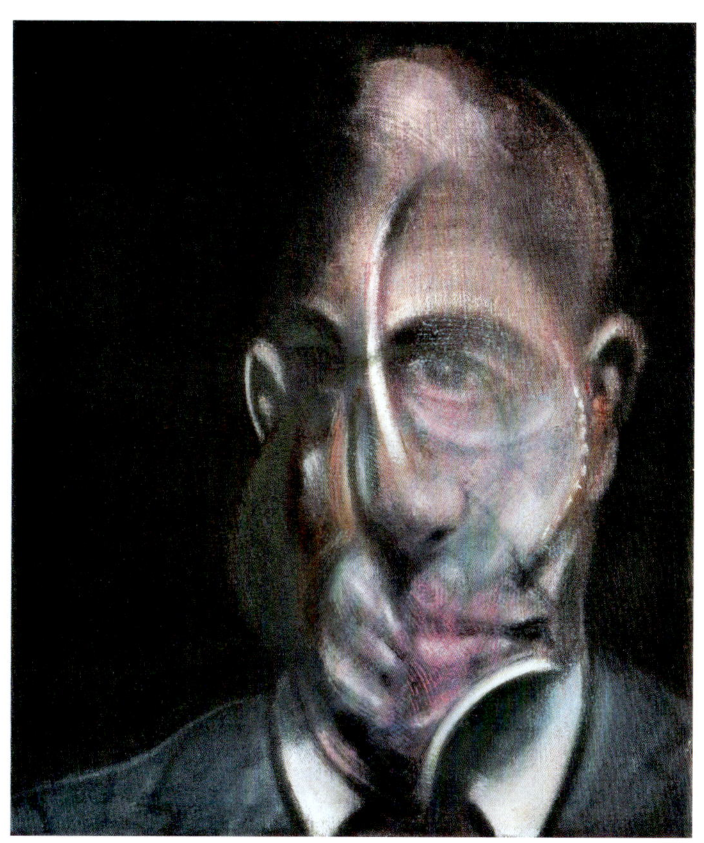

fig. 41 *Portrait of Michel Leiris*, 1976

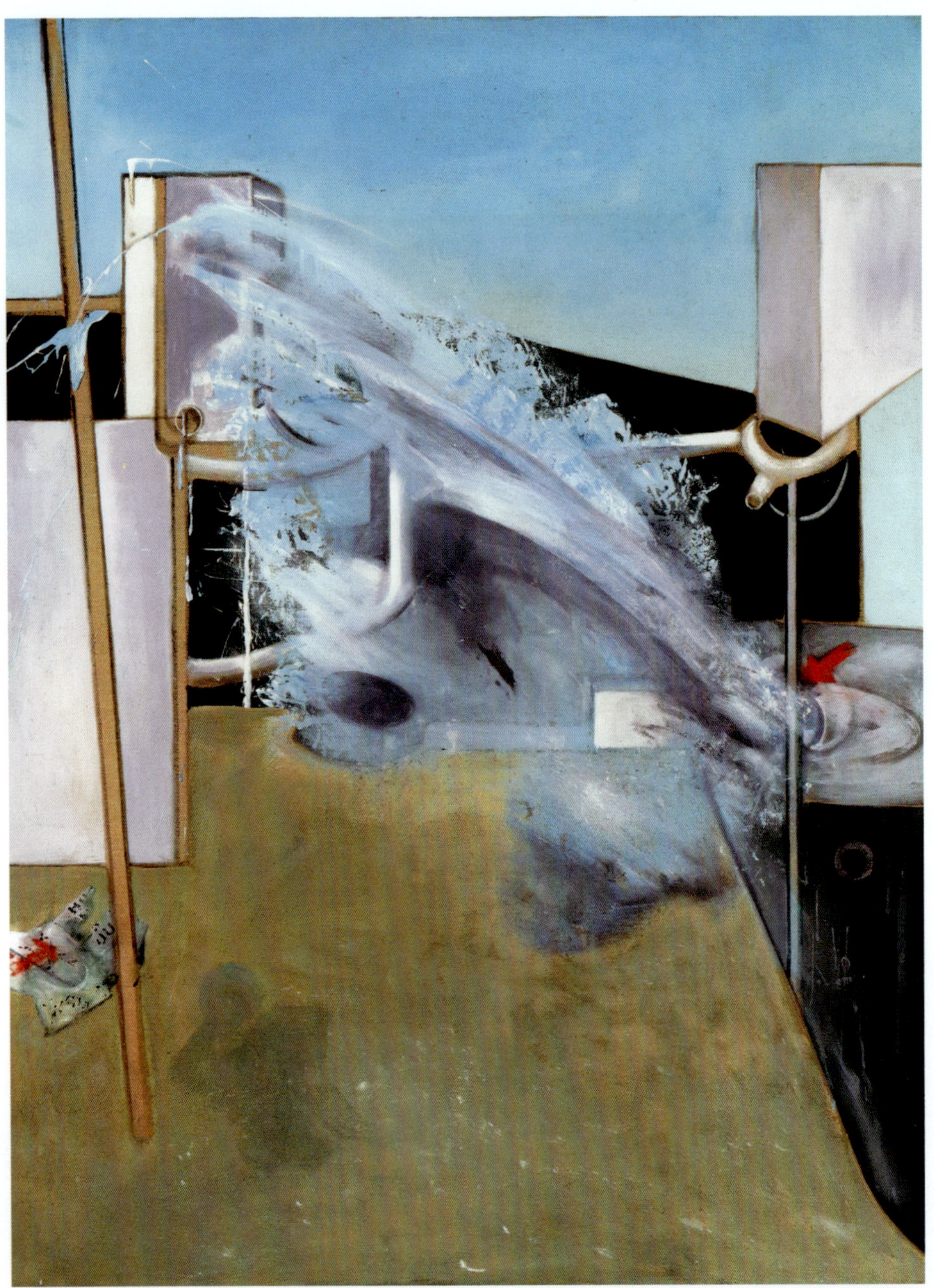

fig. 42 *Jet of Water*, 1979

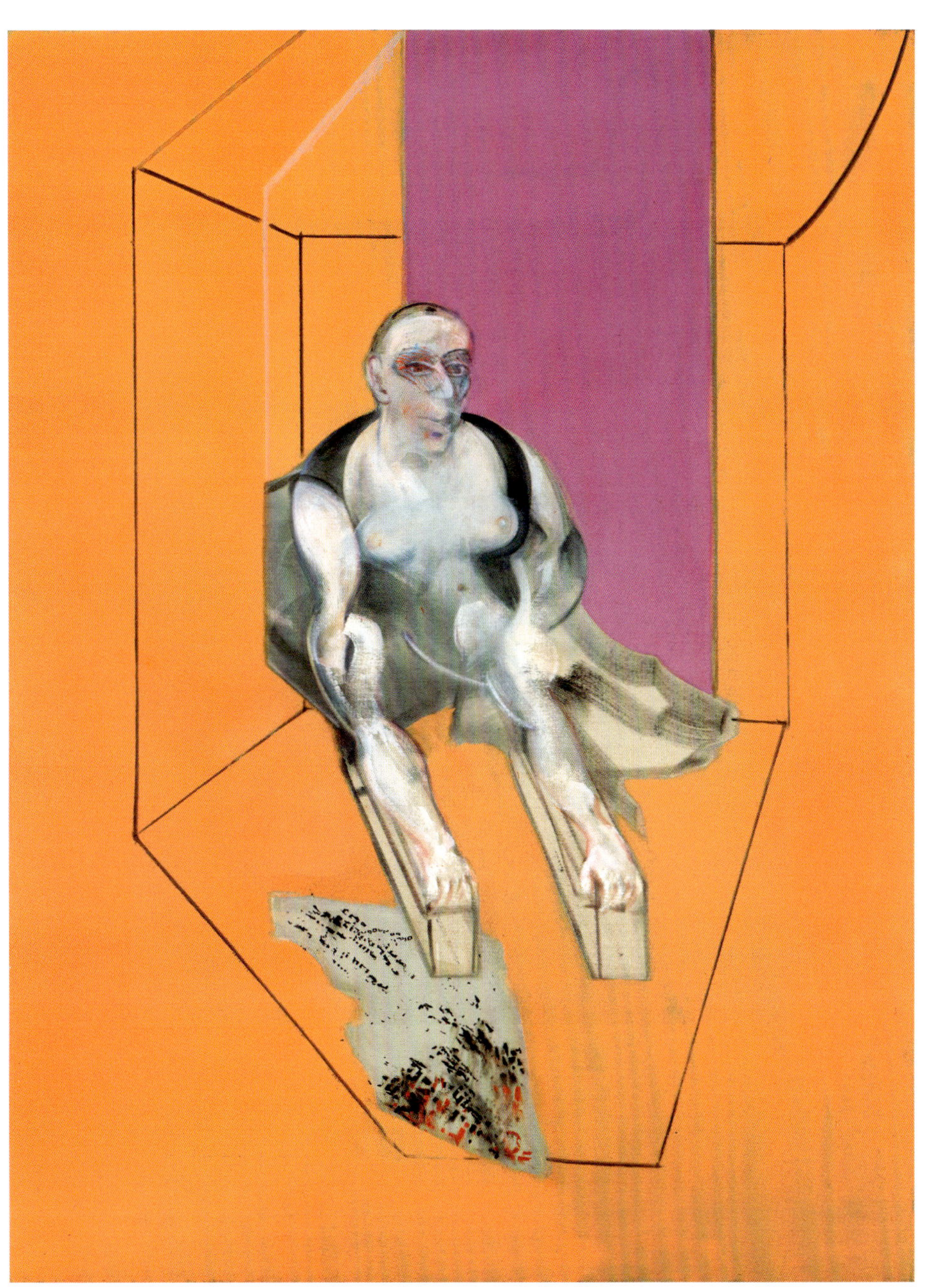

fig. 43 *Sphinx - Portrait of Muriel Belcher*, 1979

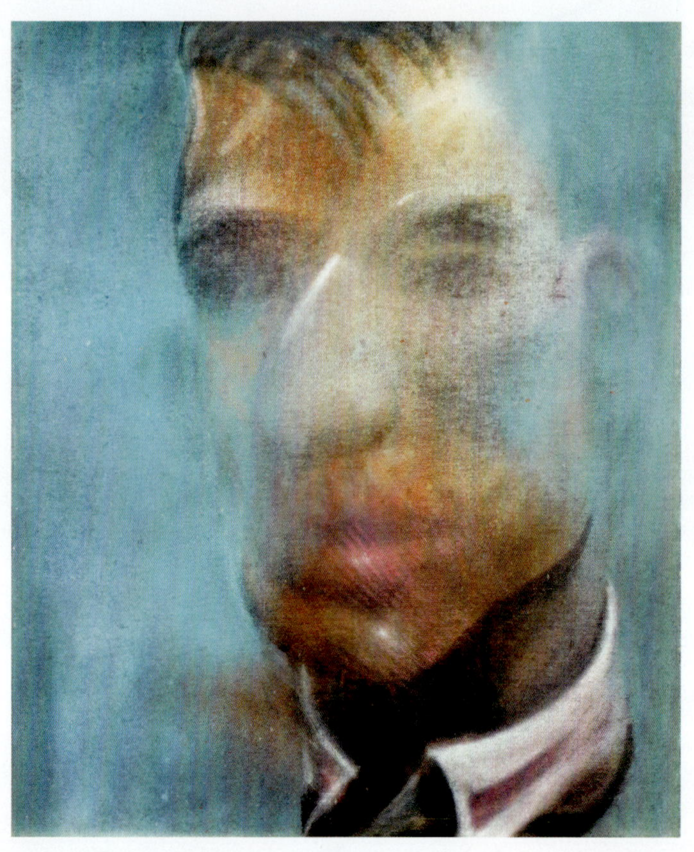

fig. 44 *Study for Self-Portrait*, 1980

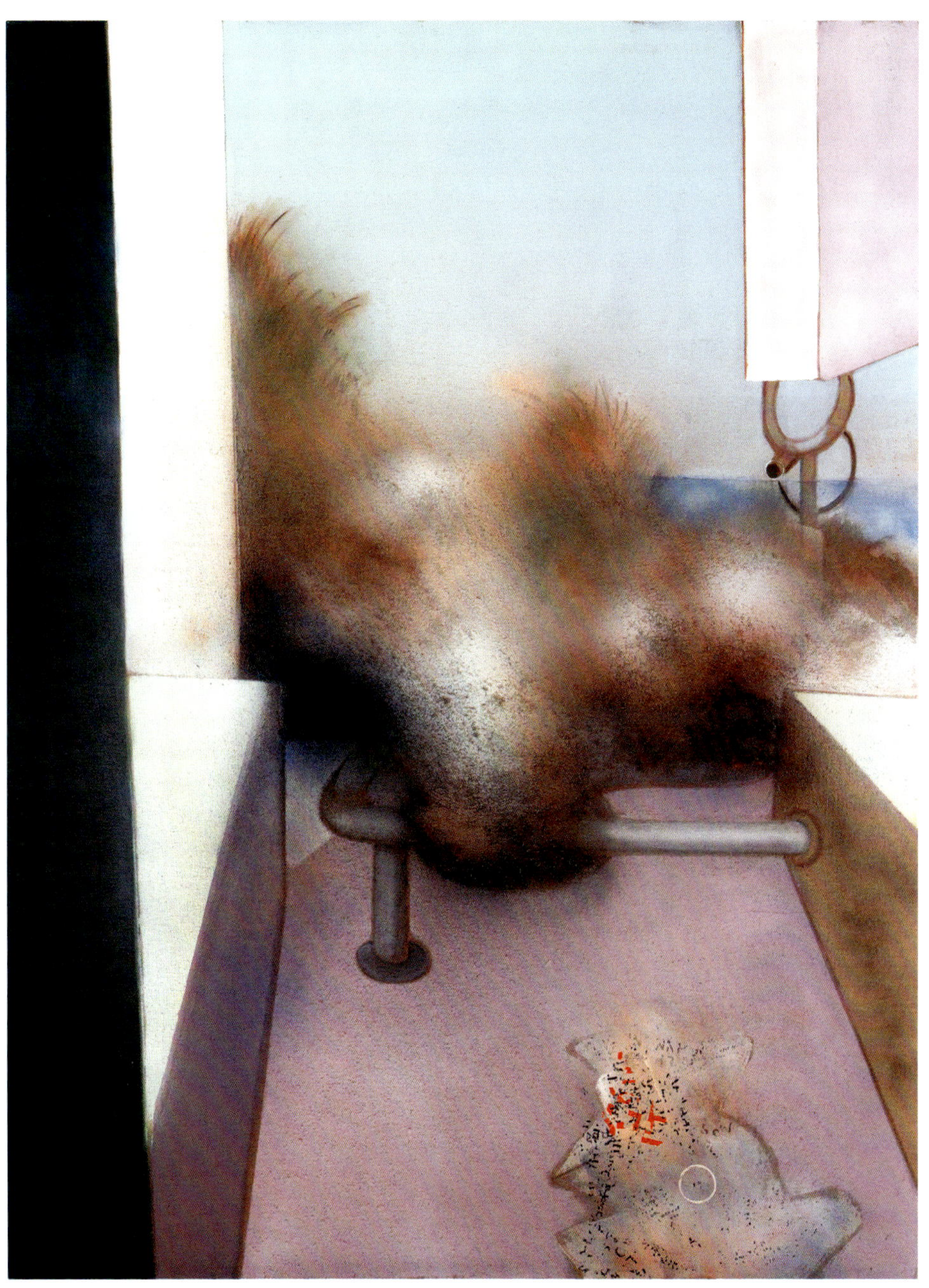

fig. 45 *Sand Dune*, 1981

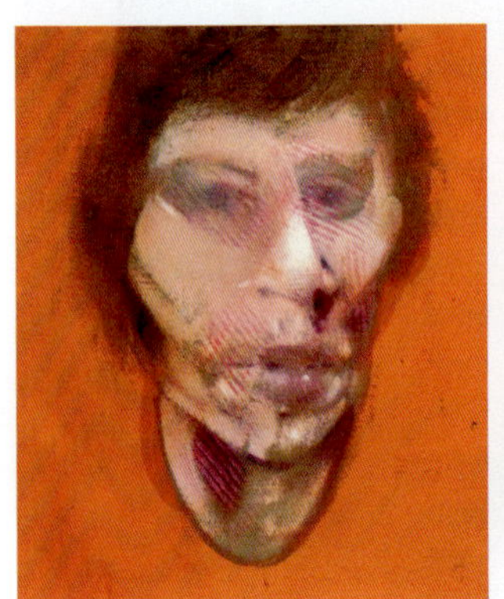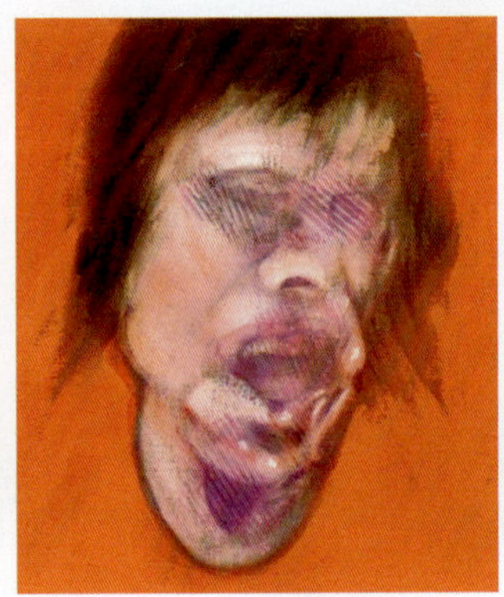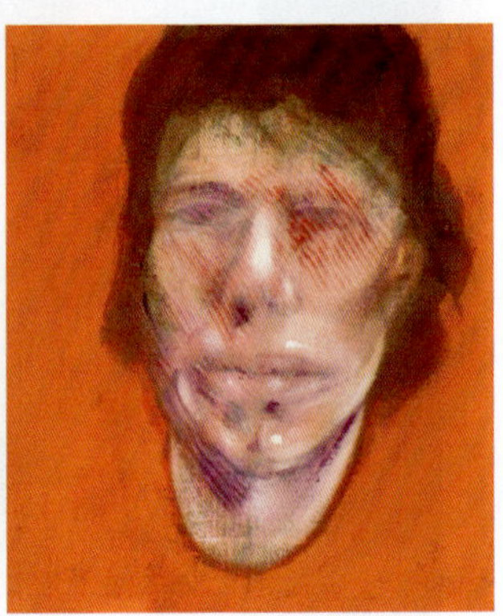

fig. 46   *Three Studies for a Portrait (Mick Jagger)*, 1982

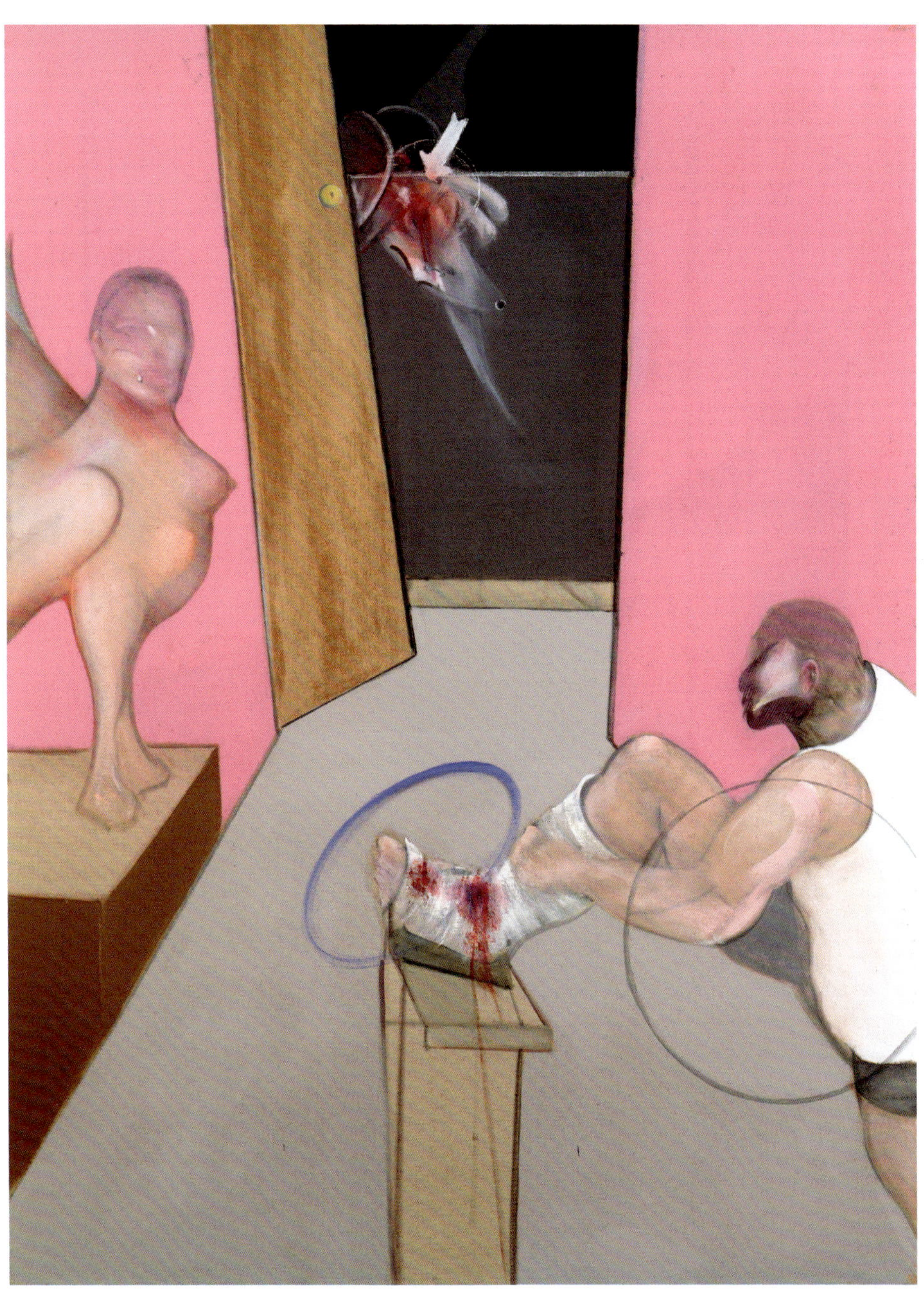

fig. 47 *Oedipus and the Sphinx after Ingres*, 1983   **185**

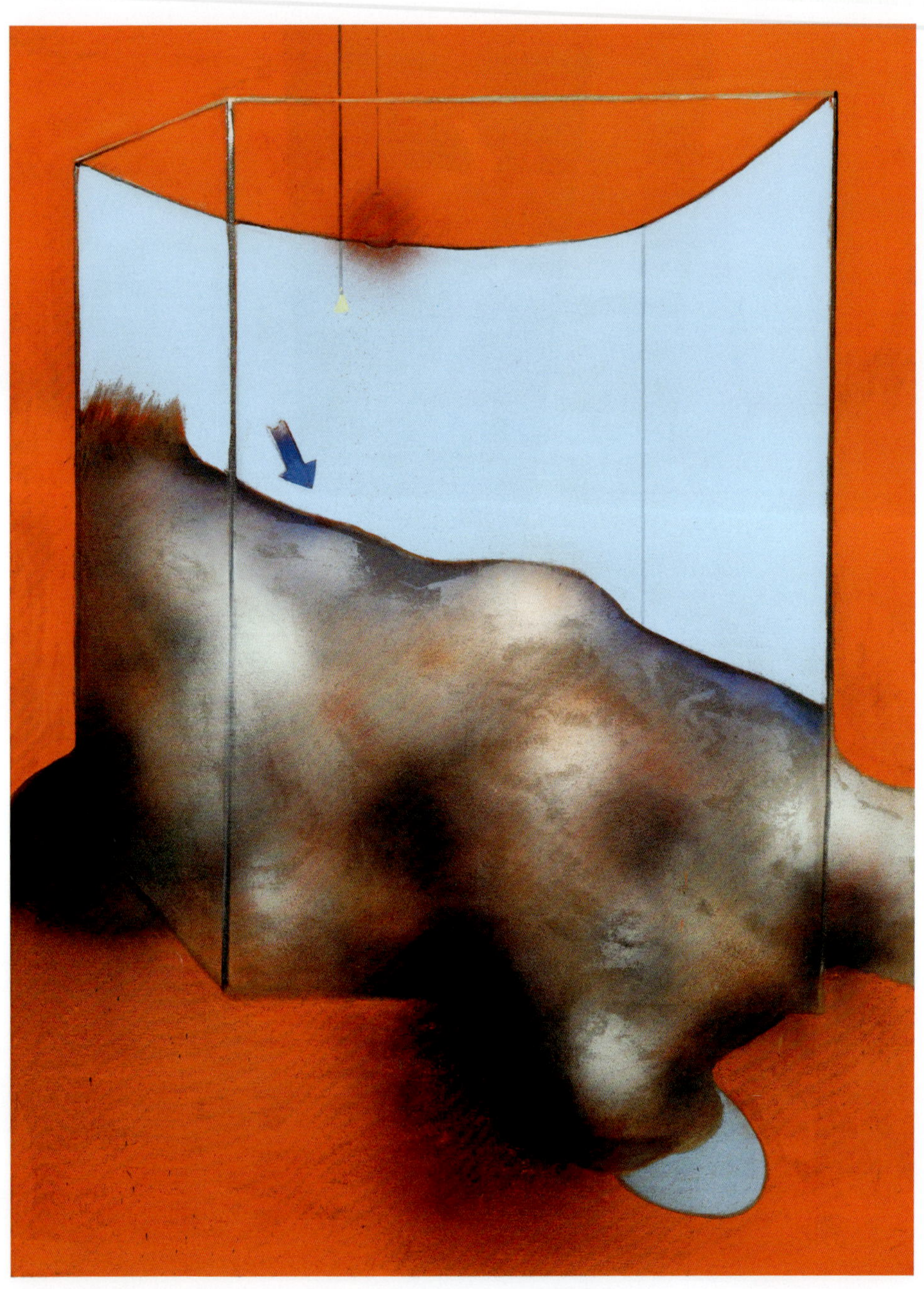

fig. 48 *Sand Dune*, 1983

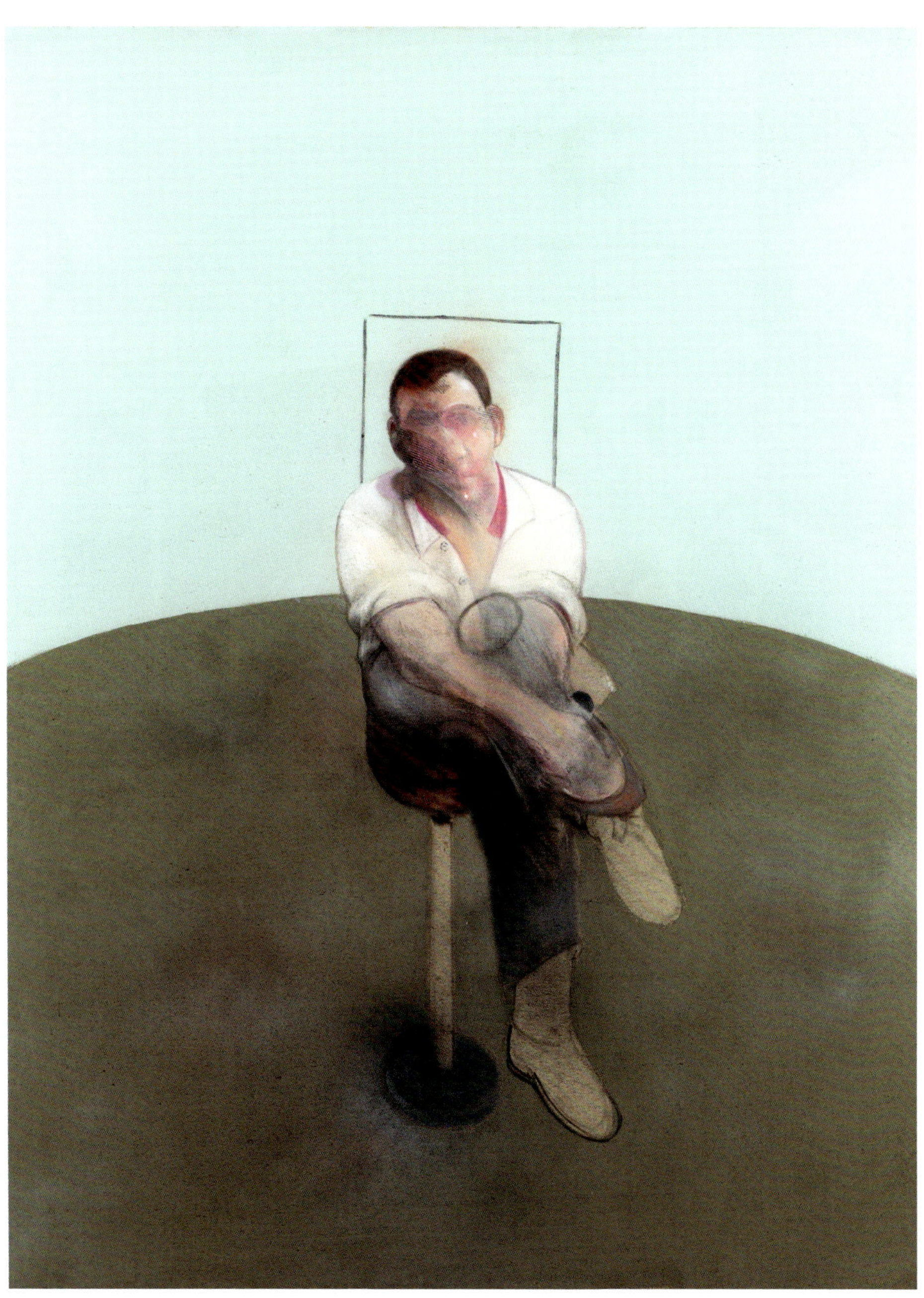

fig. 49 *Three Studies for a Portrait of John Edwards*, 1984 (centre panel)   **187**

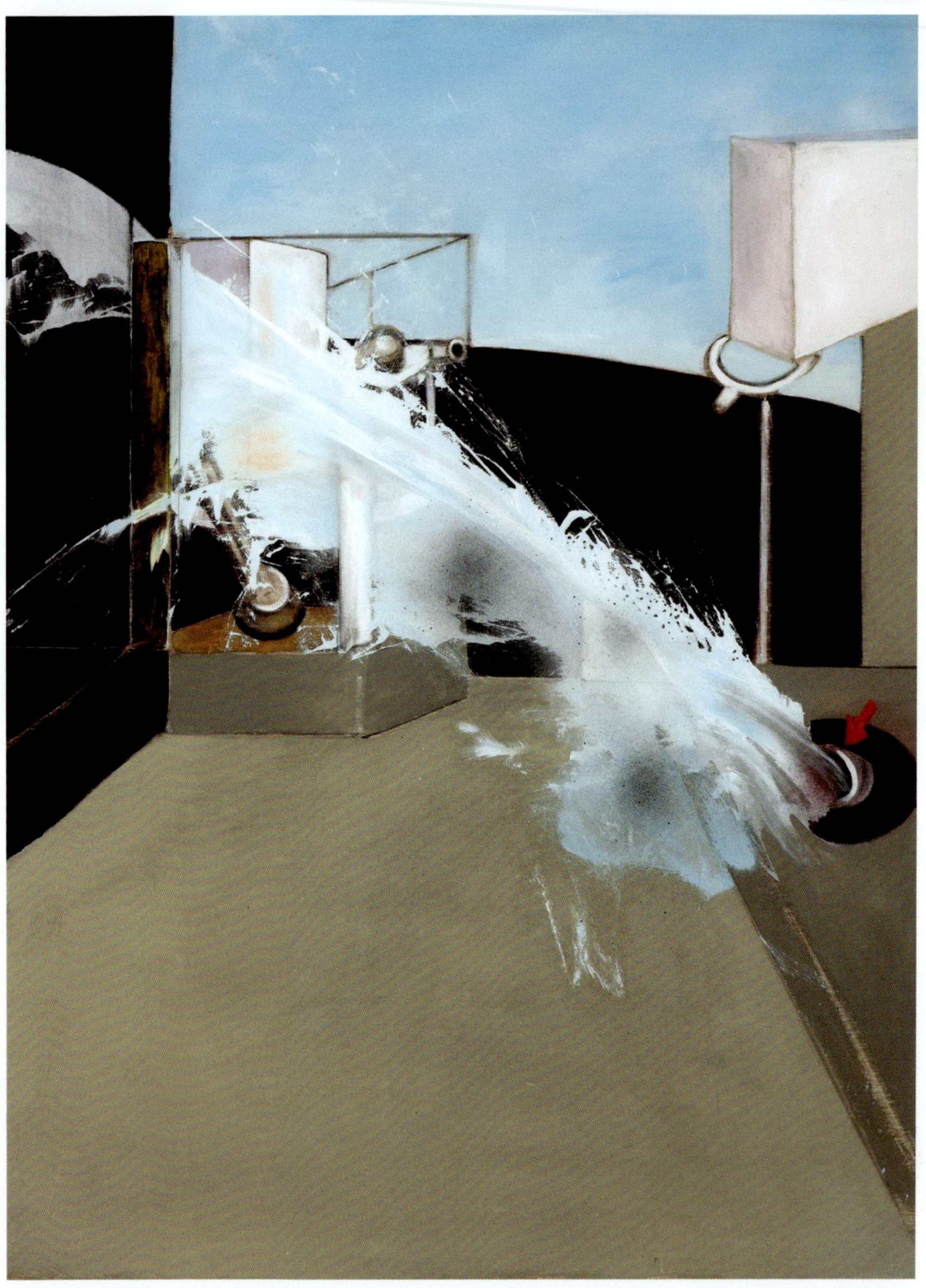

fig. 50 *Jet of Water*, 1988

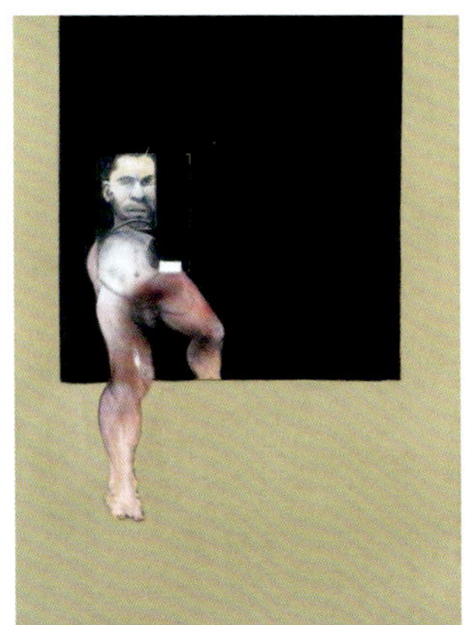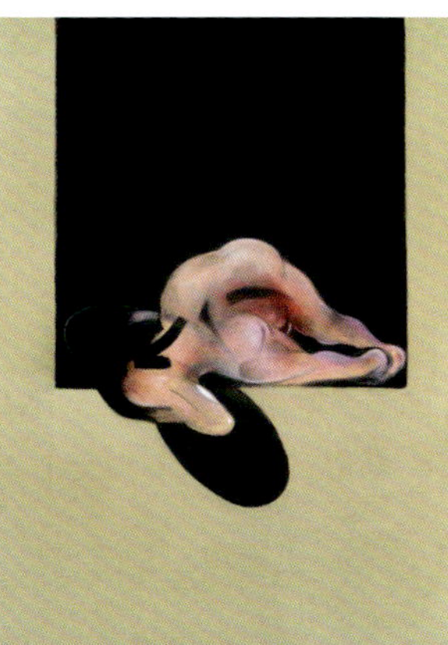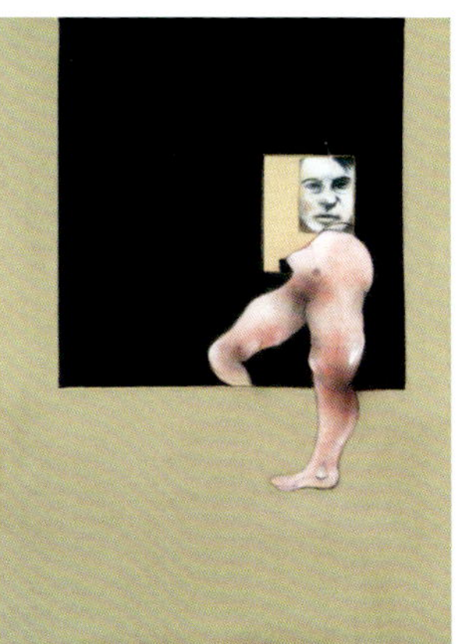

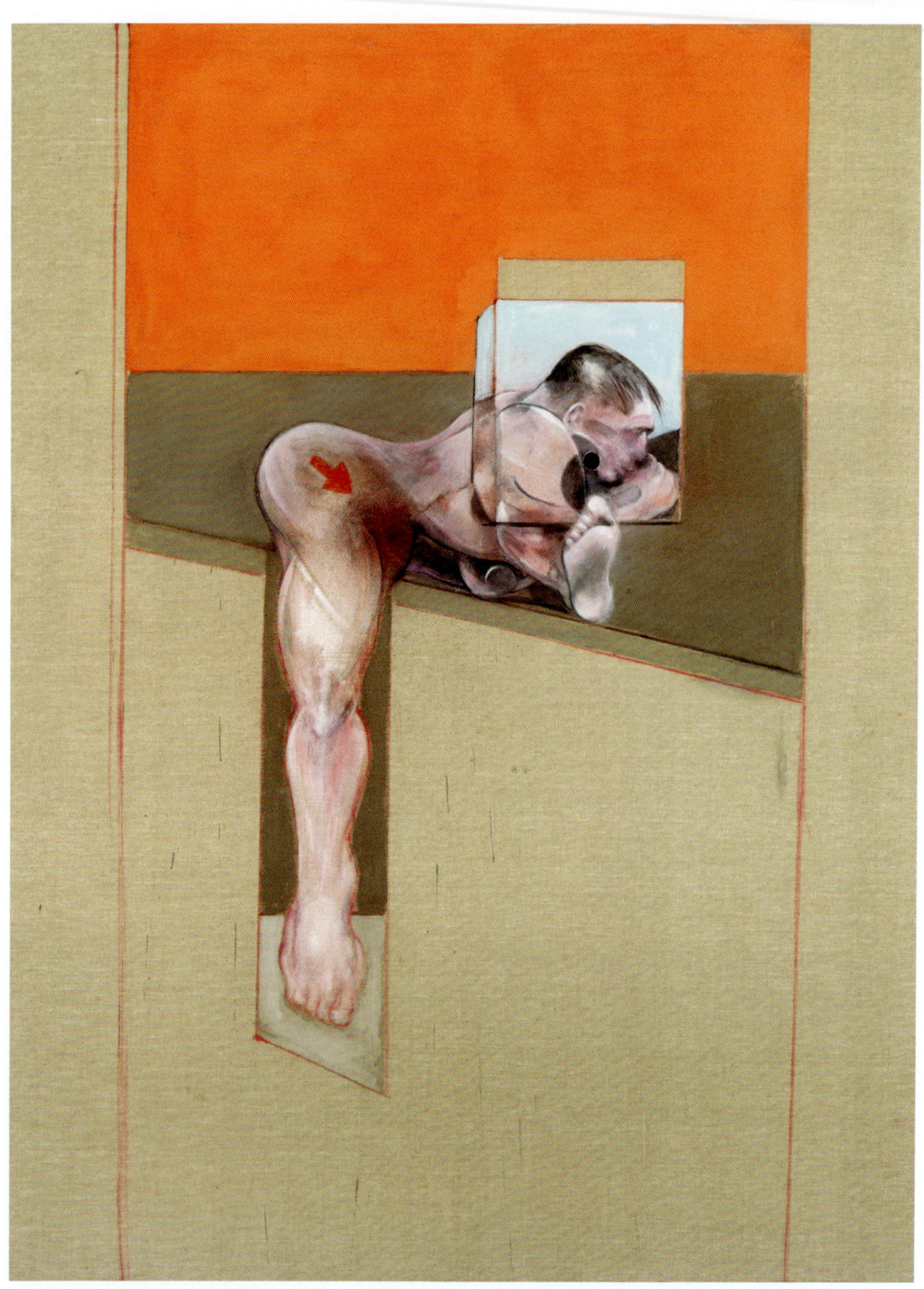

fig. 52 *Study from the Human Body*, 1991

First published in the United Kingdom in 2026 by
EFB Publishing and Thames & Hudson Ltd,
6–24 Britannia Street, London WC1X 9JD

First published in the United States of America in 2026
by EFB Publishing and Thames & Hudson Inc.,
500 Fifth Avenue, New York, New York 10110

British Library Cataloguing-in-Publication Data
A catalogue record for this book is available from the
British Library

Library of Congress Cataloging-in-Publication data
available on request

ISBN: 978-0-500-96665-5

Printed and bound in the UK by Blackmore Ltd

Design and production: Brett Harrison
Copy editor: Liane Jones
Proofreaders: Ben Harrison and Liane Jones
Print consultant: Danny Kirk

The views expressed in *Bacon Disfigured* are those of
the individual authors, and are not necessarily shared by
The Estate of Francis Bacon Publishing.